To the Unknoı

Petru Dumitriu was born in Rumania in 1924. At an early age he gained a considerable reputation as novelist and poet, at first in his own country, where he three times was awarded the State Prize for Literature, and later abroad.

For a while he served as Director of the State Publishing House, but finding himself unable to reconcile his conscience as a writer with the tyranny of the Party, he contrived to escape to the West, via East Berlin, together with his wife. He has lived there since 1960, writing in French, a language in which he has been at ease since the age of 13.

His novels *Family Jewels* and *The Prodigals* have been published in English, as has his autobiographical novel *Incognito* (available in Fount Paperbacks).

by the same author

TO THE
UNKNOWN GOD

Petru Dumitriu

Translated from the French by
James Kirkup

The Seabury Press · New York

1982
The Seabury Press
815 Second Avenue
New York, N.Y. 10017

First published in 1979 by Editions du Seuil, Paris under the title,
Au Dieu Inconnu. © Editions du Seuil, 1979.
English translation first published by William Collins Sons & Co. Ltd.,
London and by The Seabury Press, New York, in 1982.
© in the English translation William Collins Sons & Co. Ltd., 1982.
© in the Introduction William Collins & Co. Ltd., 1982.

Woodcut: Vivian Berger © 1979

Library of Congress Cataloging in Publication Data

Dumitriu, Petru.
    To the unkown God.

    Translation of: Au Dieu inconnu.
    1. Dumitriu, Petru. 2. Biserica Ortodoxă
Română—Biography. 3. Christianity—Philosophy.
I. Title.
BX699.D85A3313 1982   281.9′3 [B]   82-5722
ISBN 0-8164-2424-1   AACR2

To
Ernst and Paule Teves

CONTENTS

A DISSIDENT SPIRIT

An Introduction

Theology in Britain is something of a closed shop, like religion: the professional priests do not look kindly upon amateur outsiders, and for the most part view with horror the ordinary layman's ventures into mysticism and revelation. Theologians in particular are stern guardians of their own views of faith and dogma, and are often the most daunting and inhuman of religious interpreters – we have no Hans Küng, who was persecuted for the breadth and humanity of his views.

Perhaps this is why there are so few books published in Britain giving a deeply personal insight into religious experience. Such works are common on the Continent, particularly in France, Switzerland and Germany. These books very often take the form of novels, autobiographies, plays, poetry and essay-diaries somewhat similar to the Japanese *zuihitsu* form – an attempt to combine minute observation of daily life, contemplative prose and poetry and philosophical self-examination, often in the form of aphorisms.

The Rumanian dissident writer Petru Dumitriu, now living in exile in 'free' Europe, is one writer of such books. He was born in 1924 in the small Danubian village of Bazias, and started writing essays, in French, at the age of thirteen. During the Second World War he was studying philosophy in Germany. On his return to Rumania, he became part of the movement of Socialist Realism and his

writings received many awards of merit. He became a
reporter, edited a review, and was head of a state publishing house, though he was a communist without a Party
card. Disillusioned by the Iron Curtain régimes (a disillu-
sionment well described in this book), he fled to the West,
where he has lived since 1960, writing in French: his 1962
novel, *Incognito,* is outstanding.

Then, under the pressures and depressions of exile and
an alien culture, he stopped writing around 1969. *To the
Unknown God* is the result of over ten years of silence,
during which he has meditated deeply upon the nature of
God, and on the possibility of belief in God. He writes in a
vigorous, shapely style, rich with philosophical allusions
and illuminating quotations from his vast reading, all
presented with an easy scholarship. His five chapters on
the nature of Evil are among the finest ever written on this
intractable theme.

It was his questioning of the existence of God, and his
exploration of personal solitudes of soul and spirit that first
attracted me to Dumitriu: I, too, like so many others, had
experienced the desolation of encountering total silence
when trying to enter into conversation with God. The
tragic words of Christ upon the cross – 'My God, my
God, why hast thou forsaken me?' – are a constant theme
in the book.

But it was the vivid autobiographical scenes from the
author's childhood on a farm beside the Danube that
moved me most, and drew me effortlessly into even the
most recondite contemplations of this book. I was reminded so often of my own childhood experiences of
good and evil, of loneliness, friendlessness, poverty and
desperation in the face of a hostile world in which I soon
realized that people did not like me: the only friend I knew
was Jesus, and he was nonexistent, for he could not take
my hand in his.

Realization of the omnipresence of evil, and the ache of
solitude and silence, came to Dumitriu, too, at an early

age. He had a violent, militaristic father, an ineffective mother. Life on a farm soon taught him man's cruelty to his fellow creatures, the beasts of the field.

As he grew older, he tried to harden his heart, to be completely armoured against the horror of human existence in a totalitarian society more cruel than any farm or abattoir. He ruthlessly made his way to the top in a supposedly 'socialist' and egalitarian world that was in fact opportunistic and bourgeois, anti-religion and anti-emotion. How he broke away from that stultifying spiritual desert and found his way back to the West, to God, and to a 'freedom' that he discovered was after all only relative, even in France, is the great theme of this work. We are not spared the humiliations, the disillusionments and the bitterness that were his lot at the hands of supposedly 'free' men in the West. But he is rescued from self-destruction through the concern and guidance of a French priest whose great intellectual and human qualities make him the ideal spiritual friend and teacher many of us long for, but never find.

Dumitriu addresses himself to many of the nightmare problems of our modern world, relates them to his own spiritual struggles, and gives us no easy solutions to our nuclear dilemma. But his whole book is one that shines with the curiously happy radiance of a mind exercising itself freely, with the grace and the mastery of a superb athlete of the emotions. Its final message is one of joy, hope and faith. It left me remembering the words of another great spiritual dissident, Solzhenitsyn: 'Prayers are like those appeals of ours. Either they don't get through or they're returned with "rejected" scrawled across 'em.'

KYOTO   James Kirkup
1981

1.

CONVERSATION WITH
A NONEXISTENT INTERLOCUTOR

How can one be a Christian, how can one love God, how can one even think of God in this world, this wilderness, dominated, manipulated, ravaged by science and technology, and in which the Christian religion, its dogmas, its Church, are antiquated, outworn, decayed – a world in which we ourselves are besieged and crushed by evil, that Evil which is so obviously ever-present in us in the guises of egoism, madness and violence?

How can one be religious, or devout, or at any rate of a quiet mind, and not appear impertinent, not be villainous, confronted with the suffering of others? Confronted with the absurdity of it all, the lack of guidelines, the lack of meaning even in what is good?

Finally, to reduce all these questions to one: how can one love God when he obviously does not exist? And – putting the same question in a different way – how can one love human beings, when they are as they are, and when there is no God?

To this question there is one surprising answer. Let me give it here. It is certainly not the only answer; it is not *my* answer, it has nothing to do with me, it was given me: or, to avoid any hint of pathos, let me say I met it, as one might meet someone in the street. I would not even say I found it, though it is true I looked for it a long time: it arrived all on its own, it came to me as if by accident.

This question is already surprising enough in that it modifies the question as it is traditionally stated: how to believe in God? The answer I am talking about here requires the question to be stated in another way. We must ask, how can one *love* God? In order to answer that, the question of belief becomes almost irrelevant. I believe that it will rain tomorrow, because the sky is cloudy this evening; but perhaps it will be fine. I believe in God, but perhaps I am mistaken and there is no God. Such is not the kind of question to which an answer, in all humility, is offered here. We must not believe in God: we must love him. We must not believe in God: we must know grace. If, of course, he will take pity on us: if he will grant us the instant of grace. Having known that instant, if I doubt or even deny his existence it may be because of mental impoverishment, or illness, loss of memory, a state of shock. Otherwise, there would be no reason to doubt his existence. It is in this sense that I can say I do not believe in God.

The response I am talking about here surprises by its extreme solidity. Once established, there is no going back, no negation that can diminish its conviction, which is, in all its neat, foolish simplicity, the self-assurance of a personal experience, however trifling and modest it may be. One can no longer doubt the existence of God; and one could only forget him in a superficial manner, out of distraction, as we forget our telephone number, the name of our street, and, in chronic cases, our very own name.

I am speaking here of forgetting God, not his 'existence'; of loving God, not of 'believing' in him. Once we know the touch of grace, we shall never forget him again. The question of God's existence strikes a tiresome note of curiosity, of chill investigation. It is fundamentally ungodly, and its very postulation makes it inaccessible to the answer it claims to seek. It is more worthy of God and of ourselves to turn frankly away from him and say that he and his existence are no concern of ours. Or, on the other hand, to turn to him, to speak to him, not as we would address someone apart from ourselves with words which would equally be apart from ourselves, but as if we ourselves were the message; I am the one who sends the message, but I am also the word, the letter. I send him the message of my person, my conscience, my being. If then he grants me the grace of allowing me to pray, if he gives me what theologians call the grace of tongues, it is impossible to doubt him, impossible not to love him, for grace in its very self is that certainty and that love. But even more, it becomes impossible to hold any grudge against human beings for being as they are, impossible even not to forgive one's own weakness, though certainly not condoning it, knowing that it is God within us who forgives. In forgiveness, 'I is someone else'. For an instant of grace, he is willing to grant me forgiveness and to give me peace.

This curious response I am talking about here is also surprising because the question has to be asked without pity for God. God grants us grace, but we must not think of granting it to him, not even for the most impalpable of doubts. We must, in all piety, be as pitiless towards him as we must be – still in all piety – towards our fellow human beings. We have to show him no mercy, out of our piety and confidence in him, but not in order to put him to the test, or as a game – one does not play around with God, or, all of a sudden, he is no longer there. Out of piety, I say to God: You do not exist; and I wait for his reply. I know that that reply will not reach me in the same terms, in the same language; I know that it may well not reach me at all. We have to be able to bear the weight of uncertainty, and the even more crushing burden of the evidence that he does not exist, and yet in spite of all that go on waiting for his response. It may mean waiting ten, twenty, thirty years, a lifetime. Obviously, we must be able to turn away from him once and for all, if such is our nature. If we are equal to living in the wilderness. If our faith and our confidence are not stronger than the absence of God; if our adherence is not stronger than his desertion, and a blinding proof that that abandonment is not definitive, that it has actually not taken place. Then we must desert him. We must abandon God if we are unable to prove to ourselves that he has not abandoned us.

I am one of those who see God face to face, and they are legion: there are four billion of us, not counting the insects

I see God face to face: he is unrecognizable.

One does not see God; he brushes us with his wing – I am talking of grace, the one contact possible with God. Apart from an infinitesimal fraction of his visage – terrifying, dreadful, unrecognizable – he is behind my retina, behind what I might call my blind spot.

Man is the measure of all things; but who is the measure of man? Man is the measure of all things, of the being of all that be, of the non-being of all that are not, says Protagoras; but who is the measure of the value of things are they are? For I know by experience, each one of us knows by experience, if only for one lightning-struck instant of revelation, the sense of the non-value of things as they are.

Man the measurer stands at the centre of the universe. The Copernican revolution today sounds like a platitude, and it is wrong to say that man is no longer the centre of the universe. The Copernican revolution was an event of the greatest magnitude; the discovery of the solitude of man, in his remote corner of a very tiny solar system in a galaxy composed of millions of clouds of stars, was important, useful, decisive in enabling us to go beyond an outmoded image of the world, of the heavens in uneasy rotation round the earth, and man at the centre between God on high and hell below.

But now it is time to realize that after all man is the one centre of the universe of generalized relativity, for he is the central point of his own measurements. He projects, as a star its beams, his hypotheses and his systems of verification in all directions of space-time, in all the parameters of logical space and the mathematicable universe.

If there are other intelligent beings doing the same, then man and those beings will constitute a context of mensurations, whose centre will then have to be determined. For the centre of mensurations is also the centre of valorizations. From now on, there can be no other value judgements in the universe but those enunciated by man. In this respect, post-Copernican man, whom we may call the man of generalized relativity, both surpasses and precedes the Copernican revolution: he goes forward to link up with the man who is to come, and goes back to rejoin both Christian man, for whom man is the centre of the universe, and the man of antiquity, for whom man is the measure of all things.

Once again: man is the measure of all things, but who is the measure of man? Man is at the centre of all things, but who is at the centre of man?

Ever since I reached the age of reason I have been holding a conversation with an unknown and perhaps nonexistent interlocutor. If there is no one listening to me, no one answering me, and if at the other end of this inexhaustible one-way communication there is not one living soul, then I have been cheated, and it has been the biggest cheat in a life that has known plenty of them: a cheat that is the crowning proof of the nothingness, of the non-value, of the absolute destitution of my existence. The question must be propounded as implacably as possible. No pity for God: it is for him to have pity on us.

Later, I encountered him in Jesus Christ crucified, in every suffering human being, in every tortured child, in every slaughtered beast, and I learned pity for God. He granted me the grace of gratitude and I realized that he had pity on me, who had not had pity on him.

However, what I must call piety forbade me to shut my eyes to Evil. Piety must resist the vision of Evil, or collapse before it. May those who know only the goodness and the tenderness of God forgive me if I look at things unblinkingly. Piety forbids me to cheat with this terrible, frightening, non-human, inhuman, strange and alien God – a God alien to man to the point of not existing in the same way as man or any other object in the universe.

The absence of God, a concept with which the existen-
tialists have cleared and consolidated the ground and
opened the way for what is now an imminent renaissance
of religion – that absence of God is not of a physical, but of
a moral order. God is not absent because we cannot see
him: he is absent in the presence of Evil.

Nevertheless, piety forbids me to use Evil to set a
limitation upon God, and truth forbids me to shut my eyes
to the presence of grace. Let those who deny God, or who
know him not, or for whom God is indifferent, allow me
not to forget the few instants of gratitude that give some
sense and some value to my existence, which would have
none without them. This truth makes it impossible for me
to deny God.

The presence of God at the centre of the exact sciences,
mathematical and mathematicable, beginning with the
existentialist experience of a world of emptiness, of an
absurd universe, of nothingness and of absolute non-
value, an intellectual and moral preparation for the Christian life – that presence of God is not of a nature to be
described in words, but is a living certainty. God is not
present because we perceive him; he is present in gratitude.
He it is to whom the action of grace is addressed, he is the
action of grace; he it is who addresses his own being in the
action of grace. He is also the one who denies God, who
knows him not; he is Evil, nothingness and the wilderness,
even as he is also joy, consolation, essential amity between
myself and him. He is grace, that comes or does not come,
and which I await humbly at every instant of my life,
including the present moment.

2.

THE LONG VACATION

My lengthy conversation with that supposedly non-existent interlocutor began with my call to him, and his silence. I called him and he did not respond. My relationship with God began with the evidence of his absence.

We were in the country during the long summer holidays. The weather was overcast and sultry, with a mackerel sky. In front of me, there was the farmyard, of dry, hard clay, scattered with slabs of granite sunk in the ground. To the left, stood the farmhouse's low wall, with its little square windows and its big grey roof of weather-beaten shingles. To the right, the trees on a steep slope, so that you looked down on their crests; one or two vineyard terraces, and far below the vast, swollen, grey Danube laboured by the wind, with beyond it the high hills, almost mountains, their rocky flanks and salient ribs cleft by precipitous pits, their long spine of close-cropped grass like the back of an enormous reclining animal that had been ruminating there for millions of years under the clouded heavens.

Plumb in the middle of that pale yellow farmyard was a big block for chopping wood, made from the stump of an uprooted tree, perhaps with an axe sticking out from it. Beside it, a post to the top of which was tied a heavy block of salt: when the beasts came in from the pastures, they would lift their muzzles and start licking the salt.

At the bottom of the yard, the clay narrowed, became a thin tongue, a path climbing between a retaining wall enclosing a strip of vineyard and a fall of grassy slopes.

This path made its way up to the ridge of the hill, where it joined the edge of the sky, then turned left and rose higher, along the hedge, right to a rocky outcrop silhouetted against the sky.

And here below, right in the middle of the deserted farmyard, my sister was coming running towards me; she would have been three years old, perhaps four, and I five or six. She was running towards me with open arms, wanting to play or give me a hug. She stumbled, fell, got up and started to cry. In the centre of her forehead was a bleeding wound. It was so deep, it left on her brow a scar that never completely disappeared. Hearing our cries, our mother ran out. They started fussing round my sister. I could see there was nothing I could do, so, in a state of shock, thinking she was going to die, I ran to call on God for help.

I had heard people talking about him, and I knew that he was up there somewhere in the sky. So I dashed behind the house, leaving behind me the farm buildings, the yard, the path to the hilltop, the hedge and the clouds, the rounded tree-crests down below, the terraced vineyards, the colossal river down in the valley, the enormous ruminating animal of the hills on the other side, under the overcast heavens. I took refuge behind our house and a retaining wall covered with ivy, at the beginning of a road which climbed up into the forest. It was like a deep trench lined with great slabs of granite thickly quilted with moss and ivy. Up above, the eaves of a red-tiled roof, and the mackerel sky, empty.

I wept as I cried aloud to God. I implored him not to let my sister die. No response. Silence. No one there.

Vacations, vacuity, vacuum: emptiness; the hollow pit of the year, with hollow days in a hollow universe. Emptiness of the sky; hollowness and nothingness of everything. The clay, the granite, the tiles, the moss, the ivy, the grass, the vines, the leaves on the trees, the massive hills, the earth, the river tormented by the wind –

all that existed, certainly, and the wind too, and the clouds; but that was all. No one there. And all that existed was nothing but solitude, sadness, abandonment; it was not up to much.

A lesson in atheism in a country setting. I had started early, and with a good master. I had no faith to lose, for I had never had faith. I still do not have it. I do not believe in God. I cannot deny the blinding proof of his absence. (Blinding: we stay blind. But he is visible, or rather accessible, to the blind. I cannot see him, but I give him thanks, wordlessly, and almost without thinking.)

The long vacation, the great vacuity, the emptiness, the desert, the absence of God: I have experienced it so many times, that absence, ever since the day when my cry went unanswered, ever since the first time I saw a little animal die before my eyes; and going on to the deaths in my family, my dead friends, the war dead, the dying, my friend in his death throes, his face suddenly smaller, sharper, horribly rejuvenated, his ears either larger or remaining too large in comparison, standing out from that emaciated head, his face staring at me with a panic-stricken tenderness as his hands rose to touch my face. The sick, the poor, the prisoners of war, the victims of torture huddled in their makeshift cells, the white-faced prisoners in the dock during the ludicrous trials of the revolution; and passing on to my own people, to myself, through despair, misery, falsehood triumphant all around us, savage hypocrisy, the double standards, the black white, the white black, midnight at noon or daylight in darkness according to the caprice of parties, the gangs and the cliques, the blindness, the hatred, the sorrow, the pitiless stupidity, the contempt for the sufferings of others.

In this world in which I now exist, at this very moment, human beings are torturing their fellow men, some human being is in his death agonies at the hands of his brother, who, his business completed, wipes those hands and laughs. Soldiers awaiting execution in a distant outpost, the shipwrecked, the passengers in crashed planes during their final seconds of life, the hostages in the hands of kidnappers who tell them they are to be 'liquidated', one by one, every hour on the hour; they are all here, at this very instant, all around me. Children are being beaten to death this very instant, somewhere on the earth, and their tears cry out to heaven. From all over the world, the cry of suffering, the moaning or the silence of those who are suffering rise up to God, who is not there. It is plain to see – he is not there. And judging by the silence that answers us, he is not there. No one is there.

I know the silence of the inner desert, the inescapable fact of God's absence. I, too, have sought all round me and in me, with that mournful sense of desolation, with the absolute dullness of the extinguished soul: no one there, I told myself. *Non est Deus:* God is not . 'The fool hath said in his heart, There is no God.' Sand and stones, some sparse, thorny scrub, and the cold wind. The freezing desert. Dryness, thirst, and forgetfulness of thirst: nothing more, no more desire for anything, no more need of anything, unless of nothingness, and the only fear left is that there will not be enough soporifics, that they may act too slowly, not strongly enough, to prevent reanimation. For 'they' drag you by main force out of your coma, they bring you back to life, in the desert, they haul you back into their world, where there is no longer either God or men. They drag you back to your lack of work, to your loneliness, to your neglected old age, to your youth without future and without hope. They waken you out of that sleep, your last and only refuge – finally at rest, finally with no awakening, finally without return among them, return to their absence. And sometimes, with their help, you emerge from that sleep with a damaged mind, the human computer irremediably on the blink; a cretin, or almost. Where are you, my God? Where were you? Why hast thou forsaken me?

I know all about that, and there must be so many of us

who know all about that. It is at this point that one must speak of God, think God, and pray. It is in our last solitude that we have to see whether God exists.

He who represents us all, our one substitute, the intermediary between us and God, was himself forsaken thus. One has been forsaken oneself, or one has had a friend, forsaken, a soldier abandoned in some God-forsaken outpost, who sees the grenades raining down, and who shouts feverishly over his walkie-talkie: 'This is us, can you hear us? Where are you? Save us.' It is the very pattern of prayer, that cry in the night over the walkie-talkie: 'Hello, is that you? Can you hear me? Over to you.' And no one answers, or else he hears only an electrostatic crackling, or distorted voices croaking, incomprehensible. You know the radio message sent out by ships that are sometimes sinking so fast, there is no time to broadcast a complete distress-call. That is the exact model of a call to God in our distress. No answer: crackling, sizzling, cacophony: but in reality the silence is dense, opaque, as if the entire universe had become one solid block of granite, and as if one were encrusted, fossilised in that slab of silence, having died without realizing it, a long, long time ago.

Our friend, our representative on the cross, made that appeal, once and for all, in our name and in the name of every living thing. I do not see him from the front; I am standing a little to one side and somewhat behind that tree of judgement. Out of the corner of my eye I can see the wood of martyrdom planted in really hard, dry clay, scattered with slabs of granite. I imagine that it is towards the beginning of the afternoon, the weather overcast, and warm. I can see the massive beam of the cross rising up; I know that there is another on my left, and one more on my right, but I can see only this one, and the nailed feet. Nailed separately, because they would have had to forge an extra-long nail to be able to pierce two superimposed feet, and no one would have gone to so much trouble.

I can see the spectators, cracking nuts, chewing gum, sniggering at their own witticisms: 'He saved others, himself he cannot save!' The sorrowful, the fearful, those who have lost all hope, women weeping, followers overcome with grief, a few of them still hoping for a miraculous deliverance at the last moment. I can hear the final howl, the most important and the most terrible last words: they are in Aramaic, because this man howling at the heavens is speaking his own tongue, here and now, always some kind of tongue, always here and now: *My God, my God, why hast thou forsaken me?*

Between the childish cry of a scared little boy and that great howl, there is a direct path, and a close link: it is always the same cry and it is always the same silence that replies. For my part, I believe it was overcast and rather warm that afternoon in Jerusalem, with a low ceiling of mackerel cloud.

3.

EVIL: WINTER TWILIGHT

It is with the death of Jesus on the cross that one must begin loving God, if one can. It is with the power of Evil that one must begin praying, or else refuse to pray, and refuse God.

I had my first vision of Evil in the spectacle of the degradation of man by man. I was four or five years old, certainly no more. I have never forgotten.

It was one winter twilight, with an intensely red sky, and the melted and re-frozen snow creaked underfoot. Somewhere there was a fence of high, black planks, and the house, black also against the chill conflagration of the heavens. But above all there were two men, face to face, and one was hitting the other across the face, unrelentingly, with all his strength, while the other just stood there, motionless, and let himself be struck without attempting to defend himself. The former, the one who was degrading the other, and thus degrading himself, degrading me, too, in a way that I have never forgotten, was my own father.

I loved him. Of all the members of our family, it was he whom I loved the most, with a love mixed with pity, for he was weak, and ended his life a beaten man. But he could love better and more intensely than all of us: he loved as a dog loves, like a slave, and with a lasting love. That brute who was humiliating a man before my eyes by hitting him across the face was not he: it was the class system. When he was still a young man, he had been given the order to shoot, in cold blood, on the pretext that they had tried to escape, a dozen peasants, hostages, in reprisal for an attack by what we today would call guerrillas.

The territorial instinct was being unleashed in its full fury among all those agrarian societies in which peasants would murder each other with spades at the edge of a field because one of them, in ploughing his land, had stolen the width of a furrow from the other. Patriotic assassins would demand that a certain angle of land should belong to a neighbouring state, just as corrupt and just as wretched, but with another flag and other customs officials. The teachers of both countries would incite children and adolescents on both sides to drench the furrows with the impure blood of the hereditary enemy, that creature by his very nature deserving of their hatred: their neighbour.

Our local murderers had struck and fled to safety, as is the habit of that kind of warrior. Now, an example had to be made: the hostages had to be assassinated. While awaiting final instructions, we made them work in the kitchen garden, to take their minds off things. They were good cultivators of the soil, and true gardeners.

That evening, the final instructions arrived. My father and mother sat up all night discussing what should be done. They agreed upon a course of action: my father asked for a written command, knowing that he would never receive one, and that he had just ruined his career. For a long time afterwards, my mother would talk to me about it with pride; she would tell me how the peasant hostages, in pleading voices with a drawling accent, implored my father's successor not to take them away under escort: 'Do not shoot us, mister officer, do not shoot us' they whined naïvely. Of course, shot they were. The plots of the kitchen garden were duly drenched, as was only fitting, with their impure blood. Except that spilt blood is never impure, and the hands that spill the blood are never pure.

And it was my father, that weak, loving, good man, who on that winter evening, at sunset, was hitting his groom across the face. I recall clearly how the long tails of his military topcoat flew round his boots at every movement. I remember also that the victim, standing rigidly to attention, his thumbs along the seams of his trousers staggered at every blow he received. His coat was shorter, and he wore no boots, only puttees. That was the army class system: officers wore a coat of finer cloth, cut from a more generous amount of material; but the army purveyors had greased the palms of civil and military officials in order to be able to sell the State shorter coats, of poor quality, for the lower ranks. And it was quite unthinkable that peasants, accustomed to walking barefoot in summer and in pigskin sandals in winter (made at home by the women) should be provided with boots.

The class system. The gentlemen in that society enjoyed the unwritten right to hit peasants in the face. Less than twenty years before I was born, those peasants had risen in revolt under the battlecry: 'Land! We want land!' They had been given land: two square metres each. The insurgent villages had been shelled, and the survivors had learnt their lesson. So the soldier allowed himself to be hit across the face still standing rigidly at attention, and staggered beneath the blows, his face slammed briskly to the right or to the left by the force of the attack. I did not see his face, which was in shadow against that sky of glacial red. All I can remember is that horrible staggering from side to side, regular as a metronome, and his standing at attention, his thumbs on the seams of his trousers. I could not understand such passivity. He never tried even to run away, much less defend himself. That was in what are called the good old days.

Now, the spot where that scene took place in my childhood has disappeared. It has all been built up. The victim is doubtless dead, fallen in battle or carried off by illness or premature old age, as is often the case with those simple country folk down there, where they eat little and badly, and even when they do have something to put in their stomachs, it is bad, always bad. As for my father, he learned no lesson from what he had experienced. What had happened to him was of no use whatsoever. When the good old days came to an end and the good new days began, with the seizure of power by a party I shall not name, but with the material support of a super-power I shall not name either, my father was imprisoned along with hundreds of thousands of other people, all as innocent as he: prosperous farmers, poor peasants who were not in agreement with the powers-that-be, people holding discredited political views, members of religious sects, Roman Catholics, Jews, homosexuals, non-conformists in art and literature, scholars who rejected the authoritarian dogma of official pseudo-scientific doctrine. He came out of prison, frightfully emaciated, with nervous diabetes of which he died after years of agony, during which his toes were amputated one by one and then his right foot. He died in poverty and despair. He was not a man of any religious conviction, could see no meaning in all that was going on around him, no order of any logical kind in the universe, and would never have dreamed of accepting his sufferings as an expiation.

From start to finish of it all: where was God? The love of God should work counter to the experience of Evil, just as prayer should work counter to the evidence of the absence of God.

I followed in my father's footsteps, and I learned that social Evil is also the evil we agree to do by obeying the laws of society, or by taking unfair personal advantage of them. I had occasion to threaten a subordinate only once, warning him that if he did not carry out a certain order which he told me was impossible, he would be dismissed from his post. Under socialism, the loss of one's post at work is even more dangerous than the loss of one's job under capitalism in deep recession. It means starvation, sickness, neurosis, perhaps suicide. I had not the slightest intention of carrying out my threat, and the poor man was prevaricating, as a good socialist subordinate, as a good subject of all-powerful bureaucracy intent on preserving his nervous composure, his small private stock of energy. The order was carried out. But I can still see him standing before me, surly, humiliated, reduced to impotent silence, and constrained to obey. After assassination and sadistic crime, what I detest most in this world is rape, that rape which is always the violation of someone's will. Women are not its only victims: for one sexual rape, there are a hundred non-sexual ones.

I in my turn received an order from on high, from Central Headquarters: a certain percentage of employees were to be sacked. The State, that gigantic Beast with sullen, bleary eyes, that through sheer stupidity devours its own paws, was embarking upon a reducing diet. We all know those internal convulsions that from time to time attack mammoth organizations. Except that down there one had neither an emergency exit, nor a hiding place, nor any refuge or right of appeal: the union was one and indivisible, and cosubstantial with the State, the Party, the Five-Year Plan and the People's Police. The unemployed became lost souls. Their one boss, the State, was going to sack those employed and was not going to reinstate them in its service, and there was no other employer, there were no other positions. In the West someone asked me: 'Why didn't they protest?' One old lady even told me: 'They should have written to the papers, or to their Members of Parliament'. But there was no newspaper, there were no Members of Parliament but the State: the State was God, and there was no one else one could turn to – neither God nor man.

In a meeting with the technical supervisor, the union secretary and the president of the trade union committee (who held his tongue – yet another occasion when I learned to pity and despise that type of trade union, and when my fierce devotion to trade union ideals became if possible even fiercer), I had to select those employees whom I was condemning to starvation, to madness and perhaps to suicide. My task as works' manager was to convey to them in person the news of their dismissal. I had to tell them to their faces – men of fifty and over, fathers of families whose eyes filled with tears of despair. I was then what they call in French 'a young wolf '. Man is a young wolf to his fellow men. But then the young beast discovers that he himself was after all nothing but a man, and that there is nothing of the wolf left in him but grey hairs. In the space of a single generation, first under socialism, and then under capitalism, I have witnessed entire bands of young wolves falling beneath the axe, like a forest to the lumberjack. They cannot understand what is happening to them: the new arrivals leap to attack them, with bared fangs, and a little later they get the chop, in the form of trade recession, a new Party general line, technical revolution, subterranean shiftings of human strata; and they are laid low beneath the axe, they wither and disappear, like the successive series of young revolutionaries, *Contestataires,* protesters, terrorists, urban guerrillas, as well as the resigned, the indifferent, the 'recommencers' – having learned and understood nothing; or else repeating the Devil's antic refrain: 'There's nothing to understand.'

With the passage of time, I in my turn was thrown out onto the jobless dump and into the pit of despair by a young wolf, who now has himself had time to become human again, to suffer and understand – that is, if he has understood anything.

My sub-manager, a woman, had to announce her dismissal to another woman fellow-worker, an exceptionally fine and sensitive creature, in her fifties like herself. That distinguished woman had absolutely no hope left. She went straight home and hanged herself.

My sub-manager had been a heroine of the clandestine resistance. She had been arrested and tortured by the capitalist police without betraying her comrades, and their tortures left her lamed for life. But she did not go straight home and hang herself. She had adapted. She had become opportunist, cowardly, vile. Her husband died young. She too met a premature death.

In my own case, I chose liberty and structured unemployment. I chose to become a dropout, a jobless intellectual in structured unemployment, a nonconformist, saying 'No' to the Left, in a free society, in which the State arrogates to itself only sixty per cent of the economy, in which left and right are implacably opposed, and both just as implacably opposed to anyone who is not one of them, and in which power and property are, as everywhere else, commensurate with power and deceit – I had to go through all that. To be out of work and a greying father of a family under the cult of youth is just the same as being without work, without party, under the 'cult of the personality'.

At this very instant in which men are torturing their fellow-men in Latin America or in Africa, in which political prisoners are rotting away in the gulags between the Elbe and the Sea of Okhotsk, and in which hostages exist in timeless twilight in the private prisons of the West, the unemployed vegetate at home, dishonoured, pitied or despised by their own families, suffering psychic castration, stupefied by continuous social humiliation for months and years. They wander aimlessly, looking in shop windows, soaking up publicity for luxury consumer goods, leisure activity clubs, colour supplement photo essays on the lives of playboys, the stars of show business and famous advertising models. And for the hundredth time the politicians, looking him straight in the eye from the small screen – actually they are looking with a blind eye at the blind eye of the TV camera – tell the man without work that the recession has bottomed out for good this time. They have been telling him that ten times a year for the last ten years, relentlessly. But even if this time they were not mistaken, let alone not telling a barefaced lie, the man without work is too old now: soon a law will be passed forbidding him to work on account of his age. Work kills off the majority of those who work too long; but inactivity also kills off those who want to work. Never mind, they reject him: 'You are too old, we must make way for the young.' At the same time, his son is also unemployed, given the excuse that 'You cannot offer us the same guarantees of steady production as experienced workers, mature men...'

It is not just blows to the face that degrade a man. It is not just active malice, hatred, desire to wound and destroy that can be Evil. Evil requires no class society, no capitalist exploitation, no police terror, no Tartar socialism. All it requires is some mammoth organization somewhere, any-where on this earth. All it requires is someone with a heart of stone in a key position. All it requires is absence of heart.

I am not standing in judgement, but expressing repent-ance. For I, too, have ridden rough-shod over the suffer-ings of another, I too have despised people older than myself, I too have passed by the weak without a helping hand and the desperate without a word of comfort. I find it is right that now I should suffer in my turn. 'We cannot take you on before our own people: you're an alien.' 'You are too old, not sufficiently qualified.' Or on the other hand: 'All I have to do is step outside to find on the job market young people who will cost me less and whom I can train myself.' I accept my suffering as an infinitesimal contribution towards the re-equilibrium of a world on the skids. But the suffering of others?

Under socialism, a dozen of my acquaintances, men and women, have committed suicide. My wife was merely tempted to do so: a former militant in danger of her life, then having to face up to full-blown socialism – it was understandable. I myself was tempted three times – but here, on the job market of the free world.

The first time was a dozen years ago, when three of my friends all committed suicide in the same long, hot summer. One was a brilliant dancer from my country: an *émigré* despicably vilified by the left, he killed himself. Then the greatest post-war Polish prose writer: having sought everywhere in the West somewhere to put down roots, one evening in Wiesbaden he stuffed himself with sleeping pills and, like a true Pole, drank an entire bottle of whisky to put the finishing touch to it. The third had written the most beautiful post-holocaust poem in German, and did himself honour, for he was a young Jew from Tchernovtsy, whose parents had gone to the gas chambers and the incinerator. The poem was not appreciated: some were embarrassed by it; the left, returning from comfortable exile in American universities, objected to the beauty of the poem – something more ugly was required. He escaped, sought refuge in Paris, lived there all alone; he, too, took too many sleeping tablets, and to make doubly sure staggered down into the street as far as the Seine, and threw himself in. At our last meeting, after dinner at my place, after those heavy, over-succulent dishes that used to fill Carlsbad with Roumanian boyars and Galician Jews, we sang the choruses of revolutionary Austro-Marxist songs. Foreign dropouts...

But not all ended that way. The latest suicide was here at home, in his own country, in his own city, in his own university – comfortably off, young, with a brilliant future. But exposed every day to the humiliations inflicted upon him at every lecture by student commandos with a taste for ritual murder...The only people who, fifty years later, reminded me of my father's groom, slapped about for a quarter of an hour without relaxing his stand-at-ease posture, were the non-Marxist professors in German universities. This one did not protest. He hanged himself in his bathroom, from the hook on the back of the door where he used to hang his bathrobe

It was the fashion to proceed coldly with the business of the day, and to approve the actions of young terrorists. Now that they have begun to overdo things, it is the fashion to condemn them. But just this evening I heard that one of the young Moluccans imprisoned in Holland for kidnapping and assassination of hostages, and who was responsible for causing his chance and utterly innocent victims definite and incurable psychic traumatisms, had hanged himself in his cell. All those who hang themselves in the cells are Jesus Christ on the cross. My God, my God, why hast though forsaken us?

But to our cry of distress he could reply: why have you forsaken each other? I granted you forgetfulness of suffering and forgetfulness of offences: why do you use this gift to forget your sins? Is it just so that you need not repent, that you need not learn from your experiences, and never repeat them?

For we are all sons of the twentieth century, the age of illuminations, of the dizzying increase of scientific knowledge; the age of demystification, of the smashing of taboos, of rationalism and emancipation surpassing and making obsolete all naïve anthromorphisms, religious fantasms, metaphysical fancies, religions, dogmas. Not far from here, all round the town of Verdun, three hundred thousand Germans are buried, killed in the flower of their youth, for nothing. At Thermopylae, there were three hundred Spartans. But here, twice three hundred thousand, in obedience to the laws, in blind acceptance of the commandments of our civilization, shed their young blood on every square foot of ground, for nothing. And then, less than a generation later, they started all over again. And now, again one generation later, at least those two nations have got the message; but the super-powers, those with populations of over a hundred or two hundred millions, are ready to pounce once more. How can we not weep with grief and admiration for the heroism and the patience of the common people, and not weep with rage at the folly and stupidity of those in power? How can we not long to demolish a society that allowed, or caused, two fratricidal world wars, and that other society, down there in the East, that is coldly and scientifically preparing a third?

And already human bones are bleaching and burnt-out tanks are rusting in the Sinai desert...My God, why have we forsaken one another? At Christmas, 1914, the German and British soldiers fraternized in the trenches: strict orders were given, and those who allowed themselves to be human were shot out of hand. Sixty-five years later, socialist recruits are brainwashed into hating the foreign enemy, who is the class enemy, the capitalist, the imperialist enemy, the 'yellow peril'. Society, élites, history, the State, the army, the homeland, the Church, the Party, the mammoth organizations, the giant enterprises, the classes, the races, the people: can that really be the face of God, or is it the true face of man? I am not attempting to justify God; I am saying that we should take responsibility for a part of Evil.

A quarter of a century ago, I was contributing to the construction of socialism, by writing a book on one of those 'great useless works' which in fact have meanwhile disappeared from the steppes. At first, they were labour camps, half-heroic, half-deplorable. But then suddenly other camps appeared among them, clean, well-ordered, unapproachable: barbed wire fences, watchtowers, shoot on sight – they were the gulags. All books on the great work sites of socialism are palimpsests, with invisible writing between the lines, telling the history of those 're-education through labour' camps – what we in the West call recycling, but more drastic. The prisoners there do not drag iron balls around on their feet: but I am still dragging my iron ball and chain, and they are very heavy – the pages I wrote on the processes of socialist re-education.

Before leaving to visit the 'free' workers' labour camps – comparatively 'free' – I attended a conference of Workers for Peace and heard a speech by the famous Dean of Canterbury: he praised to the heavens that great work-site of socialism, which he had just visited. I heard him with

my own ears, I saw him with my own eyes: he looked a bit
of a freak, a caricature, like a Dickens eccentric, like some
ham actor playing at being a prince of the Anglican
Church – not without charm, of course, with his white
hair and rosy face, but perhaps too naïve.

Then I went on my tour of inspection; I returned by
train across the Tartar steppe. Outside the windows, we
could see barbed wire fences, watchtowers, a dead horse –
no doubt about it. Beside me, some young Italian comrades, returning like me from a visit to the great work sites
of socialism, were discussing Hegel. I can still hear in my
mind the marvellous euphony of those melodious voices
pronouncing *Hegal, Hegal* like *Eagle, Eagle* or *Egg-el,
Egg-el*! And there before their very eyes – their blind or
blinded eyes – were the barbed wire fences, the watchtowers, the armed guards, who killed to order. I ought to have
given those Italians a good shake; have shouted the truth at
them, had myself denounced by them to the authorities, in
naïve zeal, or in internationalist solidarity. But I stayed
silent, the train went on, there was nothing but the empty
steppe, the empty heavens, the silence. The silence of
God? Ever since then, I have come to suspect that a part of
God's silence is my own; that a part of God's absence is
nothing but the absence of our own hearts, of our humanity, of our friendship – I would not venture to say our
love, for we are not capable of love. The absences of the
human heart sometimes last a long time. Then who are we
to judge God?

I am saying that we must take upon ourselves a part of
Evil, but I am not attemtping to justify God. Evil is more
mysterious, more vast. It is our work; but we are not our
work.

4.

EVIL: CHRISTMAS PIG, EASTER LAMB

The assassination of our Christmas pig is one of my oldest memories. It was far away, at the end of the yard belonging to our house. We lived in the provinces. It was freezing hard, the ground was as hard as stone, the sky was grey; and down there at the end of the yard was the pig trying to escape. He was recaptured, thrown on his back, and a human swarm descended upon him. There were probably no more than three of them, but in the faraway of memory they seem to me more numerous: half a dozen of them, men and women. Busy, silent, dangerous.

The pig was screaming. Beasts know fear all right, they experience terror in their brief, clouded protoconsciousness with their often astonishing remembrance of sufferings and satisfactions. We are all automatons, as the eighteenth century told us, men-machines, said La Mettrie, men-plants – that is, computers. We have lucid minds, we can apply reason, we fear death, we know anguish of the spirit, joy of the soul, we have a moral conscience in addition to the computer. We have grace; but the beasts know fear as we do.

Alas, Descartes denied them a soul, and even Wittgenstein notes that 'if a lion could speak, we would not understand him.' That remark, or rather the proposition behind it, can already be found outlined in Lichtenberg: 'If an angel were one day to tell us something of his philosophy, I think that many of his propositions would seem like double Dutch to us.' And he repeats the idea in a variant about Jacob Boehme. That is perhaps true as far as angels are concerned, but the study of animal behaviour had taught us to understand lions and to communicate with dolphins. Now that we have almost exterminated them, we are at last beginning to talk to the animals. Ethnologists have recorded more than thirty different sounds uttered by pigs, creatures more intelligent than many other animal species, and cleaner than we think: in the wild, they wallow in the mud to protect their oversensitive skins. It's not dirt, but foundation cream, and we alone are to blame if we shut them up in pigsties with their own excrement.

They understand, they feel frightened; that one was howling with terror. The human beings were wrestling with him; they got him to the ground and a man got astride the victim's body. Indelible movement – rapid, vigorous, effective – of murderous australopithecus teamwork. The instrument was produced, a killing blade like a knife from the beginning of time. We have to admit the truth, we have to make ourselves conscious of the fact that we bear within us a murderous aggressiveness, and that we have to sublimate it, if we will, and as much as we can. Adam the murderer. We still survive, as a species, because we know how to control our dangerous instincts, by countering them with our good instincts – first of all the most important one, friendship, which makes man the brother of man. We have to learn to rationalize the natural process that causes us to spread out in ever vaster groups, and finally to all humanity, perhaps to all living creatures, the sense of solidarity that informs the little band of primitive huntsmen. The instinct of friendship is stronger than the predatory instinct, and it leads in a straight line from Adam australopithecus to Jesus Christ, and from Jesus Christ to each one of us.

The instrument was a blade, a knife with a grey blade, grown shorter from its many whettings. I did not see the operation distinctly. I did not really understand what they were doing to that beast howling with despair, and I do not remember when and how his screams came to an end. But I remember the jet of bright red blood that shot out of the pig's broad neck. A woman was holding a clay pot under that jet. Then she passed in front of me, running to the kitchen. At dinner, I saw that pot again, filled with dark brown blood, thickly curdled, like scrambled eggs, with an appetising aroma, brought straight from the oven and set on the table. I ate some of it. I can no longer recall its taste.

In the country, you drink milk fresh from the cow, and that still retains the warmth of the animal's body: you see buckets of milk with the temperature of a living body. You eat a dish of fresh blood. You see hens decapitated and running around without heads while thin jets of blood jerk out of the stumpy neck. You see turkey cocks and hens turning pale, the skin of their wattles passing from violet to light blue, at the sight of one of their number being put to death. You muck out the stable and the pigsty, not a very pleasant job, shovelling out piles of dung. Sometimes you have to empty the tank set under the hole in the wooden seat of the lean-to of planks that serves as a privy: you pass two poles through the iron rings screwed to the sides, a farm lad in front, you behind, and slap-bang-wallop the pair of you transport a hundred kilos of human mess to be buried, or to be spread on the vegetable garden plots, or on the potato field. Knocking muck, it's called.

The drama of little pigs operated on by the castrator is fairly comical, but the slaughterhouse is nothing to laugh at. It is done in a cold, damp room, a narrow place like a cut-throat's alley. The beast is led in through a narrow passage, into this executing hall. A man deals it a blow with an axe between the horns, or lets it have a bullet point-blank in the middle of the forehead, while another man shoves for all he's worth the already-dead body, so that it may fall sideways, instead of collapsing flat on its belly and blocking the passage. Quick, the chop, quick, give it the push, always that quickness, that silent dexterity of men who have been slaughterers since the beginning of time.

With the fat from the Christmas pig we made a crude soap for the wash, a grey, rough stuff that hardly lathers in the water, and that stinks of dead bodies. For days on end, the grease simmered in the big cauldron in the middle of the yard till the air reeked of the stuff, the stink of death and rotten corpses permeating everything. The sausages smelt of garlic. The ham smelt of wood smoke. But I can well understand that my own children, when they were very small, refused to eat prawns, because the creatures had all-too-recognizable eyes as they lay there on the dish. Boiled, but still eyes.

In that old yard where I witnessed the assassination of the Christmas pig, we made friends, later, with the Easter lamb, bought in the market a while before the festival. He was so cute, with his little muzzle, so fine, so delicate, his big round cheeks furred with tightly curled wool. He had a childlike air, and it was lovely to cuddle him in my arms. He was a child, a sheep's child, but still a child, more of a child than we, children of men.

We were not present at the sacrifice, but we met our friend again, chopped into pieces, on the table, roasted or boiled: boiling was especially favoured for the head, which remained recognizable on top of a mound of goodies – the brain, with its pretty convolutions, its lobes and its two hemispheres, the kidneys, the liver and I don't know what else. For us, the ram's testicles were also considered a delicacy, and the cow's sexual parts.

Raised like that, accustomed to feeling my mouth water at the smell of roast meat or at the sight of a juicy steak, I have been a carnivore all my life. But I had a problem with meat from beasts I had known personally, and loved as only children and animals love one another: to eat that beast, to see its beloved head boiled, the eyes boiled and then to have to eat it – that was a bit too much.

Young people who can live for weeks and months with a man they have kidnapped and imprisoned, long enough to get to know him, to discuss with him, to understand him, even if they do not agree with him, to take pity on him, even if they cannot love him, to get used to him, even if they hate him, and who then kill him, and kill him in cold blood, are deliberately transforming him, knowing well what they are doing, from an admirable living machine, from a creative computer endowed with reason and conscience, accessible to grace, transforming him into a pile of dead meat, fit only to be eaten roasted or boiled to make crude soup – such young people seem to me hard to understand.

My experience of the assassination of animals – something I have done with my own hands – makes me look with somewhat jaundiced eyes at the beauty of ancient altars and the cult of the gods of antiquity. I see upon the Altar of Augustus the bull, his eyes bandaged with a towel, so that he will not make any sudden sideways step when he catches sight of the axe. I see the sacrificer beside him, axe in hand. The temples were very beautiful, the gods were very beautiful, but their mass was massacre, with a Hup! as the axe thudded between the horns, then the push to make the beast fall on the proper side, the slitting open of the belly, the odour of bowels – that is, a stink of shit – and their reverences the High Priests examining the entrails in order to divine the future by their oracles. The ceremony of the ancients was butchery. And one must read the Scandinavian sagas to find out how it was done among the peoples of the North – the aspergillum dipped in a basin of blood, the walls of the temple splashed with blood. That can still be seen in Indonesia and in the Philippines, and in Gurka ceremonies: one blow of their little broad-bladed sabre and the calf's head, pulled forward, drops to the ground. Then they catch the corpse by the hind legs and drag it all round the perimeter of the sacred place, for as long as the blood continues to pulse from the severed neck, thus marking the boundaries of the holy area. When the first victim has been drained of blood, they decapitate the second one.

'Sacrifice', *sacrum facio*, 'I made sacred', from *sacer, sacrum,* 'separated', 'taboo'. It was fortunate for us that the destiny of the Jews sundered them once and for all from their land and their holy city with its temple and its great sacrificial altar. In exile in Babylon, then in the Exodus and the Diaspora over all the shores of the Mediterranean, they developed the custom of symbolic sacrifice, without blood – a little bread and wine, with lighted torches. If it had not been for that, we would have had butcheries on the altars of our churches every Sunday.

But to get back to our paschal lamb and our Christmas pig: I remember having seen on the outer walls of the cathedral of Etchmiadzine, in Armenia, the splashes of blood made by pigeons sacrificed by peasants, who probably do not know that these creatures were sacred not to the Virgin Mother, but to the Venus of Urartu, Anahit, Anaïtis, four thousand years ago.

The Hindus teach us that a simple offering of flowers is enough. There is also the sacrifice of things that are good to eat – but without blood – fruits, a cake, bread. In the Orthodox Church to which I belong, we place on the tomb, at a certain date after the burial, a dish of semolina, honey and crushed nuts, a neolithic rite in the cult of the dead. After the consecration by the priest, this dainty is shared by the family and friends of the dead person. We children were delighted whenever anyone died, because this cake was delicious, and was not available at any other time, as no one would have dreamed of preparing it for profane purposes.

So we have learned to simplify and purify the thing. There remains, in the last analysis, the sacrifice of the heart, as Christians say, the offering of oneself, the gift of one's soul. Instead of the slaughtered beast, we have fruit, bread and wine. Next, instead of these external symbols,

something from deep within ourselves: prayer. And finally, instead of prayer which asks for something, prayer
which simply addresses itself to God. From start to finish,
there is an uninterrupted continuity.

Unlike politics, religion has freed itself from human
sacrifices. Unlike the sporting arts, it has liberated itself
from animal sacrifices. But still we have not cast off from
our lives the most ancient profession known to man: that
of the slaughterer. The mass-massacre no longer exists;
but the butcheries of daily life still remain with us.

There is that cliff somewhere in France, at the foot of
which repose the fossilized bones of forty thousand wild
horses, hounded, hunted and terrorized by our ancestors
and driven over the edge of the abyss. What a feast at the
foot of the cliff, what a well-nourished tribe, what a
corpse-like stink in the valley, and what a waste! For the
species of *equus przewalski* is extinct. We are the extermina-
tors of animal and human races – the Neanderthals, the
Tasmanians and certain Amerindians are our most notable
victims.

I am speaking as a carnivore, as a former hunter, butcher
if necessary, according to the custom of the country, when
times were bad. True, the last time, I had turned my eyes
away at the last minute and the axe took off the tip of my
left thumb, because I was holding the beast steady with
my left hand. Clumsy, irresolute butcher, who did not
have his mind on his job, but a butcher all the same. I
respect butchers, surgeons, dentists, soldiers, scavengers,
physiologists who dissect hundreds of thousands of living
creatures every year, and then kill them, painlessly I hope,
in their research for who knows what new nostrum,
sometimes efficacious, sometimes useless. They take upon
themselves tasks that are hard, painful, insupportable, and
without which we should not be able to survive. They
carry a burden that is too heavy for the rest of us. But I
cannot help seeing before me that sort of underground
chamber, cold and damp, those hurried gestures, those

animals so like ourselves in the admirable functioning of their bodies with their traces of soul, and then think of what we do to them.

However, even if we discovered the means and had the desire to reconcile ourselves with the animals, the universe of fear and massacre would still remain almost unchanged all around us. I am not preaching a conversion to vegetarian foods; there are more urgent matters to consider, and everyone has to decide for himself. But the techniques of the slaughterer and the predator can be replaced by those of the gardener: those who say it is impracticable do not know what they are talking about. It would give us a humanity probably very different from what we have now, and no worse. But the universe of murder and assassination would remain all the same.

There are millions of animal species, every one of which ends by being consumed. I have seen a gang of lionesses around a buffalo who refused to be beaten: one of them leaped on his back and clung there, waiting until the legs of her prey slowly buckled under the weight of her one hundred or one hundred and fifty kilos. I have seen a small gnu bleating in the jaws of a lion, its head and forelegs dangling to the right, its bottom and hind legs to the left of the lion's mouth. And I shall never forget the reflex shudders of an antelope being devoured alive.

Almost all the prey of flesh-eating creatures are devoured alive; few are killed beforehand, with a blow to the spine or with jaws sunk in the throat. Certainly, the penumbra of their brains diminishes their sufferings, and men who have escaped from the jaws of wild beasts give us cause to hope that the prey is always anaesthetized by the nervous shock. (Yet another of nature's curious arrangements, an anthropomorphic entity of modern science, similar to the process of symbiosis, the sexual couplings with numerous and complex phases, culminating in the death of one of the pair devoured by the other yet still copulating even after its head has been bitten off;

machiavellian larval cycles, unimaginable mimetisms, whole colonies of insects in the form of flowers, of flowers that never existed, menacing eyes painted on the scales of fish near the tail or under the belly; all those subterfuges, all those stratagems of secondary and tertiary motivation, inexplicable without the intelligent deliberations of the species, another anthropomorphism, manipulating beings, constructing them to the specifications of some distant, indirect design, similar to the far-seeing manoeuvres of a chess player – all that incredible astuteness, inhuman and nightmarish, gives us pause. But for the moment I am confining myself to statistical causality and determinism, at the same time not losing sight of the fact that there is something more than just that.)

I shall not attempt to deny that death may be a lesser suffering than the terror of death and even than the encounter with a predator, or that pain and fear are indispensable preservation mechanisms for individuals and species, regulators of ecosystems. Even though I am well aware of the teleological flavour of the very notion of a regulator, in so far as it is not defined in a strictly determinist and causal fashion; for if not, it implies foreknowledge, or at least prevision, or at the very least the gifts of projection, of hypothesis that, so far at any rate, are proper to man alone.

Nature, the species, remain, until they can be endowed with a mathematical definition, myths, 'fantasms' far worse than that God rejected by the very people who freely employ these anthropomorphic fictions. The only principles of explanation that I can accept are, once again, causal determinism and statistical determinism; teleology is not an explanation. Yet I am not blind, I see what I see, and what I see is that there is something else there. And that something else is not 'the hand of God': we must not reduce the concept of God to these levels reserved for scientific explanation.

Nevertheless, I see what I see: and that is that the

universe of living things is permeated with suffering, and that even the spectacle of that suffering is suffering. I cannot carry on my conversation with God and ignore the constituent suffering of life. The spectacle of the mad temerity of a beast offering itself to a predator in order to save its little ones is painful to me, whether it be a gazelle of the savannahs or a water-bird in the Delta of my native Danube whose nest is being attacked by a marten. Creation has been witnessing since the beginning of time, every God-given day, the useless heroism of mothers, who in the end are themselves also devoured. And at the same time I have watched mothers of the same species of great gazelles running in zigzag courses to get rid of little ones who had lost their own mothers and were attempting to find new mothers so as to be able to suck their milk and thus survive the next few hours, to gain enough strength to run and escape the attacks of carnivores. One can read in Eibl-Eibesfeldt a report on the mechanism which transforms into deglutition the movements of mothers of certain species who are licking their young and in the end devour them: for nothing is simple, and the universe is mathematicable, but incomprehensible – really incomprehensible, and really constructed according to a plan that is not a human one. We have been inserted into this universe, we form a part of it with every particle of energy in our beings. We began by killing in all innocence and we have been killed, in all innocence, by other predators and are still being killed by micro-organisms. But our sanguinary evolution, in all its innocence, has led us to the knowledge of good and evil, of taboo and transgression, to a consciousness of sin. There is no return possible to the innocence of the herbivore, nor to the innocence of the flesh-eater. We have been led, and have come, to liberty, that hesitation in the computer. Our instincts are out of sync, scrambled, we have forever lost our innocence, that is to say our immediacy. So here we are hesitating between aggression and friendship, that age-old aggressiveness and that amity that is even more ancient and even more profound, both implanted in us by the same experimenter.

What is it you want of us? What does that something unknown, incomprehensible and supremely difficult want of us, if not the impossible itself? Why are we chained to an unbearable system, and to the ineradicable compulsion to free ourselves from its limitations? Why can we not bear our condition, and yet not free ourselves from its limitations?

The question is not just 'Why hast thou forsaken us?' It is also 'What do you want of us? Why do you insist on the impossible – that we strive always to free ourselves from those limitations?'

5.

EVIL: PLANTING A TREE

I do not care much for Martin Luther; in fact I do not like him at all. But how could I refuse my admiration, my affection, my Christian love, to a man who said: 'If I knew that the world was to perish tomorrow, I would plant a little apple tree today.' And who said too that God keeps a place in paradise for little dogs and cats. The man was a hero, and better than a hero, he was a man, and better than a man, he had in a corner of his soul a tiny flicker of the soul of Saint Francis of Assisi. Moreover, his letters to his wife are of a charming tenderness and full of humour. He remains the great Reformer of the Christian Church. May the peace of God be with him.

The proverb tells us we must plant a tree, build a house and raise a child in the life of man. Here in Megalopolis, between West Berlin and Los Angeles, Montreal and Sao Paulo, we must build a machine that functions without fault, provide an impeccable service rather than plant a tree. As for myself, I have never built any house, I have lived in the houses of the people, that is, of the State, that is, of Bureaucracy, and then in the houses of the rich who screwed a usurious rent out of me; they made my realize why Jesus said they would find it difficult to enter the kingdom of heaven. As for my children, it was not I, but their mother, who brought them up. And my profession was writing books, though I have not written a single one that pleased me. But I have planted a tree.

It happened behind the farmyard in which my sister was wounded on the forehead (and where I nearly amputated

my thumb with an axe as I played the distracted butcher).
It was where the path climbed up the hill along the hedge
towards the rock silhouetted against the sky. In the same
place, another day, I saw a snake beaten to death with a
stick, and another time I heard a dog being stoned to
death. I say 'heard': the howls of pain cut short by the final
stone, well-aimed, smashing the skull. Both times, the
killer was our tenant farmer, a big, strapping peasant, a
great hunter and poacher, who loved to kill. At the end of
the second technocratic fratricidal world war, he offered
his services as a volunteer in the execution squads which
exterminated the German farmers of the Banat region of
Yugoslavia, our neighbour. They made them dig their
own graves, for hard labour is neither as agreeable nor as
easy as killing. He crossed the frontier to take part in that
gala. Here, he had killed only what Saint Francis would
have called Brother Snake and our Brother the Dog.
Besides, the Germans – not those who were shot, but the
others, the desk-bound bureaucrats and the executioners
who found themselves trapped between the order to kill
and the threat of being hanged for disobedience – had
killed the Jews in exactly the same way, in front of graves
dug by the victims. Now it was the turn of the Germans,
with farmers instead of the S.S.; they were paying them
back in their own coin, as certain Christians of my
acquaintance say. Since then, they have been massacring
Germans in effigy in films about the resistance and the
war, as they massacre redskins in cowboy movies. Under
Hitler, I felt myself a Jew. When I see such films, I feel
myself a redskin or a German. And before that brave
peasant with his cudgel and his lumps of rock, I felt myself
a snake and a dog. So it goes, in an endless vicious circle,
and we blame the Devil for the Evil we do, and for the
Evil we tolerate, and for the Evil we do not prevent, and
which we dare not condemn.

   That was the spot where my mother made me plant a
young walnut. The afternoon was cold and windy, with

flakes of snow driven sideways, melting on my face, wetting the grass. Barely had I filled in the hole and left the little tree to fend for itself henceforward in life, with its foot in the earth and its head in the wind, than we had to see to a newborn lamb that seemed on the point of death.

He had everything, except the will to live. It was a pure death: neither from illness, nor wounds, nor out of weariness of existence; he died because he did not want to live. We carried him into the stable, then into the kitchen, in front of the fire: perhaps the warmth would revive him.

It was frightening to watch him depart this life in such a way, so simply, for no reason: he was already far gone, quite limp, his eyes clouded, his neck bent. Beasts and men die in the postures of cut grass. He was not suffering, he was just passing away; it was we who somehow were suffering to see it, to see that flicker of life, that feeble glow, dying, fading away, going heaven knows where. One of Webster's heroines says as she dies:

> My soul, like to a ship in a black storm,
> Is driven, I know not whither.

But death is often gentler, a falling asleep. But it is death. We think nothing of the loss of a future wool-bearing ram, of a future ewe, mother of a whole flock. But we cannot think just nothing of that painless departure, that with-drawal from life, erased like a faint pencil stroke on a white page, that becomes white again.

By that time, we had already had deaths in our family and among our friends. My grandmother had died, we had followed a friend of my mother to her last resting place. I knew well that curious, earthy physiognomy, that curious shut look, and the secret smile of the dead. Later I was to know the distracted look of those who had died a violent death – the sagging jaw, the rictus, or the tongue sticking out of open lips, and a dead man carried upside down by clumsy bearers. I was to see rotting corpses, monstrous bags of corruption. But that newborn lamb who let himself go as if he were being carried away by a current it was useless to fight against, and whom we were absolutely incapable of rescuing, was lesson enough for me.

Chapter two of death is when someone you love with all your heart is taken from you, on a hospital trolley, from the anaesthetist to the operation room, head fallen to one side, head and temple heavy on the pillow, in the profound slumber of narcosis, the face puffy, darkened by the intoxication of the sleep-inducing drug, with an almost sombre, almost angry expression – perhaps never to wake again, never to return. There is not only the pain of death, there is also the pain of not being first to die. It is horrible to be left standing on the station platform.

Yet we are very fortunate. God has really had pity on us. Doctors, chemists, physiologists have saved us from the horrors of physical pain, have prolonged our lives. Women no longer die giving birth, two or three children in four do not die soon after being born, their mothers no longer suffer like beasts, their maternal instinct stricken by death. All women had to suffer in the same way: one has only to read the agony of the Princess Palatine, as terrible as any peasant woman's, save that the former could write; one has only to read the memoirs of the lady companion of Mrs Longfellow on her travels in Europe, on the night of her mistress's miscarriage – the days and weeks of agony under her husband's helpless gaze. Or again, in the *Journal* of the Goncourts, the story of the young woman warned by her doctors that a pregnancy would kill her, but whom her husband forces to sleep with him; she becomes pregnant and does indeed die in childbirth, cursing her husband and her God for murdering an innocent woman, for killing both her and her child. That was in the time of my grandmother or great-grandmother, not so very long ago. God has taken pity on us, but for millions of years no one and nothing could relieve suffering and hold off the pains of death. And even now, right near where I live, that couple's child fell into the swimming pool and was drowned; another is condemned by an illness of the respiratory tracts which makes his mucous membranes swell until he dies of suffocation – he died, in fact, before reaching puberty, as foreseen, as was expected, expected for years. My God, why hast thou abandoned us to death? Life is nothing but a protracted ambush, a trap with a little pleasure as bait.

Even were I to go blind, I could not close my eyes to the vision of Evil. I am not attempting to justify God. But I do not deny him. I am asking him: why hast thou forsaken us? I ask it as an echo to the question of Jesus on the cross: and that question was a plea, not a reproach, it was not a negation. It was nothing but a cry of pain, the greatest, and the last. For only silence is the answer to that question. I am tempted to call it a terrible silence, the silence of God, a terrifying silence. But adjectives are not needed. Silence is the one reply. There is no reply.

Once again, it is Jesus who teaches us the reply, for it is we who provide it; his real last words at the end were in the Garden of the Mount of Olives: 'O my Father, if it be possible, let this cup pass from me: nevertheless not as I will, but as thou wilt.' It is the impossible that is asked of us.

6.

EVIL: DUSTY FEET

Two bare feet, grey with dust and dried mud. The left foot had a big open wound: living flesh, bleeding, with white and yellowish spots, of pus, maybe.

The whole man was grey with dust, his clothes were of the same pale grey, his face too; even his voice was grey. The dust was not the dust of our roads: or rather, though there was some of that, it was mainly stone-breaker's dust.

He had been working in the quarry, open to the sky, and a loose rock, rolling down the slope, had brushed his foot. The rock had only brushed it, not rolled over it, or the foot would have been crushed. But now the man could no longer work. He had left. He was making his way on foot, limping, straight along the road.

'And what will you do?'

He did not know.

'Where are you going?'

He did not know that either.

My mother had taken me for a ride in a car, in the motor car belonging to her close friend, the wife of my father's boss: an open-top Buick, a most impressive vehicle, with a chauffeur. The wheel spokes were of massive oak and there was a starting-handle dangling from its nose. Along the road, we had seen that grey silhouette, that solitary wanderer limping slowly along. The ladies made the chauffeur stop the car. They questioned the poor chap. They were Christians, compassionate, readers of Russian novels. In end end, we set off again, without offering that man anything, neither work, nor a lodging, nor money. He set off also, limping, all alone, without hope, without protection, without anything: forsaken.

Ever since, and for the rest of my days, I have been a union member. That man was not in any union.

Later, I had experience of trade unions under Tartar socialism. As a journalist, a reporter for the Party newspaper, I have seen, in a steelworks, swinging between the tall furnaces and the rows of wagons loaded with steel ingots radiating heat at a distance of twenty feet, turning from pale rose to soft grey, skips of ore coming in over our heads from the nearby mine, and covered with chalk marks saying: *we need dungarries (sic)*. The workers did not dare speak up in trade union meetings to ask for them. I was standing beside the Party trade union secretary of the factory committee and the president of the trade union committee of management, and they did not see what was right before their eyes; they went on talking about some production problem, like the young Italian marxists who went on talking about Hegel in front of the barbed wire fences and watchtowers of the gulags along the Danube-Black Sea Canal.

A socialist management head of an enterprise owned by the people – meaning bureaucracy, Central Headquarters, the handful of men ruling the Central Headquarters – I worked with the president of the management committee, a sad sack who had no voice in the chapter. There was the local Party secretary, there was the managing director, and that was all. The president of the trade union management committee belonged nowhere.

Ever since, and for the rest of my days, I have been a supporter of free trade unions. For me, there exist religious freedom, freedom of thought, political freedom and trade union freedom. There is the Church, there are freely elected parliaments, from the commune to the continental federation, and there are trade unions. They exist for the health of the soul, for liberty and dignity under the law, and for the protection of the workers. In my eyes, the trade unionist combines something of the dignity of the law and the sacred character of the priesthood. I know what I am talking about: not a priest in liturgical vestments, but a poor priest in a worn cassock or clerical grey, or in some indefinable collection of garments, like my very dear and reverend father and brother in Jesus Christ, Father Jean N., to whom I have just exposed my soul in all its nakedness, as I have never done with anyone else in this world, and who gave me a message of salvation. I know what I am talking about when I say 'parliaments'; I can see people smiling with pity and scorn for my naïvety, but *I* voted for the one list of the one Party, with a helmeted soldier in army boots and a machine gun across his stomach in front of the local election booth. I suffered the derision of slavery which had to be maintained by force, and the shame of being on the safe side of that weapon; and so I say, in all consciousness of the dirty tricks, the deceits and mockeries of what governs us, I say 'freely elected parliaments', and I take off my hat to the majesty of the law, however imperfect, however distressing, but still the law, and not the caprice of Politburo comrades. For me, the trade union is the same sort of thing: it comes right after the Church, after law and liberty, and resembles them.

Meanwhile, I myself became a non-unionist unemployed man on the free market of the free world. I have known what it is to go hungry and to ask the price of a brace of sausages on a railway station, and to give them up because I did not have enough to pay for them – surrounded by blocks of chocolate, delicatessen delicacies, bottles of beer, newspapers and multicoloured magazines: paradise, abundance, and the freedom to go hungry.

Three times in my life I have known hunger for months and years: under Hitler, under socialism, and in the free world. I have seen the bare backside of the Fatherland, the Five-Year Plan and Liberty.

This third time, in front of the travel provisions trolley, there was a gentleman standing beside me buying a pair of those little sausages for his small boy. When he saw that after asking how much they were I turned away without buying them, he looked me up and down in astonishment. He did not think of saying: 'Do you not have enough money? Here, take this.' I would have accepted it. But he did not think of it.

I have experienced interviews with management heads who stare at you with a cold, piercing eye, so insolent you want to kick them. You feel like an animal at a horse fair, one the horse-dealer may buy if he wants, but that he will pull a face at, and pass on to the next one if he doesn't. Here, in this free country where I live now, they call workers 'takers' and bosses 'givers' of work. That's a lie. We sell our labour, and they buy it. In this land I have known heads of world-famous large enterprises, with their dozens and hundreds of thousands of employees: I saw them as arrogant, unapproachable, sometimes victims of megalomania, delusions of grandeur, just like the management comrades in the great bureaucracies of the East, and often just as gormless, inept and destructive – the grand architects of recessions, the masters of the oil slicks, the destroyers of ecology, the men who always knew we would have an energy crisis, except that they failed to notice it: the organizers of mass unemployment, the heroes of national debt, of the balance of payments in the red, and of last-minute hard currency transfusions.

But I have also known – passionate supporter as I am of trade unions – I have known the great trade union boss who says: 'We demand *all* rights, even the right of going to extremes!' I see that thick, swollen nape, that phallocratic air, that neck with its rolls of fat round the collar: he was the financial expert of one of the best and most powerful trade unions in the world, and held, at the last count, precisely forty-nine positions of president, vice-president, director general, member of the supervisory council, member of the administrative council of societies and enterprises run by trade unions.

The right to go to extremes? There flashed before my eyes a vision of the twenty million employees in the land where I used to live, with their families, all giving themselves up to all kinds of excesses. No, it was enough just to look at that man to understand that he was talking for himself alone. He had the same monumental arrogance, the same shifty, malicious and grossly sensual look as many a member of the Politburo. Then I saw him after taking a weight-reducing cure made necessary by illness and by the sexual problems of middle-aged male menopause – just like certain high-ranking comrades after their exclusion from the Central Committee and from the Party: deflated, drained, all clapped-out and looking like a battered old leather bag: examples of different kinds of ritual castration.

The System can also easily be Evil. Evil is definitely slave labour, a beggarly wage, the curse of exploitation of the workers. 'In the sweat of thy face shalt thou eat bread': a hard fate, but not a malediction. Sometimes one would gladly work by the sweat of one's brow, but one has no work.

Yes, Evil is working from ten to twelve hours a day; it is child labour, back-breaking work, the agonizing task, the workaholic obsession – all Evil. Unemployment at the same time as Butter Mountains – Himalayas of butter kept in store and going bad to the tune of millions, Everests of jam flushed down the drain, cattle killed off by gun-toting big-bellied farmers and thrown into a common boneyard to keep prices up, the laws of free trade and the Common Market praised to high heaven (while millions die of starvation in the Sahara, in Bengal or the Horn of Africa) and extolled by people who keep our noses to the grindstone so that we can pay our taxes – those taxes with which they finance the destruction of the fruits of our labours – yes, that is what Evil is. Evil is all that is stupid, and the joyful acceptance of stupidity by those who profit by it, and by those who do not suffer because of it. Those people never have dusty feet.

In England, when the upper classes did not speak Anglo-Saxon but the French of the Norman occupier, those merchants who journeyed from town to town were not judged by the provost of their guild, but by a tribunal called the *court of piepowdrous,* the tribunal of the dusty-footed ones. There still exists another dusty-foot tribunal, a tribunal of skin and bones, of famished ribs and hollow bellies, of children with eyes swarming with flies who seem to be asking not only God, but also man: why hast thou forsaken us?

That is the tribunal that would judge God, if there were not a defendant with even stronger claims to justice. The description of this suspect is: the stupid laugh of sated appetites; the impudent falsehood of the ignorant technocrat, masquerading as expert jargon and gobbledygook; the outraged face of the rich, the happy, turning away from the importunate one, his starving brother. We are that defendant.

I know what I am talking about: having suffered hunger enough, and having lived enough in the lap of luxury, I do not need to make any effort of the imagination, like some left-wing money-maker with sinecure and servants; all I need is a good memory, and that I have. In the tribunal of the dusty feet, I have been a witness and then, I will not say a judge, but an assessor, and at present I am both witness and defendant. Before the tribunal of the dusty feet, we find we are accomplices of Evil.

7.

EVIL: ACQUAINTED WITH THE DEVIL

The devil is an attitude. I shall not touch the question of whether he is a spirit, a wicked spirit, a personal or a symbolic being: I leave all that to the professional demonologists, if such there be. The devil I am talking about is a collective name for certain attitudes. I am speaking of the devil as I know him, and because I know him.

There is the immense indifference of the universe stretching to the uttermost limits of space-time, beyond good and evil, emptiness, the stars, matter, particles of energy. It is possibly a universe of joy – I know nothing of that and I could only vaguely surmise the inhuman nature of that superhuman jubilation. It is the sublime and indifferent visage of God, his beauty, which – rarely, all too rarely – may bend itself upon us and be transformed into purest joy.

And there is the terrible visage of God, toleration of Evil, fear, anguish, disquiet, hunger and thirst, physical pain, excruciating agony. That is the dark face of God, incomprehensible, pitiless, and sometimes touched with a strange, abstracted indulgence, like the serenity of the dying, or the nervous shock that anaesthetizes severely wounded people, or those who fall a prey to wild beasts.

But there is also the more limited and more horrible zone of human Evil, of attitudes of hatred and cruelty; there is the desire to harm, the savage joy of causing suffering, the ferocious enjoyment of the suffering of another. In all creation there is nothing as cruel as human malice. There is no malice in the universe, except in man.

These words abjure the truth: 'ferocious' means 'pertaining to wild beasts': 'savage' means 'one who lives in the woods'. Wild beasts enjoy devouring their prey when they are hungry, but do not enjoy making it suffer: they do not even know it is suffering. Wanting to do harm implies a secret communion, an identification of the human being with his victim, an empathy between the two: he puts himself in the victim's place and relishes a suffering he understands. It does not happen 'in the woods' but in our cities; it is happening here, in Megalopolis. (Megalopolis is any place where there are more machines than human beings: in our house, there are twenty-four machines for four persons.)

There is suffering inflicted through thoughtlessness, through indifference, laziness – all human failings, because the thoughtless behaviour of the beasts is not a fall from grace, whilst ours is a renunciation of consciousness, a refusal of lucidity, a refusal of sympathy. There is the inert devil, and the stupid devil. But I shall not undertake here a *Complete Treatise of Demonology:* I shall confine myself to a *Digest of Devilry* drawn from my own experience.

The famous First Axiom of Devilry, 'the devil does not exist', is not just a simple refusal to personify Evil, with horns and cleft feet; it is a refusal of the very notion of guilty intent, of culpability, of sin. 'Human Evil does not exist' – at any rate, it is not the personal responsibility of any one human being.

Last year, in Hanover, a man seized four hostages in a family house: a bank director – an ideal subject for ransom and massacre – his wife and their two children. Bound with ropes, they awaited the arrival of the ransom money. Then, to make quite sure that there would be no one left to recognize him, that man took another piece of rope and strangled all four of them one after the other, in full view of one another: we do not know in what order – whether it was the father who watched his wife and children die, or the mother who saw her children and her husband strangled with that bit of rope, or the children who witnessed the killing of their parents.

The assassin was innocent; or at least, he was not guilty. It was class society, or capitalist exploitation, or the affluent society, or the family circle, or his childhood traumatisms that were the cause of his act. There was no responsibility, but only a causality, what we used to call heredity, and even further back in time, the stars.

But the causal explanation of the crime is dubious, though possibly useful. For the brothers and sisters of the criminal had the same hereditary antecedents, had also suffered the same or equivalent traumatisms: society was the same for the criminal and for those who did not yield to their murderous impulses, and the stars had shone down indiscriminately upon the birth of the man with the rope and on hundreds of thousands of other newborn beings who were not to strangle anyone.

The causal explanation of the crime is useful, though dubious. We are confronted with Evil and everything is grist to our mill: if there are social, psychological, educational or other means to try to make the free choice of Evil even more difficult for the future criminal, let us study them, adopt them, use them all. But the causal explanation of a sequence of human facts should not prevent its moral valorization. *B is the consequence of A* is a current proposition in our physico-mathematic knowledge of the universe's immense zone of indifference. It has also become widespread in the zone where we ask the question: *Is B a culpable act?* For in the human computer, characterized by its pre-ordinated hesitation that we call freedom, A can be followed by B, but also by non-B; *datur tertium,* the sequence can also be something quite different, from A to C, from A to D or to Z. In other words, there is no determinist excuse for human Evil, there is only the devil's syllogism, which says: the crime is predetermined, therefore it is not a crime. There is no crime except with culpable intention, and freely willed. But in the determinist universe there is no free will.

Except that the conviction of being free, within the limits imposed on me by the universe, is an illusion as powerful and as ineradicable as the illusion of existence, and the illusion of being myself and not someone else. Those who deny the existence of sin, of guilt, of moral responsibility, are reduced to denying my freedom, in the face of the daily personal evidence I have of that liberty. The devil, who is a great sophist and a bad logician, finds he has painted himself into a corner. Either he denies my responsibility, and then also denies my freedom and my dignity, which go to make of me the man I am. Or else he admits my freedom, and at the same time sin, Evil in so much as it is willed by me. If, as he delights in doing, he denies the existence of the devil, he is compelled to deny man, against the evidence of his existence. If he admits man, the dignity of man and his freedom, he admits sin *qua* sin.

Every minute of the day, a man who has committed several sadistic crimes and who has just left the asylum with a certificate attesting his cure, grabs a child, rapes it, disembowels it, chops the corpse into pieces. It is quite true that he is sick. It is also true that the doctors have made a mistake about his condition, and they are wrong time and time again, to the great misfortune of innumerable women and children who are raped and massacred; these doctors could defuse his sadistic tendencies by a surgical or pharmacological intervention. It might make him a little dull-witted. His life might become less interesting. He would have to renounce that ecstasy (*ekstasis,* being outside oneself), that intense enjoyment, which makes him slaver, with exorbitant eyes, as he slashes with his razor the belly of a child whose sexual parts he mutilates.

Neither I nor anyone else would venture to touch his body, his physical and psychic integrity, without his free consent. But he, the maniac, should have the choice between a measure that would render him incapable of further acts of violence, or would make them improbable; and another form of expiation.

For we are all the victim. Even the criminal is the victim. Our universe has been hurt, we are afraid, we have no confidence in ourselves any more. We were not asking for the assurance of living in a just universe, but from now on we are living with the insupportable evidence of injustice.

I heard an assassin say, during a televised discussion: 'What I did is my own affair, concerns only me; it is I who have to grapple with my conscience, with the consciousness of what I have done...' He was not altogether lost to salvation; he was not completely possessed by the devil, but only by the demon of pride. He was mistaken, the devil is always making mistakes, for what he had done was the concern of all the world; his act had broken the social contract, the non-aggression pact between human beings, the treaty of amity and co-operation between all of us, including himself. He had 'de-assured' us, if I may use that word to express the contrary of 'reassure'. He had cast us into disquiet, into a fundamental unease; and he thought he was alone with his own conscience in that? But at least he was not silent, he did not deny that something not quite in order had happened. It was not his opinion that 'hell is other people'. He knew that hell is, above all, myself.

For Evil, sin, crime do not, in the first place, concern one's neighbour, the guilty one, the sinner, my brother; they are mine. In certain countries and social groups, there is probably not a single married couple, not one man, not one woman who has not been guilty of having willed, demanded, obtained and paid for the death of a child in its mother's womb. I, you, each one of us prefer not to use a condom: women also detest that embarrassing accoutrement and the moment when the man rigs himself out in one; they do not bother to equip themselves with contraceptives, and the pill has disturbing side-effects. So it is so much simpler just to let oneself go, to tumble fully conscious of the consequences into the strange and complicated trap set by 'Nature', by the psycho-mathematical universe, by God in his most enigmatic and inhuman aspect; and at the end of three months your wife or your woman friend goes to the doctor, to have her vagina and her uterus defiled by instruments of steel, with which the doctor cuts up into little pieces the living child – so small, it is true, but already recognizable, already resembling a human being, already a human being, and who is sleeping, perhaps dreaming.

We are free, we have the choice, there is no causality, no historical, economic, social, psychological determinism or other ideology concerned. We are not even obliged to practise *coitus interruptus:* we have the means to be merciful, at the cost of a little conscience, of will power, of reflection, of tenderness of heart for the unfortunate still in its mother's womb, but that we butcher alive. Possibly one has to sacrifice an unborn creature to the survival and health of a mother; but what about the sacrifice to convenience, to laziness, to inertia, cowardice? I myself carry the blood of two or three of such infants on my conscience, together with the degradation of their mothers and of the doctors. I should like to expiate my crimes, but I do not know how. I should like to correct the evil I have done, but it is irreparable. If only I can create a little good from this evil that is too heavy for me to bear...

The Second Axiom of Devilry is that the devil is other people. I myself am never my neighbour's hell; I am innocent, I am pure, it is the other man who is diabolical. I have never been, I am not, I shall never be guilty of diabolical behaviour. I am either good, or the innocent victim of my self-determination. How can one think of oneself, when one sees the colonel at his tortures, the duty sergeant holding interrogations with his truncheon and his electrodes, the socialist executioner comrade, the State psychiatrist comrade, the bureaucrat entrenched behind his bureau, brain, heart and eyes shut to it all, saying: 'Do everything you can to obtain those confessions – the way you get them is your own affair.'

The devil is the technocrat who destroys a province, a social group, a living species; he is the imbecile scholar who says, too late: 'I did not expect *that* to happen', which is the theme song of all post-Hiroshima post-mortems. They are those learned donkeys, asking trick questions of Jesus Christ, who tried to get Jesus into a corner instead of seeing who it was they had before them – a situation which is endlessly repeated, with interviewees of lesser stature than he, but all the same recognizable as his brothers. Satan is the idiot beside us who shrugs his shoulders at Evil, saying: 'So what's it got to do with me? Why should I get involved? That's the way it is. I didn't make the world. So get off my back, man!'

Satan is the falsely intelligent, falsely realistic attitude, stoicism at the expense of others, virile, 'tough', and even 'rough and tough'. No compassion, no pity, no sentimentalism. I knew a member of the Party presidium who told you: 'Socialism is not made with fine feelings.' And then I met him again, excluded, 'denounced', so small, so humble, so stupid; but human once more, and delivered of his demon. I had a friend, chairman of a multinational concern (chemicals, fertilizers, napalm) with an annual profit of several billions – and now I'm talking about real money, the product of real work, not 'funny money', not cash that is fiddled with, recycled, 'laundered' and inflated to such an extent that it sends up in smoke the labour it is supposed to represent. 'I hate to say it, but a sound economy *needs* a certain margin of unemployment.' When I saw him again, he'd been given the boot with all the brutality that is current in the Kremlins of the multinationals, and reduced to chairman of a small sporting goods concern, no more than a dozen millions of profit a year – cut down to size, humble, embarrassed, ashamed. I had a childhood friend, handsome, adored by his sisters and his mistresses: at twenty-five, bald as a baby's bottom (he had a pointed skull), but smiling the same smile of the damned – as Hamlet says of his incestuous uncle/father:

> O villain, villain, smiling, damned villain!
> My tables – meet it is I set it down,
> That one may smile, and smile and be a villain . . .

And I too: on the heights, arrogant, proud, inhuman, obsessed; in the depths, shameful, humble, bitter, stupefied by my fall. But rid of the demon.

We must learn how to be humble before being humiliated. We must learn true humility, without social determinants. To be humble, even when one is rich, handsome, intelligent, healthy or quite simply young: for one goes in danger of the wrath of God, with the devil and inhuman behaviour always lying in ambush. To be dignified, even when one is poor, weak, ugly or stupid, or quite simply old: quite simply because one is a child of God, and a brother of Christ.

It is true that Satan obsesses us. One only has to switch on the 'idiot box' of television to find oneself face to face with him: astride the powerful, the self-righteous, the censorious, the rich, the successes, the quiz pundits: with his ferocious laugh, his contemptuous smile, his air of being deaf, dumb and blind to the most obvious truths. He hounds us, he gets his claw into us: the pornographic devil with his visceral acrobatic love-positions, parading private parts beneath one's nose, the male phallocrat and the female balls-breaker. The devil is the theoretician, negator of God, negator of evil and negator of himself, reificator of the universe, enemy of values: *wertfrei* and *wertneutral** are compliments he has invented; his slogan is always 'I pass no value judgements', and it is always a lie. He is the great enemy of anthropomorphisms such as the concept of a divinity who has anything in common with man, or of any divinity whatsoever, and one can easily recognize him by the low quality of his own anthropomorphism, by the

---

* in German in the original: literally 'floating value', 'neutral value' (Translator's note).

brutal despotism of his own implicit, unacknowledged and implacable values. Try to obtain approval for parricide, and he'll find some excuse for you; try to justify the Vietnam war, and he'll leap at your throat with slavering fangs. Now the Vietnam war was bad, but not as bad as parricide: only the devil, enemy of taboos, has decided that the latter is an archaic taboo of patriarchal class society, whilst the Vietnam war is a modern taboo invented by the left: it is recommended that one may infringe the former and fiercely forbidden to lay a finger on the latter.

The devil is the emancipator of youth: I knew a very skilful one who taught the adolescents in his charge the use of drugs and the practice of unbridled sexuality – only one death so far, at the age of fourteen. All around me I find the devils of envy, of vanity, the sniggering devil, the devil of witty remarks which, on reflection, are as stupid as certain of Nietzsche's aphorisms. Poor Nietzsche was possessed by a devil who was often an inspired genius, never wise, discoverer of implacable truths that later reveal themselves to be particularly profound falsehoods...

There is also the devil-theologian, who forgets to pardon, to humble himself, to bow the head before others, to admit: 'I do not know', and, above all, to shut up.

And there is the devil who treads close behind me and whose pestiferous breath I feel on the back of my neck: the devil-preacher, who talks and talks of God until God gives up his emptied heart – the devil-preacher who possesses those who preach to others instead of praying in silence. (So is preaching forbidden? Certainly not, but one must humiliate, humble oneself before, during and after, and take refuge as soon as possible in prayer, man-to-man with God, instead of making some self-important public monologue. This was the advice I gave myself, and I shall never forget it.)

The Third Axiom of Devilry is the corollary of the second: only others are guilty, and the guilty one is identical with his sin. If I take my sin upon me, at the same time I know that I can hope to redeem myself, to pay, and I know at least that I have the will to change myself. But not so: you must hate the criminal personally, says the devil, not just his crime: you must never forgive; the guilty one can never redeem himself, expiate, or rise above his crime. Let us hate the capitalist, not the misdeeds of capitalism; the communist, and not the crimes of communism; the sinner, and not his sin. I do not hate Evil, I only hate the man who is temporarily guilty of criminal behaviour; but I shall hound that man twenty, thirty, forty years, his whole life long, without caring to find out if he has meanwhile expiated his sin, if he has repented, if he has tried to make reparation, to square the account in some way or other: for me, he sinned once and will remain forever a sinner, he shall never be my brother and shall never become my fellow-man again. The devil relishes that kind of consequential logic.

The identification of our fellow-man with his fault reinforces our conformity to the Second Axiom: never to pass judgement on oneself, never to condemn oneself, always to have a ready excuse, and always to turn promptly in condemnation of others.

It took me the first twenty-five years of my life to discover within me the terrible power of egoistic impulses, and that Evil is the supremacy of Me over Thee. A man who is incapable of mastering his impulses does not deserve the name of man: but – I used to say with a forced laugh – impulses that allow themselves to be mastered do not deserve the name of impulses. During a second quarter of a century I have learnt the other lesson – there are two kinds of conscience: a bad conscience, and no conscience whatsoever.

I know exactly the sort of diabolical behaviour I have been guilty of up to now: diabolically cruel, sadistic, shameful, vile, asocial, immoral, unjust, insensitive, inhuman, impious. The one very feeble and insignificant excuse I had was that I have almost never acted spontaneously, but under serious or extreme provocation, or under pressures which would have annihilated many another man. I am no less guilty for that, I see what I see, in clear detail, and the only thing that stops me from talking about it here is that I suspect public confessions of vanity, of monstrous vanity, of exhibitionism. I cannot forget the awful embarrassment I felt reading that passage in Rousseau's *Confessions,* in which he relates how he had ruined the life of a poor servant girl accused of a theft he had committed himself: with what fatuous complacency he bares his heart. Complacency perhaps in his regrets, but above all in his narcissistic voyeurism; and no attempt to make reparation, to expiate his misdeed other than through the display of his sin in the bookshops of the world. No: I would rather keep silent, and try to make amends; I know it is impossible; but all the same, one must attempt, in all humility, to restore, however little, however temporarily, the equilibrium of the world I upset, the justice whose course I perverted, the harmony I destroyed, the beauty and the goodness I have dragged in the mire. I shall try to redeem my sins in a practical way, by bringing good into the real, and the good will, the friendship, the tenderness, the sweetness of which I am capable and which were missing until now.

By doing precisely that, I shall be escaping from the Fourth Axiom of Devilry, which states that as there is Evil in men, it is impossible to love them; and that as Evil is therefore also in me, there is no hope left. Evil is unendurable; but it is precisely because of that that it provides us with a way out: hell is neither others nor myself, but the acceptance of Evil. At the close of our investigation of Evil, it seems to me that we turn, like those flowers whose uplifted faces follow the sun, away from Evil, which is God under his terrible aspect, towards good, which is God, our homeland.

At the close of our trial of God, we are led to echo the Book of Job: shall I judge the equinoctial tempests, the formation of the continents, the tidal wave, the eruption of volcanoes, the explosion of supernovae? We cannot pass judgement on the plague, on pain, on death – we can only build embankments against disaster, and, within our habitable territory, we still find ourselves inextricably implicated with Evil. It is only ourselves we can judge. Or abjure all responsibility: but in that case, we can no longer accuse God and no longer talk of Evil. Unless values and value judgements return under other names (and it is indeed a great task to divest them of their disguises), it is better to call things by their names, and to see what we see.

There is only one thing more futile than judging God, and that is to deny him. And there is one thing almost as vain as judging God, and that is to justify him. The aim of theodicy is to arrive at the realization that the question of theodicy is not the issue.

8.

JUBILATE

Joy is even more manifest that Evil. If Evil is the proof of the nonexistence of God, joy is the proof of our ingratitude. I am not undertaking to justify God, but I have not shut my eyes to Evil, and I shall not shut them to the evidence of joy. The experience of Evil does not prove that God is absent, it proves that he is terrible, it unveils to us his frightening visage, alien to man, and, I would venture to add, the enemy of man. I employ the word 'enemy' in all humility, not in a spirit of rebellion, and without passing judgement on God.

Whereas joy proves that God is our homeland. In his *Journal,* Kierkegaard notes something about himself that is true of us all: 'I dwell on the borders of Arabia Felix and Arabia Petraea.' We live on the borders of desolation and joy. Bielinski says that every tear shed by a little girl under torture proves the nonexistence of God. It proves that Evil wounds us so profoundly that we become blind to good. The tears of the innocents pour down our faces, our eyes go on smarting with their salt.

But what do these prove: the laughter of a happy little girl, the cries of children playing, the orchards bristling with joy after rain, the yappings of a pair of puppies tumbling over one another as they scamper through the grass, the gambols of a litter of kittens, resembling the homeric entanglements of Gods and Titans on the frieze of the altar of Pergamum? One only needs to work really hard for six hours at a stretch – work we need to do in order to escape from neurotic feelings of futility and from the psychosomatic illnesses that causes – one only needs to contemplate one's work well done, to mop one's forehead, or take one really good deep breath. It is enough to currycomb earth's rich hide for half a dozen hours, until the sweat drops from your brow. It is enough, even, just to breathe, to make the discovery of joy.

It is enough to take one deep breath in a field after rain. It is enough to breathe, while you wipe your hands or your brow, after laying a hedge, to breathe in its smell of honey. It is enough to go outside on a winter's day, and take a deep breath, when it is very cold and the air is as dry as crystal. It is enough to breathe, to begin to rediscover good.

It is enough to be very thirsty and to gaze a moment at a glass of cold water, softly misted, before drinking. It is enough to master your thirst a moment longer and savour in advance the draught of pure water – if possible water from a well or from a fountain. It is enough to be very hungry, after having worked hard, after persistent effort, without having done anything to harm your brother or yourself; hunger after a day of work well done, at the controls of a machine, at the keyboard of a machine, behind a yoke of oxen, ploughing; it is enough to have built something that works, or to have taken to pieces and repaired a machine that was not working properly; it is enough to have planted a tree or sown a field or made a discovery or learnt something you did not know, or taught someone something he did not know. And to be hungry. And to break a hunk of bread with its thick crust, a little burnt in places, a little dusted with flour and ash; to get the aroma of that whole-wheat or fresh rye bread, and then to eat it, slowly.

Joy is here and now. It is enough to walk on mown grass, following the scythe or the lawn mower, and accompanied by your associates, a couple of inquisitive blackbirds. Joy is gardens in May, fields in June, even the steppe is in flower, even the desert is covered with a pale green mist of leaf. It is enough to swim in the sea or in a limpid river, with broad, slow movements, face plunged into the emerald water fused with sun, eyes open on the depths shot with radiant light. We can sense the joy of dolphins who dance round the bows of a ship, or enter into the slumber, the dream-life, of the swarms of translucid jellyfish, pale blue in the intenser blue of the waves. I am not forgetting the law of the finny tribe: the larger eat the smaller (unless the latter have such spikes on their backs that the big ones spit them out, as I have often seen). Nor am I forgetting the somnolent and blissful existence of the beds of animal-plants, the shoals of coral. We can see with our own eyes the love of life in animal and vegetable species as long as they have enough sun and water, and we feel the same sort of joy, essentially the same, though displayed on a human scale, which extends from sheer animal spirits to the joy of contemplative communion in prayer.

And we are not alone. I remember the trustful smile, simple, gracious, mischievous, of a young girl disguised as a gipsy in her parka, blue jeans and long, wild hair, sitting on the steps of a station in Megalopolis, listening to her companions, a young boy, or a girl who appeared to be the leader of the pack, joyful as healthy young animals. We can see the same thing with wolves, dogs, lions, monkeys, and human beings. It is enough to see your dog raise his head and look at you with absolute confidence and trust as he walks along close to your heel, to sense that he is indeed there with you, his alter ego, bigger, stronger, braver, better than he – or so he thinks, the poor fool. He is devoted, loyal, heroic; he loves you: he is happy.

It is enough to listen in on a conversation between simple folk around some joker in a tram or a bus: all the passengers are shaking with jovial laughter, without a trace of malice. I have seen that, as a student, in a suburban tram in Munich. Even here in Megalopolis I have known young people who seemed to radiate light, more especially the son of one of my friends, who, whenever he laughed, seemed to have a halo round his head. He soon lost it, what with tobacco and alcohol, which modified his cerebral chemistry; but that sort of thing is happening everywhere, and there is no end to it.

I have seen an adolescent American girl giving up her seat in a European bus to an old lady, with the sweet and tender gravity, the perfect dignity, the absolute disinterest with regard to her Me, the enchanting non-narcissism I have admired, and always with an almost religious emotion, in young girls and women, whether peasants, working class or students, in Spain and in certain other Roman Catholic countries: as lovely, as sweet and as admirable as the Virgins in their churches. It is with such beings that the universe recovers its equilibrium. They move as if they were living transmitters of celestial co-ordinates that organize creation and transform chaos into a flower radiating symmetry, like the rose window of a gothic cathedral when it unfolds into glowing life, animated by a shaft of sunlight.

Good and Evil are not symmetrical. They do not complement one another like the two sides of constituents of an equation, or positive and negative numbers. Their symmetry is purely a matter of words. Suffering is more acute than joy, and more rare. Malice, cruelty and hatred are more intense than friendship. Only maternal love could measure its strength against envy. For one human being who gives his life for his fellows, there are a hundred thousand who let their fellows die, or kill them, through indifference, lack of awareness, inertia, spinelessness, and more rarely through anger, hatred or greed. But this purulent sore on the body of humanity, murder, violence of any kind, rape of bodies, souls, spirits, kidnapping, taking of hostages, confinement of innocent victims of terrorists, threats, intimidation, looting, lies, deceit of all kinds, all more dramatic, more impressive than good, all these do not add up to that body we are talking about.

What constitutes the body of humanity, what makes it a living thing, what binds us together is the invisible fluid of good will and good faith; it is its infinite, inextricable, imperceptible tissue of tacit treaties and implicit contracts.

What is miraculous is not Evil, but the friendship between human beings. I know who we are – we are the sons of Cain, the australopithecus armed with a club. (The weapon, the first tool, which scholars educated in the hypocritical, alternative and collusive morality of immorality in its deepest form call an *implement,* for man is good, and has never dined off his fellow; or on the contrary he is bad, but this is kept quiet, for there is no hope of salvation for him.) The miracle is that I can turn my back on a stranger in the supermarket without having him kill me. The miracle is that we can count upon our brothers who give us water to drink and our daily bread, who clear away the detritus of our civilization or who save our lives after a traffic accident, bind up our wounds, repair our mutilated bodies. The daily miracle is that we do not all die like dogs of thirst, hunger and disease, and that we do not slaughter one another in response to our ancestral impulses; that we do not leap at one another's throats in the lift, and that we tell one another the truth a thousand times more often than we lie.

The miracle, the assymetry therefore, is the immense preponderance of good – imperceptible, unnoticed, received, available – on which we count and from which we seek support in order to go on existing. The miracle is that we should feel at home here in the heart of the universe, like all other beings indeed, and that for every moment of suffering there is a long period of calm and a proportion of joy that goes beyond the limits of pain, or would go beyond them if they were measurable; but they are not. Being, the ensemble of known and unknown factors, is our homeland. God is our homeland. Or rather, that narrow and ever-shifting region between joy and desolation, that zone habitable by God, is our homeland. In this sense, God is our Father, says a note by Wittgenstein in his *Notebooks,* dated 11th June 1916.

We owe gratitude to the universe, to the ensemble of all ensembles, the totality of causal chains, the sum of all structures, necessity, probability, chance, the sum of the known and the unknown – to that which we call God. Even if we become his enemies, his haters, his calumniators, even in the pit of rejection of God, at the very bottom of despair and suffering, in the paroxysm of negation, we have an escape hatch offered us by him: repose, the good deep sleep of nothingness awaits us, or at any rate that hypothesis may be allowed. If I can kill myself to escape suffering, again it is he who has offered me death, and if the hypothesis of annihilation is true, I shall owe him thanks for supreme repose; and I shall find that again in him, beyond everyone and everything, there is nothing. I shall know nothing of the exultation of energy particles, nothing of the jubilation of the grand celestial concatenations; I shall not know the bliss of the great densities of matter at the heart of blue stars, and perhaps I shall no longer know that I have ceased to exist, and that I have found rest. But joy is close at hand: it is raining softly on the garden in front of me, the fringe of the woods is like a green wall, the songs of birds shake down other limpid drops. If I am to believe existing human documents, happiness does exist. All the evidences agree and are worthy of belief: at any rate, happiness would seem to be an infinitely possible hypothesis.

Even without participating directly in the happiness of others, even in these days when, here in Megalopolis, I had no work, when my youth had fled, and I was left with nothing but a little bread and the remains of good health and indomitable hope, I know full well that I was free, in a part of the world more free than others, and free to accomplish good deeds. We all of us, including the disinherited, of whom I was a part and still would be a part without the grace of God and the power of human friendship; we all of us, even the disinherited, have more cause than Ulric de Hutten after the discovery of the new world and the rediscovery of the Ancients, to cry aloud: O *saeculum, O litterae, juvat vivere!* O atomic era, O exact sciences, what joy to be alive.

This century is not just one of technocratic wars of universal fratricide, of bureaucracies, of genocides, of extermination camps, of police terror, of terrorism, of economic crises, of environmental pollution, the century of ideologies, of lies, of stupidity triumphant. It is above all the century of the theory of relativity and quantum physics, non-aristotelian systems of logic, topology, logical algebra, cybernetics, data processing, nuclear physics, nuclear *fusion,* which will not destroy matter but create it, without poisoning the planet, and give us energy without limit and without danger. It is the century of ethology, of socio-biology, of genetics, the century which is finally witnessing the crumbling of pernicious old utopias, the century of women's liberation movements, of the liberation of races oppressed by imperial and communist bureaucracies, the century of the ecologist movement that will save the earth, human beings and species threatened with extinction. O century, O knowledge, O power to work for good! Century in which we have walked upon the moon, and prayed in the sidereal spaces with words from the Hebrew Bible, transmitter of Sumerian, Semitic, Egyptian and Hellenic continuity. And all those are my fellows, my brothers, men created in the polyvalent image of God.

This terrible century, this wilderness, this universe of suffering, abandoned by God, inhabited by Evil, tomb of God and almost of all humanity, is at the same time that shaft of radiance, that multitude of living springs of water that restore our joy, our confidence and our hope, falling from basin to basin, spreading their brims ever wider, unto the limits of the habited earth and the space explored by our machines. It is a miraculous blossoming, a garden of delights, a liberating century, an ascension to the stars and knowledge and good; a world in which each one of us has four billion brothers, without counting the animal species and all the blades of grass in earth's vegetation; a world filled with God and in itself divine and transcended by the unknown God; a world moulded by incessant palpitations of tender, faint, minuscule radiance in the hearts of human beings at prayer: nerve centres where grace is in action, centres where grace is given, centres where the grace of orison is present, that untiring talk that is the subject of my book.

But I have not tried to weigh Evil and good against one another. I know well that they are incommensurable, asymmetrical, not enemies, but stranger one to the other, not like light and dark, but like an equilateral triangle and the colour purple. And I shall not allow myself to rely upon other people's evidences of felicity, or of hope. The only evidence that can give me certainty is my own. It is possibly the humblest of all, but it is decisive, for it is immediate and I cannot deny it.

Ever since the end of my twenties, I have had occasion to know instants of pure joy, which at the same time were always moments of gratitude. They come to me at the very instant when I discover the answer to a question that has been troubling me – what we call inspiration in scientific research or in the arts, and in daily life 'getting an idea', 'finding the answer', 'the solution'. All it needs is that the question, the search, the disquiet should be as serious as anything one is capable of.

This response comes from being 'down in the dumps', in all senses of the term: the pit of depression, and the desolation in the very depths of the unconscious.

I take it on trust from fellows more knowledgeable than I that our nervous system is an auto-regulatory cybernetic circuit; my brain with its conscious and unconscious operations is a computer or data processing machine, but with the added advantage of consciousness in depth,

creative capacity, the capacity to transcend all the limitations of its functioning: a computer which has been able to
add to the sum of human life some essentially novel
things, such as the cogwheel, square roots, negative
numbers, the sonnet and card games. It will go on adding,
I have every reason to believe, more and more unheard-of
inventions. But it too is a part of the sum of things; and it
is not its own invention; and its innovations emerge from
way down in the deepest dumps, far below the level of
consciousness, right down there where 'I is another'.
There below I am impersonal and sometimes terribly
alien, and linked by all the causal chains, by all the
permutations of probability, by all the sequences and
textures of facts known and unknown, and by the logical
texture of the universe – linked to everything else, to the
All, to whatever is not I. It is from those depths that my
joy, my gratitude and grace arise. It wells up from those
deeps, it reaches the surface, it emerges in the little
illuminated zone of my conscience. It is always unexpected, always unhoped-for, for I should dare neither to
look for it nor to hope for it, unless in some very humble
way, on the verge of total renunciation.

It is for this reason that I would venture to object, with
all respect, to those Hindu and other non-Christian 'techniques' which aim at producing mystical 'ecstasy'. Grace
as I am acquainted with it – in a small way, I know, but
with certitude – comes and goes as it pleases. I could not
call it up, nor manipulate it; I could not become its master.
I cannot and would not become the master of God's gift; I
do not wish to be the master of grace, and I would not
know how to be. I limit myself to waiting – sometimes I
even forget to wait, at least consciously. Deep down
below, perhaps, the conversation is continuing uninterrupted. But 'me' and 'I' turn towards someone else,
something beyond myself, and I perform the grace of
thanksgiving, I offer it my gratitude, I am all gratitude as I
turn towards – towards whom or what? I could not say.

Since about my thirtieth year, and more and more clearly as the years go by, and despite intervals of sterility caused by suffering, bad luck, drunkenness, over-eating, sluggishness of soul, lassitude of heart: suddenly, in the midst of anguish or distress, it is there: gratitude. The response to my often unconscious but tireless interior allocution – continued probably during sleep also; the response which is not inspiration or idea or anything else but this, wholly, simply, uniquely: gratitude.

Arrested time: an instant in which the spirit, the heart and the breath are suspended. Thanksgiving without words, pure gratitude. Like a faint glow in the black-yellow of eyelids closed in the night. Like a fluorescence, a luminescence. But it is not light. It is not visible. I have asked myself if that joy is in my head – but it seems to me that it happens rather somewhere in the torso: however, that is not true, and that vague localization between the diaphragm and the brain somewhere 'at the back', is false. In reality there is no single point in space where grace is situated, unless my body is the bearer of my conscious-ness, and joy surfaces through that consciousness. I should not mention it at all, and would not dream of keeping myself under observation, for the observation of my own piety is impious, if I did not believe that by doing so I might render service to, others like myself. For if joy, gratitude, grace are all my lot – I who am of little worth – what consolation it is for those whose worth is greater than mine, for all those unfortunates, even more numer-ous, whose worth is less than mine, who are not better than I. If it sometimes comes and brushes *me* with its wing, *they* have all the more reason to feel hope, or perhaps they, too, could also hope to be touched by it.

This effusion of gratitude, this sudden state of grace, this grace of orison, has touched me, and has arisen within me I know not how often. Last year, I found myself stopping halfway down the stairs, one foot on one step, the other on the next. This month, I found myself, and above all was found by joy, in the act of taking off my spectacles. The time it takes for the hand to be lowered, with the spectacle in the fingers: and that was when the grace of gratitude welled up within me, interflowing with the response I was seeking.

It is like a small, pale glimmer. It is quite weightless, quite delicate, quite transparent. It is not the mystic ecstasy of the saints and the ascetics, which I know only by hearsay; it is only the tiny little joy of a weak and helpless nondescript, who has only this one gift, of being able to thank God. What is it I am thanking him for? For having pity on me; for giving me joy, this joy which consists in my offering of gratitude. It is not gratitude for this or that stroke of luck, of fate: I know that, and I know how to give thanks to the unknown. But the gratitude I am talking about here is identical with its motive. I suddenly love this confrontation – he is not opposite me, he is within me, right at the heart, so deeply centred within me that I cease to be myself, this interlocutor – he is not my interlocutor, for he speaks within me without words, he is identical with my gratitude, my joy, my prayer, or what I call prayer, this orison, this action of grace; and he is identical with me who am no longer of any account, who am no longer I, and who barely exist, for he alone exists, that unknown one --; yet he is not unknown, for I know nothing better than I know that infinitesimal presence of joy, nothing is more immediate to me, nothing is more certain for me, more full, more present than this gratitude, this grace.

As you can see, language is inadequate, the concepts go off course and capsize; all one can do is to encircle prayer from a distance, groping in the dark. 'Prayer.' I do not pray. 'Thanksgiving' is more precise. Gratitude, tenderness, joy. My own humble experience is not that of ecstasy, for 'here I am and here I stay'. I do not levitate, I am not transported, I am not somewhere else, nor outside myself, nor with God – nothing of that. Just a poor brute suddenly stopping halfway down the stairs, or slowly taking off his glasses. But those few moments in my life, perhaps just two or three minutes in all, two or three minutes in the life of a man, are the reason why I shall not have lived in vain.

Yes, for that alone, it is worth having lived. Even if it never returns, I can die in peace. All the rest will perish without trace; all the rest is mockery, deceit, nothingness, as I have learnt to my cost. 'Sour grapes' – but *I* say so *after* having tasted them. There are ripe, sweet ones, others green and rotten, but taken all in all, earthly sustenance was nothing very special. And God knows I had an appetite, and that I've been a good trencherman, and slavered over my meat, then vomited afterwards. All shall perish without trace, except those few instants, except that faint glimmer. As long as memory lasts, that makes up for the rest, gives all else its value, scent, savour, simmering brilliance; the beauty and the succulence of the world are reconstituted, the universe has a centre. Mensurating man, man the judge, is the measure of all things, and at the centre of the measured and judged universe; and as I am a man, I have my part to play in that social Adam, in those associate Adams; but at the centre of man, at the centre of myself, is that faint, that tiny little glimmer of adoration, of gratitude, of joy freely given, or given back to him who has given it, and which is the tenderness of the world, of the known and unknown universe, of the continuum of me-another- something-else, human–non-human, which I call by the 'technical term' of God, the name in which are associated piety, veneration, adoration, linguistic, conceptual and psychological premises of prayer.

Oratio, discourse, *adoratio,* adoration, *orare,* to pray, from *os, oris,* mouth, orifice, then face. It's pretty funny, what we say when we try to speak the unspeakable.

Neither mouth, nor face, I hold no discourse with God, I do not pray to him, and adoration is perhaps too strong a term, too vague. I should not venture to 'pray' to him, to ask him for something, to beg him to change the logical context of the universe and the infinite tissue of factual consequences, because I need, or imagine I need, such and such a thing. I thank him for the benefits of fate, the benefits of chance, the benefits of necessity; but it is not that kind of thanksgiving I am speaking of here, and which constitutes the substance of my conversation with the interlocutor considered by some as nonexistent. Sometimes misfortune pushes me too far, and I bellow in my heart, that is to say I groan out loud, meaning very softly, all alone in my room at night: 'What do you want of me? Why do you hit me so hard? I can't take it any more. Where are you taking me?' I note the curious fact that even then I do not ask: 'My God, do this, or that.' And I know perfectly well that it is all archaic as behaviour, a 'wrong attitude' of 'false conscience' concerning a fictitious personage, a personified projection of my Me, or the image of the Father, or, more seriously, of my solitude and of my suffering, a personified and compensatory personification of what is not, projecting upon it, or towards it, the normal behaviour or attitude of a conversation with a human being. My conversation with God is a false conversation; it is talking just for the sake of talking.

Only, my orison, the orison I am talking about here, the subject of all I am talking about here, is neither prayer, nor solicitation, nor invocation, nor cry. It is simply pure impulse, pure joy, pure gratitude, addressed to I know not whom, or rather, I know very well to whom – to God, the unknown, who resides, or reveals himself, in joy itself.

I know nothing of God. I do not know if God exists or not. I do not know if there is a God. I know nothing. But I know from my own experience that joy exists, and that it is gratitude. And like all my known ancestors, I call God whatever being or thing felicity addresses itself to. I am a human being and I address myself to him as if he were a human being, or at any rate a person, but I know nothing of him. Perhaps he contains all human beings, and the logical schema of all the individual persons who have been, are, and will be real, and perhaps he is in this sense a person. But I do not have the slightest intention of indulging myself in this type of speculation. One thing I do know – and only illness, amnesia, senile decay, mental trouble from a nervous shock or extreme misfortune could make me forget it – and that is that I have known the touch of grace; that joy has arisen within me and poured forth from me; and that it makes me happy to think about it, and that I consider myself saved, in so far as it is permissible to consider oneself saved without that very fact causing one to lose salvation.

I compare the joy of gratitude, the grace of orison, the action of grace, with the available documents on mystic ecstasy. This must belong to the same family of experiences, is perhaps the first step on the road that leads so far and so high. But the very idea overwhelms me: I do not ask so much of God or of life. The faint glimmer that burns sometimes at the centre of my being is quite sufficient for my lesser strength.

This pale and tiny joy that redeems my existence and gives my life all its value is something I have also compared with sexual orgasm. Not with the sensual sensation, which is intense, violent but precise – and precisely epidermic and coenaesthetic, more or less closely related to the desire to scratch oneself or to sneeze; but more exactly with that orgasm (*orgâein,* to swell, to get excited), which is massive, brutal and above all loss of consciousness, suspension of myself. I maintain that no one has ever loved his partner in an orgasm as a being at prayer loves his interlocutor, and that no one ever offers himself up in orgasm as does the being who prays and offers himself up to God. The state of orison is a state of intense lucidity; it is not a suspension of consciousness but its highest point: one does not forget oneself, one turns away from oneself, one goes beyond oneself towards the interlocutor. It is a matter of the most intense lucidity, of the clearest consciousness of things, and the most elevated, the most sublime state – not the possession of another, or possession by another, but amity. Orgasm is the blow of a cudgel, prayer is like being brushed by a butterfly's wing. It is a thousand times stronger than that faint glimmer; but a paltry little action of grace is enough to structure the life of a human being around it, and the universe around him.

I know that a toothache is enough to occupy my consciousness entirely. I know that a violent blow on the head or a glass of spirits are enough to cloud my being. I know that the brief second, or several seconds, of prayer are very faint, very weak in comparison with the fulgurant sensation that overwhelms and annihilates me in an orgasm, or with the even more vertiginous sensations provoked by peyotl or LSD.

But this brushing of wings, the faintest and the purest and the most unasked-for, the most impossible to provoke, to bring about by mechanical means, by a 'technique'; this gift of the unknown to me, this gift of myself to the unknown, this tiny instant of gratitude, the time needed just to take off my glasses, is sufficient for an entire lifetime: it is sufficient for me to feel overwhelmed by it.

I have not had much in this life, and probably more bad than good, if I do not count this; but it is precisely this, this revelation of God's pity – and, I must add, of human goodness – it is this that saves me for all eternity. I have known the friendship of God and men, and even if I forget everything, even if I were to perish with blasphemy on my lips, even if it should please God to burden me with sufferings, to teach me to underestimate Evil: even then, this will have been, this is, this can return if God wills and when he wills. But already, things being as they are, I find myself overwhelmed, my cup floweth over, and I consider myself saved.

I should never have written a single syllable of all this, knowing it is unseemly to speak of what is deepest within me, knowing that I run the risk of finding myself emptied, run dry in the way one says a well has run dry, or remaining barren, having lost the one good thing, the one value, the one thing that saves my being and my life. But I cannot shut myself up within myself and say 'That's for me alone; let my fellow-man, my brother, do his own thing; that's his business, not mine.' If I can be of the smallest service, I have done well in setting all this down in writing. Moreover, I hesitated for nearly ten years; I kept promising myself that I would do it one day, later; and now circumstances, chance, necessity, the will of God have given me no alternative but to perform this task. I have written this because I could not do otherwise, and because there was nothing else left for me to do.

I did not want to. I had to. The most spiritual short story I know, written by Anatole France, the atheist, is the tale of the tumbler in the cathedral who does not know how to pray, for all he can do is tumble; so he stands on his hands with his feet in the air before the altar. Each one prays as best he can.

9.

ABSTRACT OF NEGATION

I, too, have denied God. I am an expert in the negation of God. I know by experience the best of all negations – the worst, therefore, the most potent, the most convincing, the most sad: the negation of God on the plain evidence of the senses. I did not deny God out of defiance, nor out of bravado, nor out of indignation at the terrible evidence of Evil and of God's treachery; nor because I did not like the parish priest, nor because I had seen too many despicable Christians, nor because I had heard too many puerilities and fatuities pronounced in God's name, nor because they tried to give me a religious education during my child-hood, when human beings are least accessible to piety – (it is only towards the age of thirty that one begins to understand, because he is beginning to know life and the value of things, or their non-value).

I did not deny God because I found such and such a passage in the Bible, and especially in the Old Testament, absurd, ridiculous or horrifying - for the acts of ferocious fanaticism committed by the Hebrews are particularly revolting; and the good actions of the Christians are not to be found in the New Testament – they are elsewhere. Finally, I did not deny God, as it seems some Englishman did recently, because God did not answer his prayer that his school team should win a game of rugby – an admirable reason, which contains in a nutshell the essence of almost all prayers to God, and of all negation of God.

As for me, the more I made the personal and undeniable acquaintance – I will not say of God, but of grace, of that little touch of deeply moving tenderness, of that tiny glimmer of gratitude that flickers at the centre of my being, and that is clarified and purified with the years, with maturity, with the approach of old age – the more I was visited by 'the abomination of desolation' (Matthew 24:15). So that, much as I hope to receive once more – or, if it please God, many times more – the grace of feeling gratitude arise within me, the joy issued from the pit, from deep down inside me, from the depths of time and being, come from God and granted by him, even so much do I know that I am still threatened by the wilderness. These last years, these last months, it befell me three times, four times, to deny God in my heart.

'The fool hath said in his heart: there is no God.' He who is unfortunate, unhappy, says in his heart: there is no God. In the deepest depths of misfortune I have stopped for an instant, holding my breath, between two heart-beats, and I have 'understood' suddenly that there is no God. I shall even say that 'I have seen' there is no God. For the negation of God is an essentially visual, or sensorial affair; it tells the believer: show him to me, I want to see him.

For me, it was a vision in the wilderness. You have been cheated, I told myself, you are mistaken, don't you see there is nothing, that there is no one there, that nothing has any value? Have the courage to admit it.

An immense and sterile wasteland; dead sand, ashes, the wind of nothingness, the cold of absolute solitude. One has to imagine an earth grown cold, humanity long since dead, life extinguished: and *then* believe in God, if one can, and *then* love God.

I speak of the interior desert, worse than any other. I speak of that sudden contraction of the heart, of that instant of forsaken realization, chilled to the marrow of one's bones, frozen: 'There is no God.' There is nothing. There is no one there. Nothing on earth had any value, any being that was not perishable, illusory, derisory.

That was in my room, at the end of the afternoon, or towards evening, and it left me shaken. The second time, it was towards four o'clock in the afternoon, in the bathroom, under the shower, before turning on the tap. Dried-out, the heart withered away, the soul run dry, as one says of a dried-up well. 'There is no God.'

A fraction of a second later, I told myself: 'You who are denying God: if you had not had a friend to give you a helping hand just as you were about to die, you would now be dead.' I was like those people who reject the progress to which they owe their existence, for without it they would have died in infancy, or would not even have been conceived, their parents, their ancestors being already dead before they could procreate; or would have been carried off by plagues. Perhaps there was no God, but there was certainly man. There was human goodness. There was mutual aid, charity, solidarity – it little matters what we call it – in one word, amity, to which I dedicate these words. And that was a gift, or, to eschew all solemnity, a product, a derivative of this universe without God. I had the right to deny God, as I could not see him; but I did not have the right to deny grace, as I had experienced it: the grace of the universe, of chance, of necessity, of hazard, of the absurd – it little matters what name we give it. I prefer the greatest name of all. But just at that very instant, I only needed to remember human goodness, thanks to which I was alive – I was alive, and offering myself the luxury of denying God!

A second suffices to overthrow negation. I knew all the cute little tricks of negation. I knew how one denies the existence of goodness, how one demolishes it by means of suspicion and calumny, Freudian analysis, Marxist analysis, La Rochefoucauldian analysis or Tacitean analysis, reduction to culpability, to infantilism, to class interest, to self-regard, to lust for power and murky sensualities, down in the darkest dumps of our souls. But I was honest enough to deny the existence of God when I could not see him, and I was also honest enough not to deny the existence of human goodness when it had saved my life. What did it matter to me what concentration of impulses caused my brother, my neighbour, to stretch his hand out to me when I was drowning? He, too, like all of us, was in his every gesture governed by a field of vectors, a swarming mass of determinants; he also was a nest of serpents – but restorative ones, and that delegate of chance, of the absurd, of nothingness, of that God I had just denied, had saved my life.

It so happens that the person in question was the best, the most charitable, the most generous, the most noble I have ever known, and his wife was worthy of him. And of course, involuntarily, they made each other suffer, and suffered also because of that... I know what I am talking about. A good, noble human being is not a pure creature doing good; he is a troubled human being, a mess of obscure impulses, corrupted, but who does good and who spreads around him sweetness and peace. The wicked man is perhaps a pure creature, an innocent, an immaculate, an incorruptible being, but who kills me, lets me drown, lets me die of hunger or anguish, lets me commit suicide; who slits my throat for a little cash because he urgently needs a fix; who sends me to the gas chamber and to the crematorium ovens because of my foreskin (or lack of one), to the stake because of my faith or my lack of faith, to the guillotine because I have an aristocratic name; who looses a round of machine gun fire in my belly because I belong to a certain social or political group, according to a very bad and superannuated sociological theory whose exponents only raise laughter. Repression, sublimation, exploitation, alienation, call it what you will; but here we have on the one hand someone who murders me, another who passes by indifferent, and a third who saves my life. I know that all three of them are suffering. I know that Jesus Christ commands me to love them, and I cannot reject that commandment without weakness, cowardice and malice.

But Jesus Christ does not ask me to call the good wicked and the wicked good, nor to call them *wertfrei*, 'floating values', determined by neutral determinations, indifferent, free from all moral valorization: and truth forbids me to deny what I see, or to call it by its opposite name, and to falsify language, my one link with reality and with human beings. I am not of the left, after all. As for the one who passes by without helping me, without seeing me, or who sees me and turns away his head – that character so well known on the motorways – whether he does so because of the stars, because of class society, because of his libido, I know only this: he could save his fellow-man, and he lets him perish.

I know goodness, having experienced it myself; I was given the grace of orison, people were kind to me, I was offered friendship; I have known man in a way that does not allow me to deny his goodness, and consequently I feel an insurmountable difficulty in denying God who created him thus.

Negation mounted an attack again. Reality mounted an attack again. A third, a fourth time, as suddenly as the state of orison, my eyes were opened on the terrible nothingness of the world. 'There is no God.' All at once, everything withered, nothing had any more colour, scent, savour or sense; nothing had being any more. There was nothing left for me but to lie on the ground and let myself give up the ghost like a sick animal or a famine victim. Ardrey speaks of man's essential illusion, that of having some value and some importance, whether it be in a universe so measureless that if man found himself reduced to his real dimensions there would be nothing left for him to do but lie down, fetch a final sigh, and pass away. Deserving of praise as he may be for revealing to the profane the twentieth century's ethological revolution – concealed, passed over in silence and denied by the new obscurantists, the academic behaviourist, Marxist and Paleoliberal or Rousseauist obscurantists – he is not a good

philosopher. For who is it measures the value, the importance, and indeed even the reciprocal dimensions of the
universe and man? Who is the mensurating animal, the
valorizing or the devalorizing animal? Ardrey is only
describing a value crisis, known to the devout as negation
of God. A fossil skull one million years old is the image of
my value; even worse, the flank of a mountain with the
strata of coral limestone well displayed, which once was an
atoll in a vanished ocean, replaced today by a chain of
mountains: *that* is my portrait, that cubic centimetre of
limestone, which was once a living being, a pulsing
animalcule in warm, sunny water, eating whatever came
within its reach, excreting in the same current of blue
water, and injecting it with its sexual secretions: a dream
existence, then extinction, and millions of years of
nothingness.

The evidence of the absence of God is visual; the
negation of God, the death of God, the death of values, the
devalorization of the world, the devalorization of man are
operations with a visual base. 'Did you see God up there?',
N.S. Khrushchev asked his country's first astronaut. He
could have looked for himself, and in himself, instead of
making such inane remarks of a Mr Gradgrind seated on
the throne of Gengis Khan. He might have seen God there,
and if not God, man – he who had revealed unto Tartar
socialism the technique of ministerial shuffles without
massacre of unseated ministers, and those bizarre, extraordinary, but so beneficial verities: that one must not kill
everyone on earth, and that bread is preferable to terror.

I lived under his predecessor, in the days of terror, and I
know how the more or less positive reforms brought
about by Nikita Sergeyevich were a benefit to a large
section of humanity. But the question, primitive as it was,
was nevertheless a good one, and pertinent, as was to be
expected from a man who had the greatness of simplicity,
and who, rustic as he was, called a spade a spade, blessed
be his imperfect memory.

For the negation of God is the negation of a visible God. There is no object, no being in the universe, no concept in the logical universe, that I can identify with God. Every attempt to trace the outline of God ends in disaster. God is the projection of my being, or of my intellect, or of my anguish, or of my ignorance, into nothingness, emptiness, the unknown. God is always anthropomorphic. Nature, History, the Social Classes, the Subconscious, the Unconscious, the Id, the Thing In Itself, Necessity, Chance, Nothingness and the Species, as well as all manner of Systems, including the Ecosystems, those crucified victims, are equally anthropomorphic beings, that behave, in the contexts in which they appear, like Homeric heroes, or the Homeric gods, in all their humanity. Fabulous beings, God at their head, acting in mimodramas and melodramas worthy of the Duchess of Death herself. What I found particularly amusing were the caperings of capitalism, that Gentleman Crook, and of the Punch and Judy of the Proletariat, 'having at its head the Party of professional revolutionaries who...', etc. But my laughter fades away as I remember the melancholy and the tedium of a world in which that fiction, 'God', has been replaced by fictions so much inferior.

But can we call man heterogeneous, in relation to the universe? Is there such a solution of continuity between each of us and the causal chains, or the distributions of probability, or the vector fields, or the genetic sequences, between us and the history of matter, of living matter, between us and the history of humanity, between us and the physico-mathematical structures of the universe, between us and the logical tissue of the real – including the real in the sense of scholastic realism: is there such a solution of continuity that anthropomorphism has to be radically eschewed? Should not this interdiction be limited to naïve anthropomorphism? And would not the great abyss between man and the universe forbid also, symmetrically, all interpretation of man from the point of view of the universe, hence all knowledge of man with the means and according to the categories of the exact sciences?

Let us reject anthropomorphism, and let us reject the universe. A galaxy and a football team have this in common – they do not exist. They are both myths, descriptive decisions undertaken by myself. There are only individual stars. The galaxy is a myth. There are only players, the football pitch, the goals and the goalkeepers – and the referee – but there is not and never will be a football match. The game does not exist, it is an empty word, *flatus vocis,* applied for ease of description to all individual matches. The team and the match are beings as fictive as God, and as invisible as he. Winning is an empty word, the will to win the match a bizarre disposition of our psychosomatic computer, an instruction we have fed into it under the action of incompletely cognizable determinations.

But I have no wish to come to the rescue of God with irony. There is no God. I must resign myself to that truth. The fourth time, the last or the one before the last – yes, alas, I know it is only the last so far – when the negation of God, or rather the evidence of the nonexistence of God, struck me like an apoplectic fit, I took the second step: I accepted that negation. Yes, there is no God.

O the solitude, the sadness, the desert! God was all I had had. Nothing in my life and in my person had had any worth, save through him. Save as thin, dark rays issuing from a luminous centre, like that heavenly body which hangs over Dürer's *Melancholy,* and which is not a 'black sun' – they are simply rays which are darker than he. With that radiant centre gone, all that was left was the spider's web, the black rays, a faint stain on nothingness, as insubstantial as ash. I had nothing left.

At this point a utilitarian temptation presented itself: to cling to God through solitude, through essential non-value of being. We know the pitiable reactions of the sort 'if God did not exist, all would be permitted', or, to express myself with a cruel irony: 'If God did not exist, what would become of us?' What does it matter what would become of us? Is his existence a fiction or not? That is the question that has to be answered, without regard for any interior comfort one might lose if the answer is 'No'.

But for me God is not some fiction of my own impotence. He is not, as Nietzsche says, a stopgap, nor, as narrow minded scientists claim, an invention of my ignorance, nor, as Hobbes wrote, a fiction of my fear. I am not inventing him. And certainly I would not invent him in order to give myself courage, as one whistles in the dark. Nor is he a fiction of my desires, for I would not invent him in order to address requests to him. None of the classical critics of scepticism and unbelief, from Euhemerus to Russell, has any power over the relationship between me and God. He is not found in explanations. For the explanation of the universe, eternally incomplete and in infinite progression, I put myself in the hands of the exact sciences, with their critical commentary tempered by philosophy. He is not consolation: I do not ask him to console me. I ask nothing of him. He is not escape: I am not running away from anything. He is not hope of eternity: I live on the hypothesis that death is repose, sleep, extinction. And despite all that, I was not going to treat myself indulgently, and I was not going to spare or excuse God the severest scrutiny. It is true I was running away from the feeling of absolute non-value, of absolute non-sense, of absolute solitude. I was running away from nothingness, the absurd, all that was hollow and base, the experience of radical devalorization of the being. I took refuge from the icy breath of that evidence in an absolute reality, an absolute certitude, both illusory, manmade, or made from man's anguish. Flight, panic, next-best thing; masturbation, rambling talk to reassure myself. Courage, man: there is no God, nothing is, nothing has any value.

For I do hope that no one will ask me to see that value and that being unpossessed by God in trivial fictions and paltry caricatures like Society, Country, Class, Party, Humanity. I do not see God, but I can see those all too clearly. If I resist being intoxicated by God, I am not going to let myself get drunk on the cat's piss of those words which are really somewhat inferior to the name of God.

There is only one thing left: truth. Courage, I told myself. Set yourself free. Tear out your heart. Live without God. You have nothing left, but at least you will have had the courage and the dignity of truth. Grit your teeth, and die like a dog.

I know the most subtle and terrible of temptations: to cling to God out of weakness; because I would not know how to go on existing without him. (I should continue to exist, certainly, but I would be dead.)

I resisted that temptation, too. I was ready to accept nothingness, and to perish miserably in my heart; without stoic pride, I must confess that the satisfaction of truth and heroic dignity leave me cold when confronted with my death, when I see myself dead, incinerated and scattered like ash on the wind. But that is just how I want to die. I am prepared, and I am so at every moment. Nothing certain, no value, except the mathematicable knowledge of the universe, and a little predictable activity – to the second or third collateral effect, when there arrives the unforeseen catastrophe: 'that's not what we intended'. The rest is entropy. Very well. I don't mind. I accept.

Negation would have triumphed – she would still triumph – if I had been suffering from amnesia.

My eyes tell me that God is nowhere there, that there are only individual objects, and systems of movement. My wounded heart tells me that it is being suffocated by Evil, and that we are crushed by Evil, that there is only suffering, and a few paltry pleasures, mainly physical ones, and no God. My sovereign intellect, which thinks as if it were cut off from space-time, from history and the duration of the universe behind it, and from the tissue of the universe around it and in it, tells me vaingloriously, with a nasty snigger, the saying of Laplace: 'I have no need of that hypothesis' (after which, the republican Empire baron – what did he want with such trivialities, he who was so contemptuous of God? – invented the Genius of Laplace, a description of God conceived by a mathematician). All our Graeco-Latin, humanist, scientific, positivist, philosophical intellectual formation based on the blinding evidence – it does indeed blind – of our own eyes, turns us away from God. And I will not mention Jesus Christ.

But what can it be, this memory, difficult to eradicate unless by amnesia, senile decay, mental powers diminished through nervous shock, illness or accident? What can it be, this tiny, faint, delicate glimmer of tenderness, this rush of gratitude, this marvellous instant of the free and disinterested gift of oneself, addressed to the unknown, with full lucidity, in the clear light of the intellect, in pure and sweet fullness of heart?

I deny no evidence, not even that of the absence of God. All the same, I am not going to deny the evidence of grace. It was here, a few days ago, as I was gazing abstractedly at the Lake of Zürich, one evening, through the window of my room in the clinic, as I was absently, slowly, taking off my glasses; as long as it took for my hand to fall, holding the glasses in its fingers.

Thank you, God, I should have thought, if I had thought or felt in articulate words, in concepts equipped with their verbal signals. But there were neither words nor concepts, there was only joy, gratitude, affection, that gift of myself. According to my trifling powers, my humble means, my narrow limits: I cannot be other than what I am. But what is it, this spark of grace that glows, flowers, blossoms? Who is it? It was not I – it came from deep behind me, from the depths of the universe and of time. It was a gift. It was I, in me, but certainly someone other than I, something other than I. It was a contact with the tissue of the universe – the logical, mathematical, physical, biological, affective, intellectual universe; the briefest instant of rediscovery, of reconciliation, of re-identification.

Nothing much; a poor thing; cannot be seen, is not good to eat, not good to play with for enjoyment and pleasure, nor to use as a club, a tool, a drug – to kill, manipulate, manufacture, buy, sell, dominate, direct, impose one's Me: that is of no value whatsoever. Adam the ape asks his anthropomorphic God, his pithecanthropomorphic God, for a banana, and tries to manipulate God with his hands, in a rite. I do not despise Adam the ape; he is my ancestor, my father, he is myself, and his clumsy piety is mine: there is an age-old continuity, through evolution and sublimation, but still a continuity, between the rite of offering God a banana, prayer which asks for a banana, and my simple thought of God, and my offer of myself. I saw an Amazonian Indian, clothed in a piece of rope round his loins, arranging two or three pebbles and two or three waterlilies on the bare earth: he was celebrating his mass. He was addressing himself to God. With his couple of pebbles and his couple of flowers, he was I, who arrange a few concepts and sequences of verbal symbols as reverently and in the same intention of conversing with God as he his childlike cult objects.

I will not give in: if it is not a projection of my fear, nor the image of the Father, can it be an aspect of my solitude? Is it a projection of those pleasant little moments that a benevolent Nature saw fit to give me? Is God an invention of my little moments of euphoria?

Rather deny God than deny doubt; rather accept negation, than to make faith easy for oneself. God can be denied. What cannot be denied is the action of grace, adoration, orison, prayer; for me, very modestly, it is thanksgiving. Thanksgiving to whom? I do not know. Can there be someone there? Or something? So I am alone, in a solipsistic universe composed only of myself and my fantasies, and I am addressing my gratitude to one of those fantasms, the most fantasmatic of all. That is an hypothesis, it is not evidence. There remains the evidence of grace. It cannot be seen, it cannot be verified, it cannot be induced, it does not come whenever we choose to experiment with it, but it is there – grace, the instant of gratitude in which the great unknown context itself is found again in my consciousness and in my heart, with perfect intellectual clarity, in perfect emotional transparency. Am I going to deny it, I whom it has sometimes brushed with its wing?

Here once more is found that strange asymmetry of opposites which verbally, superficially, are as symmetrical as the two sides of an equation. The negation of God is not symmetrical with the action of grace, or with orison. I am not speaking of 'faith'; I do not have it, and I do not know what it is to 'believe' in something that might not exist. For me, that something, then, is the object of an hypothesis, and not of a belief. Thus death as annihilation: hypothesis, one that seems probable to me; but 'believe' in it?

Negation is common, prosaic, a question of visual evidence: we meet the absence of God wherever we go, whatever way we take. He is nowhere visible, nor palpable. All the objects stand there before us, but God is absent. As I indicated above, concepts, mathematical relationships, things as real as a football match, are not there, they are not visible and palpable except through the interposition of individual concrete objects assigned to them. But I am not concerned here with analyzing levels of reality. I accept negation as it is, in all its brute stupidity. It is a question of the evidence of the senses; one falls back on their evidence, a surrender takes place, we bow to the evidence, passive and vanquished by it.

The action of grace is active. One addresses God; instead of opening one's eyes to let oneself be invaded by things, one closes them in order to concentrate oneself upon the leap, or rather to concentrate oneself *into* the leap of the soul. There is nothing equivalent, nor homologous, corresponding to the platitude and the triviality *(trivia,* something found at every crossing) of negation, for grace is rare, exquisite, fragile, interior, hidden, and hard to put into words.

And more evident. I do not need the evidence of my senses to convince myself of my gratitude, nor in order to address that gratitude to my unknown interlocutor. The evidence of grace is stronger than the evidence of the absence of God. His absence is a discovery that leaves me without a leg to stand on, floored, crushed. His presence is neither a surprise, nor a shock, nor a discovery; it is the action of grace addressed to him in all simplicity and in all felicity. It is outside and beyond the question. It is not the affirmative response, opposed to the negative response: it is the shrug of the shoulders at such a question ever being posed. Grace, and even the memory of grace, is stronger than despair, stronger than sorrow; I have just experienced it, and it is stronger than negation and the evidence of the absence of God. For negation can be maintained only by effacing the memory of former states of grace. Negation of God is no longer possible for me, except through forgetfulness.

Which does not mean to say I am not threatened. Forgetfulness is possible. The terrible lassitude of the heart, the impotence of the soul, the death of all affection, the exhaustion of all tenderness and of all sweetness: in one word – the loss of God remains hanging over me. At any moment, the evidence of the nonexistence of God may reimpose itself upon me.

My God, save me, do not abandon me, give me the strength not to forsake thee. Nevertheless, not my will, but thy will be done. If I must lose thee, let me at least not lose the memory of thee. But even if I lose that, even if I lose all, I give thee thanks for these few instants of grace that thou hast given me. For one man's life, that is grace enough.

10.

THEOLOGY OF
THE NONEXISTENT GOD

Apart from the certitude of the heart, there has been granted me the certitude of the spirit. With my humble means, clumsily, I transmit it here, hoping that perhaps it will be of service to someone. I have collected in a schematic survey the various stages of my progress.

1

I know nothing about God and I would not know how to say anything about him. I can only grope my way, stammering, as I do here. My strength is not equal to saying anything coherent and adequate about him, and if I had that superhuman strength, human language would betray me, disintegrating as soon as it leaves its legitimate universe: the reality beyond prayer. But I shall keep on; I cannot and will not stop myself addressing that presumedly unknown interlocutor, to whom I offer in actions of grace the grace of orison that I have received from him. I am blind, but no one can prevent me from feeling my way. I am lame, but no one can prevent me from crawling towards that source of light that I cannot see, but that I sense as they say blind people can sense light. Even if I know in advance that I shall stop somewhere along the road before reaching it; even if I know that one cannot reach it. It is the road that matters.

2

My situation makes me think of Pascal's wager. That, of course, has a strangely, one might almost say a basely, utilitarian aspect – let us make a wager with chance: if we lose, we shall have lost nothing, and if we win, we shall have gained a blissful immortality. If at least there had been a risk of serious loss, that would have been more noble; if the mathematician holding the bank had said that if we lose, we face eternal damnation. But Pascal's wager – I count him among my saints – is redeemed in my eyes by its other appearance, of wild dissipation, even debauch. It has a Dostoevskian, or more precisely a Tolstoian air, the air of a mortal wager and the English Club in Moscow: one plays for one's soul at Russian roulette, using a pistol with two barrels – one loaded, the other empty. It wasn't too bad, for a man of the age of Louis XIV, and a native of Clermont-Ferrand.

But of course, the point of the wager is the frightening, despairing feeling that one must throw one's all on a 'yes' or a 'no', with no possible retreat, no withdrawal, no reason.

But I cannot believe in God. I cannot 'believe'. I cannot throw myself into the void. I cannot *wager* my being. The game implies the very opposite of all that is serious. Even if the game, should one lose, is mortal, another dimension of existence remains, the one which is not a game. Now if there is anything serious in my being and in my existence, apart from sorrow, it is those few instants of felicity. At those times, I did not seek for him, I did not doubt him, I did not believe in him, I did not even have any certainty of his existence: I quite simply addressed myself to him, without words, and without naming him to whom I was speaking; without even identifying him, as that did not come into question; and certainly without knowing him.

Once again I find myself faced with that curious asymmetry of things which verbally seem to be the two contrary directions of a same straight line produced from a single point of departure, like good and Evil, and which in truth are completely alien to one another, more than opposites: absolutely heterogeneous; still like good and

Evil, but also like sleep and dancing, the *analysis situs* and the digestion of a too heavy meal. The negation of God and 'faith' are, even in Pascal -- who moreover can hardly be accused of a geometrical turn of mind – symmetrical; when they are only so verbally, and not in reality. The wager seems to be a wager with two chances, one white, one black, with a fifty per cent probability on either side: but this is not so; the absence of God is proven for me by a myriad sentient facts in my daily experience, millions of unities of phenomenological duration, if such unities of measure existed.

And set against them, there is only an instant, or several instants, of 'faith', that is, grace, the state of orison. It is not one to one, it is a million to one. No quantitative symmetry. No qualitative symmetry either, for it is not the evidence of God's presence that is opposed to the evidence of the absence of God, but, in those people who have known the same experience as I, something asymmetrical, heterogeneous to negation: something beside the question. There is no problem. I do not seek to know if God is there. I address myself to him, with affection, with filial affection made intellectually possible by a philosophical proposition to which I shall return. There is no problem, and so no solution, but a dissolution. I am no longer interested in the problem of the existence of God.

I wrote 'certainty' and 'certitude'; but it is not a question of 'certainty'. It is I who address myself to God; but it is also another, who comes from elsewhere, from 'down in the dumps' and acts in me and through me. He to whom I address myself is another; but truly I know no other being in him nor other sojourn for him but in my heart and in the thoughts I direct towards him: in my prayer, or more precisely, in my action of grace. He is in me, but he is not me. God knows, and I know, that there is no question, at that instant, of 'my' heart, of 'my' thought, of 'my' prayer, or of 'Me'. They belong to him, I belong to him, I have no other existence than that. A friend who read these notes tells me that there is a passage in Saint Theresa in which she jokes with God, with all filial love; that reassures me, for I believed myself, with some trepidation, to have been the only one to have said to him, laughing, in the night: 'I thank thee, but it has to be said, you know, that it is to yourself you do it...'

But he is not there. There is no one there. The conversation I have with him, that conversation with one voice, and one way only, is the monologue of a halfwit in his padded cell.

3

That critique of my conversation with God, the most thorough-going of all, is essentially that of Bertrand Russell, and it errs by excess of logic.

The greatest logician since Aristotle was Gotthold Frege, and since Gotthold Frege, Bertrand Russell. Two thousand five hundred years after their discovery by the school of Eleatic philosophers, Russell gave the solution to the logical paradoxes. As befitted the twentieth century and that falsely liberal spirit, secretly thirsting for power, it is a police regulation. It is forbidden to the Cretans to pass an opinion on the veracity or the mendacity of the Cretans. Forbidden to state anything about their own class of statements; all must be done in the immediately superior metalanguage.

After that, the greatest logician of this century invented the most famous dilemma of the century: *Better Red than dead*. The middle was not excluded. To humiliate us even further, Russell lent his name to enterprises of political paranoia, or of political charlatanism, which have as little in common with justice as with logic. He was the offspring of a great aristocratic family, and I have observed among fifty- and sixty-year-olds coming from great historical families in my own country the same attitude towards life, that of a well-brought-up little boy, but full of high spirits, irrepressible, because raised in the profound conviction, the unthinking conviction, that nothing irreparable could ever happen to him. Russell was a great mind and a vain and frivolous creature. His critique of prayer as a wrong connection with an unknown interlocutor whose existence cannot be verified ignores the essential. Prayer is not a communication between two equal poles. It resembles the one communication that can legitimately bear that name, that between two human beings; but in prayer, one of the two poles is identified with the other in a state of grace. The distinction between the two poles is swept away. And from the start it is made between the part and the whole, and not between two 'wholes' that are autonomous and equivalent.

Once again, Russell's critique errs by excess of logic. It fails to perceive the fact that it is a question of paradoxical relationship, of the relationship between God, who is exterior and interior to men, and man, who is not autonomous before God. Or if he is, or believes himself to be, prayer cannot take place. It would be making an affirmation that radically prevents prayer, makes it essentially impossible. All description of prayer, with full awareness of what one is talking about, is paradoxical and so it has no logical sense. All logical analysis of prayer is absurdity and foolishness before personal experience of prayer: it is like a blind man pronouncing on the colour in a Van Gogh.

4

The only sort of relationship that can exist between us and God – the only sort that can be true, incontestable, uncontested, a factual truth, though unverifiable by experiment – prayer is a relationship that escapes negation because it is inaccessible to it in so far as negation is thought and language. This relationship goes beyond the limits of language and distorts logical thought – that is, thought as we know it. Logic rules the relationships between the parts of the universe and between their mental signals; it could not properly be applied to a being apprehended as transcending all limitations.

I make my way towards God. I address myself to him. I allude to him by means of symbolic constructions or constructs, pebbles and flowers disposed in a certain manner, victims with their throats slit according to this or that rite, statues, painted images, concepts, propositions composed of concepts and ligatures. But nothing more, never. I cast my prayer into the void.

The void? The void, emptiness, that space-time curving and turning back upon itself, or that is structured from an even stranger, and yet unknown matter, and traversed by swarms of particles of energy like the flakes of snow in a storm on the steppe? I know that 'energy' is a word which only makes sense by the equations in which it is placed, and that these equations only make sense by this pos-tulated, indicated, accepted concept: approaching its limits, logico-mathematical thought, experimental thought, is distorted and denatured as language is de-formed and denatured when it approaches the concept of God.

I cast my prayer into the void; I cast my prayer towards God, projection of my unmotivated jubilation; my prayer is nothing but a small psychosomatic euphoria cast into the void.

The void? The known and the unknown, the all and myself, the sum of beings that transcends it, the speakable and the unspeakable, the knowable and the unknowable, the light in supernovae and absolute blackness, the fra-grances and the sounds and the play of colours in the sensible universe, and the cold of the interstellar night at a temperature of absolute zero, the void of those great holes in space and the monstrous density of matter at the heart of heavenly bodies where it has its birth, the absurd, the void, the desert of the world and the logical tissue of the universe in which two and two make four – in galaxies, in rosebuds, in pairs of animals, in finger-snappings – but also in which, on the frontiers of that logical universe the statements on their own class terminate necessarily in paradox, and in which beyond Newtonian space-time geometries no longer tolerate the Euclidian axiom of the parallels – is that it, the void? It is towards that fundamental postulate and whatever transcends it that I turn, humbly, clumsily, and call God. I did not write that I call *it* God. I know nothing about God. I cast my gratitude into the void, I want to call out in the void. If there is no one there, I want to address myself to that strange absence.

However, may I be allowed to find audacious the negation of all this. For it is of all this I am talking, and of what goes beyond all this. 'There is nothing that goes beyond all this.' I allow myself to find that negation a risky one. To deny God, a God about whom one has not thought in any rigorous way, a God who one imagines more or less consciously to be a human personage or a humanoid being situated somewhere in the atmosphere of the planet Earth, is one thing. But to deny all this, the sum of things and everything beyond, immanence and transcendance: that is an enterprise whose temerity, presumption and frivolity surpass those I may be afflicted with. To deny God – fair enough, or unfair enough; but to deny everything I can see, everything I know, everything I am permitted to infer? And to deny – qualifying it as unmotivated psychosomatic euphoria – that supremely motivated leap of tenderness, of gratitude, of friendship, of peace, which turns me towards all this, and which is the one thing of value in my life, arising from the very depths of my being, from those profoundest deeps where 'I' is no longer me, but only the culmination of the very thing that surrounds me in space-time and projects me out of the past, in accordance with all thinkable and unthinkable dimensions? To deny all this? Deny God? I cannot do it.

5

One cannot deny the God of pantheism. All one can do is refuse him our prayer. To deny the God of pantheism is an incorrect way of uttering the proposition: 'I have no inclination for spiritual things.' But it must be said openly, and nothing said about God.

6

I owe it to the exact sciences to be able to pray. The exact sciences are for me the first preparation for prayer. Today, for all of us, they are the first and decisive 'Introduction to the Spiritual Life'. The exact sciences invite me to consider the whole of being. The philosophy founded on the exact sciences invites me to prayer. And a definition of the concept of God, formulated in 1078, just over nine hundred years ago, tells me to whom I should address my prayer, whose general direction had been indicated to me by the exact sciences and logical empiricism. I am sketching the stages by which I arrived at the impossibility of doubting God. Moreover, when one has reached that point, one rediscovers what one already knew, and I write this in the depths of sorrow, but awaiting patiently the return of grace. For it is not a question of knowing if God is or is not; one just has to love him – and that comes, or does not come, as God alone wills.

7

The exact sciences take me back to God. I am speaking here of the Aristotelian logics, not the non-Aristotelian, of the whole of mathematics, of generalized relativity, of quantum physics and microphysics, of cosmology and astronomy, of chemistry based on nuclear physics, of biology and genetics based on chemistry, of sociobiology and ethnology – experimental and mathematized as far as possible – of ecology, and to a lesser degree of the historical sciences; as for the social sciences, they are either mathematized or contemptible.

The exact sciences give me the world held in the grip of mathematical expressions, of programmes of experimental verification and of infallible predictions, verifiable experimentally, of the type *given A, then B.* They weave across the abyss a tissue of equations as solid as a steel floor, and like the steel floor, composed of particles separated by immense voids. Through each of its holes, the net of propositions which the exact sciences weave above the unknown gives glimpses of the abyss.

Step by step, tirelessly, the exact sciences thrust forward their line of advance positions, teaching me at each step that beyond this line of advance positions in constant progression there is Something Else. The experience of four thousand years of exact sciences, ever since the surveyor-geometers, the arithmetical warehousemen, the priest-astronomers of the valleys of the Nile, the Tigris and the Euphrates, the Indus and the Yellow River, teaches us that beyond the line of advance positions of the exact sciences there is always Something Else; that beneath the unyielding territory won and consolidated by them, there is Something Else; that in their very texture, in their bearing, their vocabulary, the syntax of their propositions, the schema of their methods, their point of departure, their point of arrival, and their collateral results, there is always Something Else, discoverable, and, perhaps, beyond that, Something Else, undiscoverable.

The two hypotheses of the most general kind in the exact sciences are: a) the existence of the world; and b) the existence of the unknown. The exact sciences take me back to transcendence. The world in their grip is the one firm ground in the universe; consolidated, cemented by them, it is infiltrated by the unknown, invaded by transcendental cells; their All This is the other side of Something Else. The exact sciences are the most trustworthy and only indubitable indicator of transcendence; the ground of their certainty is the launching-pad of prayer.

8

I consider the world strictly and exclusively according to the data and the methods of the exact sciences. This consideration of the world gives me: a) the world in the grip of the exact sciences, and b) all that goes beyond them. The exact sciences give me mastery of the known, the desire for the unknown, and make me question my attitude before the known-unknown continuum, immanence-transcendence, All This and Something Else. This is the way in which they are the introduction to prayer. They are the intellectual preparation for that leap of the heart, of the whole being gathered together in a powerful emotion, and addressed to God. The exact sciences clear the ground for that leap.

The current gross prejudice bequeathed to our century by that of Mr Gradgrind would have us believe that the exact sciences make religion impossible. It is the contrary that is true: the exact sciences make religion possible, necessary and inevitable, because they demonstrate the continuity and therefore the unity of being, its infinite depth in all conceivable dimensions, categories and qualities; and because, making ourselves the masters of that portion held firmly in their grip, they tell us: 'For the rest, and also for the sum of what we give you and what we do not give you, you must address yourselves elsewhere.'

It is true that Christians, and in the first place the Church, the hierarchy, the theologians, have lived for three centuries – those of enlightenment, progress and ideologies, as if Pascal, Descartes, Newton and Leibnitz had never existed. The greatest mathematicians since Al-Khwarezmi and before Gauss, the creators of analytical geometry and the differential calculus – the one a constructor of a world system, the other a constructor of a system of the sciences, two precursors of cybernetics and data processing, the one through his calculating machine, the other through his research into the *ars combinatoria* – they were Christians, and the first-named was a great mystic. As I am very ignorant, I know only one scholar in our own times who was at the same time their equal and a man of the spirit – yes, I do mean Einstein. It is not religion that the exact sciences make impossible, but murky, superstitious, lukewarm, lazy, intellectually dishonest religion, the religion of tradition, of habit, of convenience, or on the contrary the religion of enthusiasm and frenzy, without intellectual effort, without any rigour of the spirit, without unity of intellect and soul, and thus without the whole man. The exact sciences do not make prayer impossible: they only make prayer impossible except on the most elevated level to which my intellect can aspire.

9

The perception of the sensible universe is naturally atheist: I do not see, feel, smell, hear or taste God, but only the chaos of things. Intellection of the universe through the exact sciences invites to prayer. The exact sciences reveal to me in the chaos of things the subtendant and the constituent, the order of abstract relationships, skeleton of the concrete, and to which the structure and the functioning of my intellect are so strangely related, so strangely adequate. It comes about that an abstract game of my intellect, apparently functioning in a vacuum, is revealed after centuries or even after thousands of years to correspond with the mathematical scaffolding of the real universe: as if the world were thought, and as if my thought were the thought of that thought, the mind of that mind. The atoms of Democritus were still true two thousand years after Democritus. Anaxagoras of Clazomene affirmed in the fifth century before Jesus Christ that the world is reason, *noûs*, and that the universe is composed of whirlwinds, as Descartes affirmed twenty centuries after him, and as nuclear physics proved three centuries after Descartes; in an infinitely tiny universe, particles of whirling energy, and in an infinitely great universe, galaxies and spiral nebulae, their arms bent by the wind of rotation. I amuse myself with metaphors, because my reader knows better than I the history of mathematical hypotheses confirmed by experiments in astronomy, physics, genetics, sociometry.

(Anaxagoras dared claim that the sun is a burning stone bigger than the Peloponnese and more than forty thousand stadia from the earth. And Athenian democracy accused him of impiety, as it accused Socrates a little later. Anaxagoras escaped execution only by going into exile. He was also a metic, *métoikos,* 'outsider', second class inhabitant, resident, noncitizen so he could leave Athens without losing his homeland, which he no longer had. Republican, democrat and outsider, I am determined not to forget what I am and what we are.)

The exact sciences purify piety by forbidding it to take heed of anything else but God. All research, investigation, curiosity, experiment, distraint, manipulation, domination, reduction to the known and the predictable – all that is not prayer, nor can it nor ought it to be. The Me of the exact sciences is the adversary of things, and then their master. The Me of the prayer is not the adversary of his silent interlocutor, and in the end he is no longer Me. Prayer enriches me, comforts me, directs me, not by a seizure of power over things, but by the indelible memory of joy.

However, it is rather surprising to find the exact sciences so powerless before the proliferation of a new kind of superstition centred round them. I am speaking of the folklore of the half-educated, of the semi-scientific, those primitive peoples of industrial society, with their ectoplasms, flying saucers, visitors from outer space and secret and absolutely unimportant messages entombed in the

Pyramids, in the ruins of the Incas and on Easter Island. I have heard a minor savant proclaiming before the television camera his belief in the existence of life on the planet Mars, with a tone of blind fanaticism that revolted me. I should be ashamed to 'believe' in God in that way. 'Faith' should not be an eruption of irrationality. One does not expect to find an energumen in a laboratory, but he would seem to be not uncommon there.

A few years ago, a capsule was projected into space, containing, beside a drawing representing an unclothed man and woman, both very plain-looking, just physical formulae, a recorded tape with two messages. The first was composed of platitudes given in Basic English, and with an Austrian accent, by a functionary of the so-called United Nations – a name that now seems a pitiable attempt at nostalgia, not so say comedy. The second message contained the words 'Hello, here's the Earth', croaked out by a little girl with a Brooklyn accent. I like space capsules, naked men and women when they are good-looking, and physical equations; the Austrian accent amuses me, the Brooklyn one also, and I adore children; I can overcome my disgust at the spectacle presently offered by the United Nations, and I have nothing against extra-terrestrial vegetables and animals. But how lamentable it is, that solitude which opens its arms to the first cephalopod it meets, even hypothetical. And even if it is only a lichen, even less sociable. They invent anything, dream of anything, fraternize with nightmare beings provided it is not serious, not true, not committing us in any way. They invent a Jesus falsified as a hippy, they transfer the Saviour to an imaginary ante-historical period, into fictitious worlds; they believe with passionate faith, the wicked zeal of the fanatic, in all the spatial Tarascos, provided it does not distract us from ourselves, such as we are, from God in us, such as our praying hearts adore, from our fellow man such as he is, concrete, present, close beside us. Those people who say hello to octopuses to whom they have not been introduced would not so much as bother to say good morning to a stranger in the lift.

The exact sciences are guilty of that kind of superstition, because they have forgotten to make themselves available to the general public. The age of enlightenment, the era of progress, even the century of ideologies had a didactic thrust, an intellectual democratism which today have been lost in scientific technocracy. There are fewer and fewer works of popular science written by first-class scholars for the instruction of the general public, and couched in a language accessible to the general reader. The pretext of the difficulty of the subject is nothing but an expression of the lack of love for one's fellow man, a loss of human solidarity, a sluggishness of the intellect, of language and of the heart. They talk about conversing with the thinking lichens of Venus, but they do not think about making themselves understood by their fellows here below.

However, the greatest reproach must be addressed to Christians. It is we, Christians, who have been unable to display the splendour, the strangeness, the sacred character of the real of the those poor souls athirst for the miraculous, for veneration and worship. We have obviously not opened our arms to those people who open their arms to the tentacles of the noble monster, modern version of the noble savage. They did not find their arms filled with our friendship. As in the Goya engraving, 'the sleep of reason engenders monsters'. The sleep of faith, too. Ideologies and superstitions, concentration-camp utopias and interplanetary folklore occupy the void left by the withdrawal of the Christian soul and scientific humanism, by the ebbing of Christian intellect and the élitist encystation of men of science in their special languages, waterproof compartments.

But it is also obviously for Christians to reveal to us the fascinating drama of Christian existence, that adventure often too serious, too dangerous, too difficult, but with instants of exaltation incomparable in any other; and to make others see what is before their eyes, the majesty and sanctity of the intelligible world, resplendent in all its pied beauty, the presence of the divine abyss behind more and more transparent figures and ciphers; and finally its emergence, blazing with light, or in my own poor, humble experience, infinitely delicate and sweet, at the centre of our being – so close, and much more fascinating than the most distant of worlds (whose plurality is not in doubt, but that does not change the terms of the problem).

The exact sciences send me back to transcendence. They prepare me for prayer. Philosophy, in so far as it is a critical commentary on the exact sciences, shows me the general direction in which I should address my being, and forbids me to speak of God, or – which is the same thing – to think of God. It teaches me to pray in silence; what I call the silence of thought. As follows.

10

Five propositions make up the sum of my philosophy. What is special about them is this: once enunciated, no one would dare to doubt them. They are among the rare statements composed of words which have the same restrictive force as mathematical expressions. The first is the aphorism of Pythagoras already quoted, according to which man is the measure of all things.

I shall not concern myself with determining the context of that affirmation, nor the precise meaning Pythagoras gave it; I take it as it is, and I imagine, perhaps wrongly, that he meant much the same as we mean by 'man', 'the measure' and 'all things'. For me, mensurating man is he who measures the infinitesimal intervals between particles of energy, flakes driven by the hurricane of the electromagnetic fields, the man who measures the distance between him and the quasars and the pulsars, the man of the exact sciences, man *par excellence,* at the centre of the universe measured by him in human measurements, formerly inches, feet, steps, miles, *mille passus,* nautical fathoms, cubits; more recently, prudently, he simply calls them metres, from *métron,* measure. He measures in 'measures', with his measure, to his measure. He is the measure of all things. His power over things is expressed in mensurations, before and after the experiment.

The knowledge and the domination of the world by man is achieved by the reading of dials and scales with graduated markings. He measures the day and the night, his day and his night, in hours, *hïrai,* 'rounds', dances in a circle, and minutes, *minute,* 'small', and seconds, *minute seconde,* 'second order of small'. Protagoras also had a mind that worked like this regarding the qualities of whatever exists; at any rate, we understand him so; lost in the crowd of four billion human beings, that is how I interpret him, for my personal use. The sole value judgements expressed in the universe so far are those expressed by man, if one excludes the tropisms, the preferences, the attractions, the appetites of the animals and vegetables. The fundamental value judgement, the one that gives meaning and value to the universe, was formulated by man.

But who is the measure of man? Not the universe, the sum of things, *ta panta:* that would only be a sterile inversion of the proposition. Who gives meaning and value to man and reciprocally to the universe? Man is the judge of all things, but he is not judge of the composite ensemble of all things, of himself and of transcendence. Judgement on man and at the same time on the universe is uttered within man, but not by him. I am only helping, in the role of defendant and assessor, or as a witness. Man, Pythagoras states, is the measure of all things, of the being of those things that do exist, and of the non-being of those things that do not exist. He was probably thinking of the gods, and of their non-being; today we would say he was thinking of God, and of his nonexistence. The question that forms a necessary appendix to Protagoras' axiom, irrefragable in itself, becomes therefore: Who is the measure of man, of his being and of his value in the measure of his existence where he has some kind of value, and of his non-value and of his nothingness in the measure of his assumed existence where he is rendered null and void?

11

The second proposition in my little Table of Axioms is the prescription of William of Occam: we must not invent superfluous concepts. *Entia non sunt multiplicanda praeter necessitatem,* 'Entities ought not to be multiplied except from necessity.' This definitive maxim is the law of exact sciences never to accept a concept which is not the name of a class of objects, or the name of an individual object, or the name of an operation linking individual objects or classes of objects. There are things, the relationships between things, the concepts that name things, the propositions that link concepts. The rest is nothing but empty noise, mere voice sounds, *flatus vocis,* unsupported by reality.

This can be applied to all the objects of metaphysics and theology, and to the concept of God himself. Occam, a devout Christian, was certainly only concerned, like all Franciscan scholastic theology, with placing the concept of God above the ascendancy of the intellect, where only the leap of the heart can reach it. But he had whetted his razor rather too well, and not only cut off the Eternal's beard, but also his head.

We have never deprived ourselves of the most murderous weapons nor of the most efficient tools, and we shall not deprive ourselves of Occam's razor. I use it every day. However, I know by experience that it is impossible to amputate all metaphysics, all theology, to the level of thought; a stump remains, from which grow deformed shoots, excrescences of ideologies, the monstrous proliferation of the stump of Christian theology and of ancient metaphysics grafted upon it. No matter: a fig for Hegel, a fig for Marx, a fig for the existentialist *en-soi* and *pour-soi,* a fig for the arrangement of derangement and of the nought that nullifies: I shall continue to shave myself with Occam's razor till I draw blood.

Only, my little anthology of irreversible maxims includes also a modest compendium of their attendant interrogations. *Qualisnam est summa entium?* Concepts must not be multiplied unduly, that is, without support in reality; but the real is inexhaustible. I accept the law of thinking nothing and giving a name to nothing as long as the concept and its name are not legitimized by a thing, or a class of things, or a relationship between things or classes of things. However, I cannot shut my eyes to what I glimpse beyond the line of advance positions set up by the exact sciences, and through the holes in the net of equations stretched below my feet. Nothing distinct, certainly: a faint glimmer; Meister Eckhart could see a 'spark', Pascal saw a 'night of fire', others the whiteness of a flash of lightning, still others the darkness of God, and finally those who could see joy, or the friendship of God, or peace.

Certainly there are things and their intelligible relationships, but also Something Else, present within them without being identical with them, nor limited to them. Postulate of the beyond, axiom of the beyond-bounds: *entia non sunt circumscribenda citra limitem.* One must not stop before, but pass beyond. Not through speculative folly or frivolity, through philosophical pride, through unbridled invention, but in all humility of spirit and piety of heart, and only to find out there, at the limit of the sum of legitimate entities, and beyond that limit, nothing and no one other than God alone.

12

The third of the five aphorisms that nourish me and that I offer to anyone who wants them, as if I had caught the crumbs of bread and fish by the Lake of Tiberias, is the major proposition of the seventeenth century. Ignorant as

I am, I know of no other axiom which would present man in the same strong light, in the same definitive way, and also give him a solid base in thought. As you may already have guessed: 'I think, therefore I am.' Man is at the centre of the universe measured by him; he strives to measure only what is; and he himself is constituted by the act of thinking. Descartes is looking for the way out of that interior universe, perfect but closed, by the construction of a demon which offers it a cinema performance, and by the most majestic and powerful construction of the concept of a perfect being. He is looking for the way out, but that is not it. There is no way out of the *cogito*. There can be no subsequent proposition to 'I think, therefore I am'; it is the victim of its own strength, which cannot be equalled by a second proposition.

The version that Spinoza proposes to us is *ego sum cogitans,* 'I am thinking'. I have read with astonishment a commentary that judged it superior to the original. The blinding truth is not that of a Me only perceptible in a secondary position, with total self-apprehension, through return of the action upon the thinker; the blazing reality is that of thought in action. Spinoza's version deforms the original and makes it unrecognizable. 'I think, therefore I am' is a perfect circle, but a restricted one: its circumfer-ance, equally zero, coincides with its centre. The only way out is by the entrance: Who is thinking? *Quisnam est iste qui cogitat?* or rather: *Quidnam est istud,* etc. What is this thing that thinks? An impossible question in Descartes' day, and very easy to ask today, when Freud has taught me to see what has always been within me, the operation of the profound layers of the soul, and if the hasard of birth has afflicted me with an irregularity of interior life which leaves me with no illusion regarding the fact that I am not the master, and that it is from the Me behind the scenes that thought springs. Descartes had just made the most considerable enrichment to geometry since Euclid, by basing man on thought and science on method, the greatest forward step made in the constitution of man since Protagoras, and in that of science since the days of Socratic ignorance, henceforward resumed with precision under the form of methodical doubt. In every life a little rain must fall. However, I may be permitted to recall that night, the eve of Saint Martin in 1619, when Descartes had a dream in which the marvellous discovery was revealed to him as if by a miracle, that possibility of reducing physics to mathematics and linking the sciences to one another as if with a chain... In a dream, in sleep – as good an example as ever was of creative thought arisen from 'down in the dumps'.

Descartes knew. He had experienced himself, at the culminating point of his interior history, the passivity of the lucid Me, witness of his own thought, and the spontaneous dynamism of that thought. In *Madame Bovary*, Monsieur Homais readily uses the epithet 'Cartesian' to express the glacial clarity of an excessive lucidity – one that is moreover mythical. He should be told that the man who was the spirit of geometry, the man of method, the man of the rules for the direction of the intellect (and even of the creative spirit, *ingenium*), had received his major creation in a dream, like a pythoness, like those Ancients who went to sleep in the temples in order to solicit on waking the interpretation of their prophetic dreams by oneiromancers. Descartes knew, and yet he did not try to dig behind the scenes, behind the brightly lit stage's back wall. The unknown personage, author of the play, director of the theatre, producer, actor and public all at once, as well as Freudian prompter and machinist or scene-setter in the secret understage, was not identified by him. He believed he recognized him in that actor on the lighted stage, wearing a royal cloak and a crown: the concept of a perfect being. It was not a bad choice; where he went wrong was to have made any choice at all. He who makes a choice is the ruler of his choice. It is true, he could have thought of something worse than that, and preferred the actor who plays the ghost: the Thing-in-itself; or the acrobat, otherwise known as the Spirit in his dialectical progression; or, even worse, the same as Robert Macaire, economic History; or the sword-swallower, Will to power; or finally the Libido, in its indecently-revealing tights.

However, as soon as the I hovering over the lighted stage had chosen among the actors, *he* was the real king; the cloak and the crown of the perfect being were no more than his theatrical attributes, and that being a creature of comedy. One thing remained assured for ever, unshakeable as a tautology: I think, therefore I am. The concept of the perfect being was still not quite the concept of God.

13

The penultimate maxim from my little portable personal table of irrefutable Axioms is by Henri Poincaré. It takes up the aphorism of Protagoras, the deicidal prescription of Occam and the definitive constitution of man in thought, by Descartes. Thought, says Poincaré, is only a spark in a long night; but that spark is everything.

He takes up also, naturally, another aphorism, that by Pascal on the thinking reed, but in D major. In the silence of those infinite spaces, which frighten me, man is only a reed, but a thinking reed. In the long night of the universe, thought is only a spark, but it is that spark that is *all*. I think, therefore I am; I think only the real; I am the measure of all things, the one judge of their existence and their value; and I judge that my thought is all, the one thing of value, and the rest – darkness, frightening silence, infinite and empty spaces, void of value.

They are obvious and constricting like tautologies, my five irrefragable propositions. I do not expect anyone never to affirm that it is not man who is the measure of all things, nor that one must multiply concepts without support in reality, nor that I think, therefore I am not, nor finally that thought is more than a spark in a long night, and that this prolonged light is not all.

Only I find on my list of interrogations appended to the unassailable maxims, the question of finding out the source of thought. I am certainly the centre of the universe, the supreme tribunal of values, the departure point of the electromagnetic soundings of the universe measured by me – feeble being on my little peripheral planet. But Greece was a small part of the ancient Orient, Europe a small part of the continental mass, England a little planet of Europe: these marginal situations are quite in accord with ascendancy over distance, by navigation, astronautics, landmarks, faraway bases... This is the control room of weights and measures, the court of arbitration, and the altar of prayer. It is my own thought that is all. But it is the all that thinks my thoughts in me.

Poincaré's value judgement bases its value on truth and its morals on knowledge. He does not wonder who produces thought. For him, as for Descartes, the I that thinks is a complete wall at the back of the lighted stage on which is played the comedy of thought or the ballet of the passions. There are no wings, there is nothing behind the stage, no mysterious machines below it. The actors, concepts or propositions, come from nowhere, they materialize as they enter the stage. The separation of the Me and of its object and adversary, that which is not Me, and that the Me subjects to its investigations, is completed by the separation of the Me and the Backstage Me, whence thought comes. The first operation of the exact sciences is the scission of the world.

The result of this is that the leap from value knowledge to value friendship cannot be made. There is no friendship between the exact sciences and their object. There is no friendship between the wisdom of reason and the object of that wisdom. Even the gentlest, the most amiable goodwill expressed by reason is essentially foreign to reason, adventitious to it; it comes from another universe of values, that in which the premier value is not knowledge, but reconciliation between Me and that which is not me.

In that universe, prayer, or love of one's neighbour (which is the same thing, whether turned inward and towards God in us, or turned outward and towards God in our neighbour), is only a faint glimmer in deep night; but that glimmer illuminates everything. In that universe, man is only a reed, but a praying reed. There, I pray, therefore God is. There too, man is the measure of all things, but God is the measure of man. There, finally, one must not multiply unnecessary concepts; but neither must one limit the sum of concepts this side of God, who is the limit of that sum. (Whereas the converse is not true: the sum of beings is not the limit of God.)

14

The last of the Axioms to direct my Being is proposition number 7 and the last in the *Tractatus logico-philosophicus* of Ludwig Wittgenstein: 'Whereof one cannot speak, therefore one must be silent.'

There are statements of fact. They tell us what's what about things. There are logico-mathematical expressions. They tell only about themselves. They are the rules of the logical syntax of the universe, which is the logical syntax of language. Any proposition about God, being, value, is neither a statement of fact nor a logico-mathematical tautology. It has no meaning. It does not belong to language. Whereof one cannot speak, thereof one must be silent.

I accept this verdict and I make it my fifth rule *ad directionem animae versus Deum*. It is the interdict of all theology, of all metaphysics, of all ethics. It is not interdiction of prayer, nor of moral action, but only of discourse about God, being or good. As such a discourse is impossible, one must be silent.

To this absolute commandment, which could not be disobeyed, as a tautology could not be proven false, I append only my little complementary interrogation. Whereof one cannot speak, thereof one must be silent. To whom shall I address my silence?

15

Wittgenstein's axiom is the Second Commandment of a Table of the Law, which has only two. The first is Occam's razor. Both of them say the same thing. They are the first and last word of nominalism, philosophy implicit in the exact sciences.

There are things; there are the names of things and the classes of things, *nomina*, the concepts. There are the relationships between things, and the relationships between concepts, and between statements that link the concepts to one another according to the same logical syntax by which things are linked with one another in the universe: the logical syntax of the universe is one for both things and the names of things. There are things, their names, and the rules of the logical syntax of the universe. The rest is idle chatter, *flatus vocis* and the nought that nullifies.

Moritz Schlick, a philosopher of the school of Vienna, whose most illustrious representative is Wittgenstein, demonstrated that the major proposition of Heidegger is an abusive use of language and signifies nothing. A Nazi student murdered Schlick, shot him to death with his revolver, just as he was arriving to give his lecture. At that time, violence was on the right. Heidegger, who was a Nazi in those days, died full of years and surrounded by the superstitious reverence of German writers and media. Shamanism is not the sole preserve of the Ostiak Voguls. Spellbinding by the use of mysterious language is a recognized method in Germany and elsewhere. Swabian shamanism is particularly virulent, witness Hegel and Heidegger, both of them great poets, whom I admire as I admire greatness in everything, even in crime:

but I prefer *Jabberwockey*.

In 1888 and 1900 there appeared the two volumes of the *Critique of Pure Experience,* by Richard Avenarius, a German born in Paris, professor at the University of Zürich, who died at the age of fifty-three between the publication of the first and second volumes of his work. In 1906 there appeared the original edition and in 1908 the French translation of *Knowledge and Error,* by Ernst Mach, professor at the University of Vienna, better known because people gave his name to the speed of sound taken as the unity of measurement of aviation speeds. He deserves greater fame for having founded, with Avenarius, that movement which presently dominates, unknown to the verbal philosophers, scientific thought.

Their most important successors were the philosophers of the school of Vienna and their friends of the Cambridge school, of whom Bertrand Russell is the best known. Wittgenstein taught at Cambridge. His friends left behind in Vienna, all Jews and all with little indulgence for the abusive use of language, were for these two reasons obliged to flee Vienna and found refuge in the United States, where the Chicago school continued the school of Vienna. Quite recently, a scholar from Harvard – Cambridge again, but in Massachusetts – ended his book on philosophy and the results of the exact sciences almost in the same terms as Poincaré in the conclusion to *Science and Hypothesis,* but on a more bitter note. The universe is absurd and inhuman, there is but one certitude and but one value, that of the exact sciences. It is not much perhaps, but it is everything.

I note in passing that Poincaré's book belongs to 1903, and I would draw attention to the promptness with which Mach was translated into French. At the time, the French were still great mathematicians and with a passion for the exact sciences. Today, there are great French mathematicians. It is an important nuance. For between the appearance of Wittgenstein's *Tractatus* in 1921-1922, and that of the French translation in 1961, there was a gap of forty years, dominated by philosophy-incantation.

For the laser beam of Wittgenstein, which is Occam's razor and Laplace's guillotine (you will recall that atheist too proud to accept the universe from the hands of God, and the republican not proud enough not to accept a bogus barony from the hands of General Bonaparte masquerading as Charlemagne), cuts the tongues of all the Pythians and pythonesses. He, it, cuts the beard of God the Father. 'I imagine the master of the island like a handsome old man with a big white beard, seated on a cloud, with a golden globe in his hands. – But that's the portrait of God you are painting!' (Jules Verne, *The Mysterious Island*). The portrait of God! There is nothing as anthropomorphic as God conceived by unbelievers. In passing, Occam's razor also slices off the beard of Marx.

A well-known student joke tells how a Cambridge logician was travelling in a train with a friend. It was summer, the fields of Cambridgeshire were radiant under the beaming sun, the English landscape was tender and luminous, and a flock of sheep was grazing between clumps of oaks. 'Look, those sheep have been shorn,' said the friend. "On their observable side,' replied the Cambridge man.

We have never given up our most murderous weapons, nor our most dangerously efficacious tools. Lenin instinctively sensed the terrible efficacy of this intellectual process; he guessed what it signified for socialism, abusively and absurdly called 'scientific'. After he had read the book by the chief Russian disciple of the 'empiriocriticists' Mach and Avenarius, Bogdanov-Malinovski, Lenin vented his spleen in helpless rage against them in his work entitled *Materialism and Empiriocriticism,* whose presence in the history of thought is of a purely material order and on the level of cheap stationery. The refutation of that implicit philosophy of the exact sciences was also of a purely material order in those countries where marxism or

Hitlerian irrationalist technocracy triumphed: it springs from the same source as ballistics, physiology (blows and wounds, sub-alimentation) and psychology (intimidation, fear). But one does not refute statements of experimentally verified facts on their own ground, nor logico-mathematical tautologies, nor the rules of the logical syntax of the universe, and, implicitly, language itself: there are no others.

In liberal lands, the repression was more muted, where marxist irrationalism dominated through pressure groups and 'literary terror'. But the result was almost the same: a gap of forty years. Sixty or one hundred will pass before one can freely apply Occam's razor in Tartar universities. (Between the two wars, the contribution of Polish logicians to the development of polyvalent logics, or non-aristotelian logics, was decisive. Since then, they are restricted to dialectical logic, which has only one, but serious, fault: it does not exist.)

My experience of marxism can be contained in two words: disgust and indignation. Studying at a German university between 1941 and 1944 – Freud, Wittgenstein, Spinoza, Bergson, Husserl, Einstein were forbidden as they were Jews – I refused to swallow Heidegger because of his philosophical style, repugnant to philosophy, though magnificent from the incantatory point of view. My professor guided my steps gradually towards the *mathesis universalis* of Leibnitz and arrived at symbolic logic, at one remove from logical empiricism, from Russell and the school of Vienna, when he was beheaded for having expressed disapproval of the second fratricidal World War, which ruined Germany and Europe.

My second professor made me study Jacob Boehme, the Teutonic philosopher (1575-1624), the master of the enlightened philosopher Louis-Claude de Saint-Martin (who signed his works 'the unknown philosopher'), and of Balzac. I admired with polite consternation that tumultuous theosophy, enjoying the magnificence of its images and language. In it, God goes coiling like a serpent, almost like the procession of the divine gnostic triads seized by a Titanesque upheaval. In the Gnosis, the Abyss, Bythos, and the Night, Nyx, engender Sigé, Silence, and so on, from triad to triad, to our world here below. The 'procession' of the triads operates by 'emanation', 'self-apprehension', and production of a third term, following the schema invented by Jamblicus: A produces non-A (B), is actively resumed in B, which produces AB (C)...

More ancient, hieratic and magical configurations of thought can be divined within this schema. Ammonius Sakkas was Egyptian; his great disciple Plotinus a Greek of Egypt; the latter's disciple, Porphyrus, was called in his Syriac mother-tongue Malchus, of which the Greek name is a translation. Finally Jamblicus, the creator of the 'procession', was from Chalcis, in Coele-Syria. The last great neo-Platonist, Proclus, was born in Constantinople, but of Lycian parents, and was brought up at Xanthus in Lycia. Jacob Boehme proceeds from that remote Egyptian, Syrian and Anatolian ascendance. In his work, the Abyss has a primitive and magnificently coloured German name, the *Ungrund*, 'without ground'. He goes beyond himself and produces his Heart or his Humour, the *Gemüt*, and apprehends himself in it again, etc. God and his hypostases in the form of a dragon go coiling along. Dialectic is named *Qual*, 'torture'...

Schelling was a pupil of the famous theological school at Tübingen. In his work there appears already, more frankly and naïvely, the *Urgrund*, a primitive base or first reason. *Grund* means both 'ground' and 'reason'. Adequate reason is *zureichende Grund*. *Ur*, prefix equivalent to the adjectives 'primitive', 'archaic', 'original', is found in *Ursünde*, original sin – already contemporary German. Schelling did not read properly or did not wish to employ Boehme's archaic and much more powerful form. Hegel, his friend, proceeded more casually: he only took on the formal skeleton in which the cosmic dragon unfurls its coils.

A few years later, on the university benches of Tartar cadres, I found myself confronted with the theosophy of the genial cobbler of Goerlitz, travestied as dialectic of history and class struggle. Uncoiling its form here was matter, techniques of merchandising and production. Michelangelo theosopher had become a socio-metaphysical Vautrin.

It was grandiose, but scandalous. Marxism promised me 'scientific socialism' and I found myself confronted with Jamblicus and Proclus. It promised me a classless society and I was seeing society re-stratifying itself before my very eyes according to the criteria of the bureaucratic hierarchy. It promised me in a ridiculously imminent future the satisfaction of an infinity of desires, through 'collectivization' – that is, the Nationalization of the means of production, which I knew to be limited. It promised me the liquidation of the State, and I felt myself crushed by the most monstrous State in human history. Marxism promised me the end of man's exploitation by man, and was replacing it, before my very eyes, by the same thing, baptized 'direction of the economy' by the Party. It promised me the 'disalienation' of man, and was drowning me in the masses under the whip-hand of authority, the spur of agitators and the prison chains of the cadre sections. It promised me the fulfillment of all human potentialities according to ridiculous modalities. (Marx: 'In the morning, I'll go hunting or fishing: in the afternoon, I'll write criticism.' Trotsky: 'Everyone will paint like Raphael.')

At the same time, marxism was forcing me to participate, directly or indirectly, in the persecution of scholars, writers, devout Christians, artists, individualists, homosexuals and all non-confirmists, of marginals and minorities – or become a victim myself. The first task that was entrusted to me – still a young cadre – was a purging of the library, and at the present time, thirty years later, my own works in their turn are banned in my country's libraries. Marxism polluted and tortured my youth by making me participate in its crimes; it sent me, in my maturity, into exile, kindly termed emigration by the Western left, and in my exile I found again marxism reigning by intimidation, insinuation and the conspiracy of silence. And indeed I fear that in my old age that world in which I sought to escape from it may be reduced to slavery by the world from which I escaped.

However, this is a story of reconciliation. It must not be forgotten that marxism was born out of revulsion at the inhumanity of capitalism in the nineteenth century and that today it still encroaches upon those societies which resemble that capitalism. Nor must it be forgotten that it is a shout of defiance against the villainy of liberalism without scruples and the desert left by the dismantling of Christian values, called pluralism by its beneficiaries. Marxism succeeds infallibly in agrarian societies in which the rights of man and of the citizen are unknown, or are not guaranteed, and where they do not know how to make use of Occam's razor in intellectual life. It fails infallibly in industrial societies where the rights of man and of the citizen are known, certain, and protected by everyone, in his own interest of course; where, moreover, intellectual hygiene is assured by the use of Occam's razor. But marxism has reminded us that we cannot live in a desert of non-values: inevitably, pseudo-values grow there, wild and poisonous weeds. It has also reminded us that even liberty, even tolerance of the broadest kinds cannot survive in total pluralism, completely invertebrate, and that it requires the consensus of the majority on questions of truth, freedom, friendship, good; otherwise, there too cohesion will result only by an eruption of irrationality, by violence and repression.

Finally, the greatest service marxism has performed for us – alas very indirectly and at what a price – was to draw our attention to the most ancient, the most extensive and the most durable form of government of human societies, which is better than nothing, but is the curse of our race, capable of doing better than that: oriental despotism, the *aziatschtchina,* the totalitarian techno-bureaucratic State, invented in the valleys of the great rivers at the same time as civilization itself, and which Marx stopped mentioning as soon as he perceived that the true dragon is not his Hegelian contortionist, but this thing that cannot enter into any marxist categories and cannot be included in the 'dialectic of history', in the class struggle and the future inflexible sequence of primitive communism-slavery-feudalism-capitalism-socialism-communism. The dragon runs parallel with this system, and it is still there today, as it was in Egypt, as in Sumer, as it was in the State of Tsin, as it was with the Incas and the Aztecs. It is a threat to all mass societies, because it is their most elementary form of organization. The bureaucratic State is the entropy of the mass societies. Even in today's liberal societies, the old dragon is sniggering in our faces underneath moderate, constitutional and very human exteriors. It must be sacrificed. If I am not mistaken, the technique of all monster-killers consisted in 'decentralizing' the Beast: they cut it up into little bits.

Through the relativization and the politization of truth, through State lies, the dialectic lie, official effrontery, persecution of the truth, denial of evidence, marxism has done much to give us back our faith in the truth. At the age of twenty, after reading Nietzsche, nothing had any value for me any more. Then I learned to recognize the force of truth through the traumatizing experience of falsehood, and, in particular, through what is called 'the difficulties of the transitional stage', and to discover the absolute moral postulate: do not make your fellow man suffer.

Marxism has recalled us to our duty, to our fundamental Christianism, to our ineradicable humanitarianism, to liberty, to solidarity with our fellows here and on all other continents. Marxism has been a blessing. My blessings on it, but please do not mention it to me again or I shall start to scream.

16

Believe in marxism? I would not even 'believe' in God. I only believe in what I see, and in the rules and conditions of thought. I keep silent about the rest.

But the frontier between language and silence, between me and God, is not watertight. It is not a barrier, but a fluid zone, always in movement, like the sands of the Delta where the Danube enters the sea. Language gives way beneath my feet; but it remains the general direction in which I look, the general direction in which, silently, I cast my troubled heart, my imperfect being.

It is impossible to speak of God; but it is impossible also not to make allusion to God.

Wittgenstein taught me the general direction in which I should cast my silence. He was the penultimate stage of my intellectual journeying towards God. (And we must not forget that he is only a preparation for prayer, before which he clears the ground, and for which he provides a launching pad. But he is nothing without prayer, and prayer is nothing without the grace of orison, which either comes or does not come, as God wills.)

In 1930, Wittgenstein wrote a preface for a projected book. The book and the preface were not published until ten years after his death, a generation after they were written. I shall quote the final paragraph of that preface because of the moral attitude it expresses: it is of an ascetic severity, and lets us know what kind of man Wittgenstein was. But I am quoting this paragraph also because of its first line. It shows of what nature was the asceticism of that man who ordained that one should never speak of God: it was essentially religious:

I should like to say that 'this book has been written to the glory of God'. But to say such a thing in our times would be unscrupulous, because I would be misunderstood. What those words mean here is that this book has been written with goodwill. In as far as it has been written without goodwill – that is, wherever it has been written out of vanity, etc. – the author would wish his work to be condemned. The author could not purify it of such ingredients to a higher degree than he can himself be pure.

'Goodwill' is will pure of all egoism; will directed to truth is will 'to the glory of God'.

This is the aim of that will, and the aim of all philosophy, indicated by proposition 4.115 of the *Tractatus Logico-Philosophicus*: 'It [philosophy] shall signify the unspeakable by representing clearly the speakable.' And proposition 6.522 explains: 'There is an unspeakable effect. That reveals itself. That is what is mystic.' The primal, philosophic and religious amazement before the universe, before being, anterior to the wonder before its intelligible structure, is expressed by proposition 6.44: 'It is not the *how* of the existence of the world that is mystic, but the *fact* that it exists.' Mystic means both relative to the adoration of God, and vowed to silence: *muein*, 'to keep silence'.

God is the source of all value; he is value itself and the very meaning of the world; from which the world 'has a meaning'. I am saying this now, following the great company of myriads of devout people who have said it already, as a consequence of our common experience of the non-value of the world without God, and of the value of existence and of the world *with* grace. Wittgenstein says: 'The meaning of the world should be found outside the world... there is no value in the world, and if there were one, it would be without value. If there is a value, and if it has any value whatsoever, it should be found outside all event and all quality.... For all event and all quality (*Sosein,* 'to be thus') are contingent. What makes them non-contingent could not be found *in* the world, for by that very fact it in its turn would become contingent. It must be found outside the world' (6.41).

The philosophy implicit in the exact sciences keeps God in immanence and has kept me in his train during twenty or thirty years of pantheism. However the formidable thrust of the Jewish soul towards transcendence is activated in this logician descended from a family of converts: '*How* the world is is of absolutely no importance in what concerns the All-High. God does not reveal himself *in* the world' (6.432). The aim of all philosophy is to transcend language, and that in the one direction in which one can transcend it, for transcend means 'to rise above'. That is exactly, even to the concrete metaphor, what Wittgenstein says in his penultimate proposition, 6.54: 'My propositions illuminate the subject insomuch as that he who understands them realizes finally, when he has risen as it were above them, that they have no meaning. (So he has to throw away the ladder after having climbed it. He has to go beyond those propositions: then he sees the world correctly.)' 'They have no meaning' signifies here that they are tautological, that is, only unfold what was folded, quite simply name the necessities and the necessary conditions of logical language,

What follows is the interdiction to speak of the sacred, of the unspeakable, of that which goes beyond the universe of logical language. The 'last commandment' of Wittgenstein is the disguised repetition of the third commandment of God to Moses, to the Jewish people, and to all of us: thou shalt not take my name in vain. In the final analysis, that means: thou shalt never speak of me. (But thou shalt think only of me, and thou shalt do nothing but pray to me every instant.)

Behind the text of the *Tractatus* can be found the notes of the diary kept by Wittgenstein from the summer of 1916 to the beginning of 1917, while he was working on his book. They say more openly what the enigmatic sentences

of the *Tractatus* refer to. On 1st August 1916, he notes: 'As
it is of all things, so is God. God: that is how it is of all
things.' That is immanence; in proposition number 6.432
he had gone beyond, and under the number 6.41 he had
stated that the meaning of the world has to be found
outside itself. On 8th July he writes: 'To believe in a God
means: to see that the fundamental idea of life has meaning... Whatever we are dependent on can be called God. In
this sense God would simply be destiny, or – what is the
same thing – the world in so far as it is independent of my
will.' We can see that the powerful thrust towards transcendence is reversed here in the same brief sequence of five
aphorisms: departing from the meaning of the world,
which is exterior to the world, he returns to the one
evident God of the exact sciences, the world itself. I am
not surprised that Wittgenstein should have helped me to
pray, but that it should only have been the God of
pantheism. But I *am* surprised that I should not have come
to realize earlier the necessity and the possibility of going
beyond. It took me twenty or thirty years, the experience
(not experimental) of prayer, the advice of a Christian, my
Reverend Father and Brother in Christ Jean N., and a
definition of the concept of God that was awaiting me and
awaits every Christian since the year 1078.

But even if he does not transcend the world, Wittgenstein knows that the secret of felicity is to live 'to the glory
of God'. For the same diary note of 8th July 1916
continues: 'In order to live happily, I must live in accord...
with that alien will on which I seem to depend. That
means that "I accomplish the will of God"... We are
certainly right to believe that the conscience is the voice of
God... When my conscience is upset, it is because I am out
of harmony with Something. With what? Would it be
with the world?'

That ascetic man, driven by the thrust towards transcendence, relapses into the essential and constitutive temptation of the exact sciences, the temptation of man the

world-investigator, that is, the sin of dissociation, the sin of analysis, the splitting of the world in two, the investigative Me and the world, its object, its adversary, its conquest, its victim (and secretly, with the return of the unknown, the monster that finishes by devouring it). He had departed from the point of God transcendant, of a meaning in the exterior world to reach the sum of things and their relationships; in less than two months of thought, burning with intensity and burning with fever, he finished up with – the sin of pride.

On 11th June 1916, he had written: 'The meaning of life, that is, the meaning of the world, is what we can call God... I know that the world is. That I am here within it as my eye is in my field of vision. That there is something problematical, which we call its meaning. That this meaning does not reside within it, but outside it.'

On 1st August, after having written that 'God must simply be the world in so far as it is independent of my will', Wittgenstein records the split: 'There are two divinities: the world and my independent Me.'

Heir to a great fortune, he had renounced it in favour of his sisters. All his life he lived like a monk. We have seen what he thought of his vanity. He had the stuff of an ascetic, of a mystic and perhaps of a saint. He was no Luciferian, he was not possessed. That is why it did not occur to him to take the final step, something at which wretched Nietzsche would not have balked. For when 'there are two divinities, the world and my independent Me', there is only one: the Me. The sin of pride is the constitutive sin of thought and therefore of man, who is constituted in his thought. We are constituted in separation, in delimitation with God and our neighbour. That is why knowledge is solitude and sadness. We are dedicated to it, we are not human except through it, between the innocence that precedes it and salvation that goes beyond its integrity and makes it happy. That is why the story of Paradise and the tree of knowledge of good and evil is not a fairy tale but the abstract of our condition. 'Ye shall not surely die: For God doth know that in the day ye eat thereof, then your eyes shall be opened, and ye shall be as gods.' The world and your independent Me. Your eyes shall be opened, and that spark shall be all.

Thought is separation, and there is one thing inseparable from separation – sadness. The thinking reed and the sorrowing reed. The solitude in the midst of the eternal silence of infinite space frightens it. But pride remains: it is sadness that is all.

Here we must return to the shut character of the Me of thought, of separation, of pride. There is no way out of the *cogito,* towards the so-called other divinity, the world, or towards a God exterior to the Me – exterior to the autonomous Me, to the Me of pride, to the Me of sadness, to the Me of thought. My consciousness of that essential bitterness should not lend itself to misunderstanding: it is not a repudiation of thought; I remain the man who lives exclusively in the universe of exact sciences, and who knows himself to be constituted by thought, therefore by them. But I am conscious of the fundamental sadness of our condition. Our dignity is in thought; our original sin is in knowledge; our condition is separation – from God, from our neighbour, from the world, and from ourselves. But we have the recollection of lost innocence – paradisal, childlike, vegetable; and we have the thrust, the invincible thrust towards a going beyond of what we are, in reconciliation – with God, with our neighbour, the world and ourselves. In that reconciliation thought is not suppressed, it is integrated; our dignity is not lost, but surmounted in peace, which it will carry on its shoulders, as the exact sciences and philosophy – their critical commentary as well as that of my own existence and of my own condition – will carry on their shoulders prayer.

The essential problem of the table of values constituted by knowledge is that it is not a 'table', a list of several values. 'Article One: it is that spark that is all. Article

Two: H'm... er...' There is no level crossing from the value knowledge and the value amity, nor is there one to any other value – unless it be that subordinate value, that false value, efficacity, the fundament of technocratic hell. No passage from *cogito* to the perfect being cogitated by me, nor from the spark that is all to goodness, friendship, the love of men; but a leap over a precipice, and a drop into the abyss. The way out is still somewhere at the rear, made by piercing the wall against which the Me is backed. Neither God nor love can be deduced from an anterior principle: they *have* to be first, or they remain absent. Love for human beings, so often noticed in the man of the exact sciences, is grafted on knowledge, as a foreign heart is transplanted into a body that no longer has one. For let us not forget the interdictions of the exact sciences: we must demystify, de-anthropomorphize! That is, we must desacralize, dehumanize. Which is anyhow just and justified at every step: knowledge is always superior to mythic interpretation, even if as too often happens we see 'nature', 'species' or 'organism' acting out their roles like characters in a melodrama, or even a farce.

However, despite such imperfections which are inherent in any philosophy critical of language and of first concepts such as are used by the exact sciences, I fully approve of 'demystification' – that is, desacralization, desecration, profanation; I fully approve of 'de-anthropomorphism' – that is, the dehumanization of the universe by the exact sciences. Sacredness is not the miracle of Saint Januarius. Humanity is moral action founded on amity. God is not an explanation, nor is man; God is the aim of prayer, man is the interlocutor of friendship.

The post-Christian value crisis, euphoric in the Age of Enlightenment, pseudo-joyful, nervously exuberant and visibly anguished in Nietzsche, reaches its apogee in the century of ideologies with a very tiny, weak groan of agony. When he had collected all the materials for his future *Tractatus,* Wittgenstein ended his diary. Since he

had started it, within half a year three hundred thousand
Frenchmen and three hundred thousand Germans had died
prematurely at Verdun, dying violent deaths of their own
volition, for the homeland and its laws, like the Spartans at
Thermopylae; only those Frenchmen and Germans were
two thousand times more numerous than the Greeks, and
they died uselessly. A little later, civilian soldiers betrayed
by their superiors were to mutiny – with the result one
knows. At the other end of Europe, in Russia, the
common people, betrayed by their superiors, rose up in
revolt. Again, with the result one knows. Man is the
measure of all things, and one must not add a God to the
sum of things; I think, therefore I am, and it is that
thought that is everything.

On 10th January 1917, Wittgenstein drew the one true
consequence of the *cogito* considered as primary, unique
value, enthronement of man all alone and sad in an empty
universe. The last note in his diary reads: 'If suicide is
allowed, all is allowed. Or else is suicide in itself neither
good nor evil?'

But Wittgenstein did not leave me without having made
me a gift perhaps even greater than that of having taught
me in what general direction I should address my silence.
At the beginning of that half year that was to conduct him
to silence, he noted, on 16th June 1916: 'The meaning of
life, that is, the meaning of the world, is what we can call
God.' And: 'Prayer is thought about the meaning of life.'
The first aphorism, which I have already cited once, is a
signal towards transcendence, but also a limitation and
therefore unsatisfactory. The second, too, does not satisfy
us much, because it does not admit its own incomplete-
ness. Prayer is also, but not only, *amor intellectualis Dei*.
Between these two propositions lies the marvellous gift
from Wittgenstein, who was not happy, to me, an obscure
stranger living one generation after him, and whom he
made intellectually capable of being happy, whenever it so
pleases God to take pity on me. For the full passage reads:

'The meaning of life, that is, the meaning of the world, is what we can call God. To which we may append the parable of God as father. Prayer is thought about the meaning of life' (my italics). Here, in a nutshell, is all the little philosophy I know, the one way open towards the conception of God as father. (Conception and concept are of course improper terms – the words derive from capere, captum, 'to seize': all one has to do is to direct oneself, in thought, towards a point that is found beyond thought.) Love God; love him as a father; how can we love transcendence as a father? Wittgenstein gave me the answer to that.

I have never addressed God with those archaic terms signifying social and political superiority – Lord, Adonai, Dominus, Kyrios, Ichvârâ. I cannot call God sire, master, chief, comrade secretary or mister. He is God, and no other name befits him. The Semites called him God quite simply, El, Il, Al, Eloah, Allah, and it would appear that this word derives from a root which signifies duration. The Indo-Europeans say: 'light of the day', deus, dies, Diespiter, Jupiter, Dyauspitar, the Day-Father; they say déva, daéva, théos, Zeus-Dios. They also say something like 'fullness, richness, distributor of richnesses', bhaga, bog (bogatyi, bogatstvo). They say numen, that is, nomen, 'name', a being of the neuter gender, and God, Gott, also originally neuter, from the hypothetical root eghou, 'I call'; In-voco, 'I cry towards'.

Thou shalt not make any graven images, nor mental images; thou shalt not create for thyself a mental concept of God; thou shalt not make for thyself a God. I suspect that Jewish and Protestant scholars who reject the concept of God are obeying, at the bottom of their hearts, and unknown to them, the fourth commandment of God to Moses.

Freud discovered the strata of the soul and the mechanism of their tectonic movements, their irruptions of igneous matter, the cooling and hardening of their lavas, the sedimentation of memory, the metamorphism of gestures and speech. He named the things he discovered, and which ever since have borne the names he gave them. But like another discoverer of new worlds, he thought he had discovered something else, which people had already heard about. He thought he had discovered the route to the Indies, the libido, the predominance of the sexual instinct, the instinct of death or the death wish. He discovered America, the mechanism of repression, the chemistry of sublimation, and that the soul is stratified. He was the type *par excellence* of the scientific hero: truth, work, stoic courage in suffering, death and all the absurdity of the world without God, and finally the truth – and one or two falses hypotheses. The inventor, the discoverer of the Father image recognized this in his mental image of God. Thou shalt not make unto thee any graven image. He rejected God, and that illusion, the religious relationship between an infantile Me and a nonexistent God.

Having loved my own father with a pity that was mixed with embarrassment and contempt, I am refractory to the Freudian critique of religion. The dissociation between an investigative, observant and experimentive Me, and a Something Else which is perhaps God, but which until further convincing proof is nothing but the chaos of things, forgets or ignores that God is not something that can be split into two parts, nor something whose boundaries I can mark out for myself; or else that was not the God that was meant.

And the life sciences, right up to the most recent ethology, teach me that the universe is the matrix of the living being, its mother, its homeland. That is more fundamental than infantile regression. The microorganism in its maternal ocean, or man at his mother's breast; the severance, the break, the separation, the loss of paradise, the green paradise of childhood loves; the drama of man the real man, that is separate – a Senecan tragedy; the rest is silence, the brute silence of death, or silence illuminated by prayer, and the return to the breast of the Father or the Mother, an appellation as valuable and as incomplete as the image of return to the lost homeland.

I owe Wittgenstein the clear and distinct knowledge of the fact that the only possible apprehension of the universe is logico-mathematical, and that once the limits of the logical universe have been reached – which is also the universe of language – one must go beyond words and pray in silence, addressing one's prayer to God as Father.

But for twenty or thirty years I did not succeed in going beyond the God of pantheism, *Deus sive natura,* 'God, or destiny, or – what is the same thing – the world in so far as it is independent of my will', 'God, that is, how all things have their being'. For twenty or thirty years I was a religious man whose concept of God cut him to the quick. I am astonished that Spinoza, son of the Jewish people, should not have sensed the terrible thrust of God within us, a thrust that wants to go beyond all limits in order to find God in transcendence; that impulse which we have inherited from the Jews, or perhaps at the same time as they did, and as all human beings did.

I finally discovered what had been cutting me to the quick for decades. The God of pantheism is a limited concept. He is identifiable with something other than God alone, that is, with the world; he can be named with a name other than that of God alone, that is, with the name of the all, that repertory of things; he is conceivable, and therefore less great than the thought that thinks him; identifiable, and therefore exterior to him who identifies him.

In Wittgenstein's *Tractatus* there is a pointer in the right direction, but an inadequate one – something I did not realize until later. It points in the direction of definition of the concept of God made by Saint Anselm, by reproducing his celebrated ontological argument, severely generalized, but still recognizable. Proposition 4.123 says: 'A quality is internal, when it is unthinkable that its object should not possess it.' I had reached the final stage of my long journeying.

17

This is the final step before prayer.

During my conversation with my unknown interlocutor, I conduct, in an aside, a conversation with the exact sciences, philosophy and theology. They are my counsellors, who prepare me each time I speak to him.

The exact sciences tell me: 1) the world is; 2) the unknown is; 3) the world and the unknown are one and the same continuum. From this point on, contact someone other, not us, but do it in silence. As for us, we are getting on with our job; 4) there are constants. They must be discovered.

Philosophy tells me: 1) language apprehends the world; 2) language does not apprehend that which transcends the world; 3) from this point on, contact someone other, not me, but do it in silence. As for me, I am getting on with my job; 4) the critique of language by language knows no end.

Theology tells me: 1) the concept of God indicates the direction in which you should address your silence; 2) from this point on, address yourself to God. As for me, I am getting on with my job; 3) the concept of God is the object of an elaboration without end.

The concept of God is found in the ontological argument, and the ontological argument, in the second and third chapters of the *Proslogium* of Saint Anselm, and, consolidated, developed, illustrated by metaphor, in the third and the fifth *Meditations* of Descartes.

Man, even the most benighted, conceives something which cannot be considered as nothing, and which is superior to him. There is a superior limit to my thought. That which is found at the superior limit of thought cannot be nonexistent, for then something else would be found, which would be superior to it in so far as it exists, and which would then be situated at the limit of thought.

I am translating from medieval Latin into our language which is accustomed to the notions of limit and going beyond that limit. The letter of the text says that a being conceived as perfect could not suffer from the supreme imperfection, that of not existing. I conceive God, absolute perfection, therefore he exists. Or, in Wittgenstein's terms, 'a quality is internal when it is unthinkable that its object should not possess it'.

The *Proslogium* was written in 1078; just over nine hundred years ago. Still in the lifetime of Saint Anselm, Gaunilon, a monk of the Abbey of Marmoutier, attacked the ontological argument of the existence of God. Later, Saint Thomas Aquinus took up this critique. Finally, Kant submitted it to an examination which apparently annihilated it. He argues that existence is not one quality among others, but a predicate in apposition to all existing things: it is the prefix to all the statements made about existing things. I think one hundred dollars: they exist in my thought, but not necessarily in my pocket.

Already Gaunilon had made the observation in his *Liber pro insipiente* that an island conceived as perfect must, according to Saint Anselm, exist necessarily in the middle of the sea. Saint Anselm answered him in his *Liber apologeticus* that it was not a question of one thing among many, but of an absolute and unique being. In his case, logically necessary existence in the *ordo idearum* was necessary in the reality of the *ordo rerum*. But, says Kant, the statement of the existence of God is not an analytical judgement, which unfolds a tautology, it is a synthetic judgement, which tells us something new about the world.

Saint Bonaventure, Duns Scotus, Descartes, Malebranche, Leibnitz and Hegel supported, defended, consolidated and renewed Saint Anselm's argument. Descartes enriched it with the distinction between the concept of the infinite and that of the indefinite, and with his discussion of the concept of perfection, which I could not deduce from my own physical experience and which nevertheless I possess. Existence, he adds poetically, is as inseparable from the concept of God as the valley is inseparable from the mountain. Leibnitz, partisan of the ontological argument, weighs it down by affirming that it is necessary to precede it with the concept of the *possibility* of a perfect being.

Hegel finally appears to have rescued Saint Anselm's argument, and for that reason I owe him my gratitude and my friendship; for I had nothing else to offer him than the same awestruck and somewhat horripilated admiration with which I contemplate the gigantic visages of Angkor Wat, both supported and devoured by the dialectical proliferation of the vegetation springing from their crevices. Our good philosopher says that the conception of the perfect and necessarily existent being is at the origin and centre of all thought. We think that which is; we think with necessity that which *is* with necessity; all that follows may well be contingent, this or that, existent or nonexistent: at the source, the order of ideas responds to the order of things, thought to existence, and the origin of thought like existence is the concept of God and of the being of God, which are one and indivisible.

Not being a scholar, I shall not attempt to criticize the apparent sophism of the ontological argument, nor to combat the ill-founded critique of its adversaries. I confine myself to stating, firstly, that those medieval theologians were very hellenist; what a central role the dimension of beauty played in their thought, through its value-limit, the concept of perfection. Perfection no longer seems to be a category of our thought.

I would remark secondly that Saint Anselm sets God at the head of the hierarchy of all his values, as supreme value and source of all value. He is *ens perfectissimum,* the most perfect entity, and consequently *ens realissimum,* the most real entity – everything flows from that absolute perfection. The twenty-three chapters of the *Proslogium* which come after the ontological argument are occupied exclusively with divine perfections. His existence derives from his perfection. He is not as in the burning bush: I AM THAT I AM', he is 'I am that which is perfect'. 1) God, 2) perfect, 3) necessarily exist. In order to bring out the articulation of the argument better, let us set out what precedes it in Descartes: 1) *Ego,* 2) *cogito,* 3)*sum.* – 1) *Erus,* 2) *perfectissimum,* 3)*est.*

Despite everything, Saint Anselm's argument, 'unfolded', does not help me, What saves me is that of which it is the unfolding.

It is neither altogether acceptable as tautology, nor altogether satisfying as synthetic judgement, and highly suspect as a syllogism, to be nothing but a vicious circle. But behind the ontological argument and its philosophy of perfection and its false airs of proven demonstration, there is the definition of the concept of God by Saint Anselm, a unique source of certainty. It comes after the five axioms I took for my viaticum, it crowns them and goes beyond them. It has, as they do, the appearance of a tautology, irrefutable by definition and reducible only to itself. But I have no question to append to it; at most a humble commentary.

A definition of the concept of God is not a definition and the concept of God is not a concept. To define means to trace limits, *fines.* To conceive, concept, is *capere, captum,* 'to take, to seize, taken, seized'. A prisoner, *captivus, is captus.* The intellect takes, seizes, manipulates like a prehensile hand. God has no limits; neither the intellect nor the hand can seize, can grasp, can apprehend God. The 'concept of God' is only the general direction of prayer; the 'definition' of the concept is only a tentative attempt to indicate that direction.

The definition of the concept of God in Saint Anselm is: 'that which is such that one could not think of anything

greater.' *Id quo nihil majus cogitari potest.*(Such as that
nothing greater could be thought.' *Id quo majus cogitari non
potest?* I'm not sure, and it's the same thing.) It must be
remembered that *majus* does not just signify quantitative
superiority, but also qualitative. In modern speech, the
equivalent would be: 'beyond which thought cannot go'.
It is the limit, but also going beyond the limit. For
everything I name has been apprehended and overtaken by
my thought, at least virtually, at least formally. Even God.
That is why one must not name him; that is why to name
God is irreverent, as the Hebrews sensed so strongly three
thousand years ago, and after. Apprehension and overtaking in words only, nothing more – real apprehension and
overtaking being excluded – or else it was not a question of
God – already irreverence is there.

('God is dead' is the most frivolous proposition in the
history of the human spirit. Obviously, it was not a
question of God being dead. Here he is, God, in my heart,
in the memory of grace, in our leap towards him, and
before us up there at the end of our ascension. Poor
Nietzsche. No one has been more brilliantly mistaken, and
with greater genius, about the most serious questions. The
Germans do not have a reputation for frivolity: but when
they put their minds to it, it is God himself they lay hands
on. My place is beside Nietzsche, in that street in Turin:
his arms around the neck of an old horse on the ground,
and mine around that man weeping over a beast that was
dying, and less despairing than he.)

Id quo majus cogitari potest. That which is such that one
could not think of anything greater.

I like the *relational* character of this group of signs. It
does not contain one name of a thing, a being, a class of
things, or beings. Only names of relationships. *Id,* 'that',
is the sign for the relation between him who indicates and
that which is indicated. *Id* is 'that which I indicate here', as
God was originally 'the one whom I call to', or rather,
'that which I call to', neuter. *Quo majus* is the relationship

of superiority between the second potential object of a comparison and the first. *Nihil* is the negative sign that forbids all designation: 'nothing'. *Non* is the sign that bars all operation whatever it may be. *Cogitari,* that is the sign of the process of thought, of thought as action: 'to think', 'to be thought', verb, name of a movement, of a passage, of a logico-temporal rapport with certain spatial characters (exteriority, inclusion, separation, addition, etc.). And again, in the passive mood, applied to that potential object which I indicate indirectly: *nihil majus,* that which would be greater, if it were thought, and thinkable, but is not, *nihil,* halt the operation. Finally *potest,* the sign of that which is available, at one's disposal, but not yet in operation.

It would be interesting to translate this text into Chinese and to seek the original concrete signification of the ideograms that correspond to those signs. In our languages, there is nothing but a tissue of relationships between a sign open to everything, *id,* and a sign which bars everything: *nihil.*

One could transcribe that *id quo nihil majus cogitari potest,* 'that which is such that one could not think of anything greater', as follows: (open indication) (identifying liaison) (going beyond) (halt the operation) (to think, passive) (possibility). (*Id*) (*quo*) (*nihil*) (*majus*) (*cogitari*) (*potest*). (I indicate something) (that something in relationship to another thing) (relationship of superiority: overtaking or going beyond it) (halt the operation) (making possible) (thought).

This admirable degree of rigour in abstraction is the first lesson: we find ourselves on the confines of thought with the unthinkable, on the edge of language; beyond, there is nothing but silence.

The second lesson is even more important. It is decisive, vital, in the exact and proper sense of the word: it decides what my interior life shall be, in so far as it concerns the orientation of the intellect in relation to the soul, to the heart, and to the whole being. In those six Latin words, which designate six different operations of thought, including the 'halt', *nihil,* Saint Anselm inhibits, or spurs on, our leap towards God. Any attempt at definition of the concept of God is a devout tautology. 'God is' signifies 'I pray'. We can translate thus: 'I establish between Me and non-Me a relationship of amity, of reconciliation, of peace. At the limit, I am commingled with the non-Me.'

But 'I am commingled with the non-Me' is translated as 'God is'.

For that is what God is: Me and non-Me, not at all like 'two distinct divinities, the world and my independent Me' (the world is not all, the all contains me, and it contains the world and that which transcends the world; and my Me is not independent), but like a single being that goes beyond the Me, integrates the Me into the non-Me without destroying it, fulfills it and liberates it from its limits, from its separation, from its solitude, from its sadness, from its sin.

Tautology: God is. And even here, there is one term too many: 'is' – that is irreverence, impiety. To say 'God' is enough; that is, to call to him is enough. And even that is too much, and on the threshold of irreverence. It is enough to be silent, with him.

All statements about God are either false, or insufficient. That one is insufficient.

Statements about God which are false do not concern God, but something less than he: graven image, mental image, *flatus vocis.* That too, like all things, is in God.

The irreverent who speaks of God does not speak of God. He knows not that of which he speaks.

When I speak reverently of God, I do not speak of God, I speak in the general direction of my prayer.

He who prays to God knows nothing of God, unless it be that God has given him the grace of orison, and that it is this love of God that returns to God. This is not a truth of experience, nor a mental image of prayer, but the one way in which he who prays can speak about prayer, and know that of which he speaks.

One can only think of God as present. To think of God absent is not to think of God, it is to think of the desert. To think of God not existing is not to think of God, it is to think of nothingness.

To tell the truth, one does not think *of* God, one thinks *towards* him. One can only think towards God by thinking towards *God*. Otherwise, one is thinking towards a graven image, or a mental image, or an empty word; or towards an image of a desert world.

The 'dialogue with the unbeliever' is absurd and ridiculous. We have no language in common with him, nor concepts in common. He speaks of an image of God that he knows and that we do not know, and that he is made to overthrow. We are speaking of a God that neither we nor the unbeliever know, but whose grace we have in our hearts, or the memory of grace, or the hope of grace. We are speaking of a God *towards* whom we think, towards whom we think with necessity, towards whom we think by going beyond all, always, in all ways, dimensions, categories, actually, always in action, always in power...

But I must pause. We think towards God by means of the apparatus of thought called, for want of a better name, opening towards God. It is a general disposition of thought, the most general possible: that of being open. It can be expressed also as follows: all statements about God are insufficient, including this one. Or also by the proposition: 'Man thirsts after God.' Or: 'Man tends towards God.' Or quite simply by the sign (an arrow) which represents a vector.

Veho, vectum, vehiculum, vector, 'I transport, transported, means of transport, that or he that transports': a vector is that which transports: man as vehicle of love towards God, man who transports the grace of orison towards him from whom he received it, or prayer that transfers man towards God, towards God who thrusts man forward and attracts him to himself.

But all that is insufficient. Language is lacking. One should perhaps draw, not a vector in the form of an arrow, but a circle, and somewhere on its circumference, an arrow head. Of course, that too would be insufficient. There is a point beyond which thought (language) cannot go. From there on, thought falls by the wayside. There is nothing left but prayer, prayer from the heart, prayer of the whole being gathered within the heart, and offered up. And that only if God so wishes it: grace comes, or it does not come. Without it, all the rest is nothing. However, we must sweep the floor, wash the walls, set the masonry firmly right at the start, cement the ground well. And wait for grace to come, and then all this will become transparent, luminous and trembling like a flame. If it does not come, all this will fall into dust, a little handful of ash falling in the void. But I am waiting.

While waiting, I comfort myself, reassure myself and take heart and hope again through the memory of instants of grace. *Memory and reality should occupy* one single *space* (Ludwig Wittgenstein, *Philosophical Remarks,* proposition number 38).

And, dedicated by me in total gratitude, reverence and in all Christian love to the memory of Saint Anselm of Canterbury, of René Descartes, of Georg Friedrich Wilhelm Hegel and that of all their defenders, but also of all the critics of the ontological argument in favour of the existence of God, the second half of that remark: *And also, representation and reality occupy* one single *space.*

NOTE ON SOLITUDE

Note on sadness. To whomever is still seeking, to whomever knows no more than I do about it, I allow myself to offer him this consolation. In the night of our solitude, in forsakenness, in anguish, contemplate yourself, contemplate the universe. At this very moment as I think into the night, thousands of beings the same as I sleep the sleep of the just, or like brutes, or simply sleep. At this very moment, children are coming into the world amid their mothers' cries of pain, and with howls of rage at having been thrust out into the cold. At this very moment, couples are making what is called by synecdoche 'love', for it is often done without love, and then it is taking, if I dare say so, the parts for the whole. At this very moment, prisoners, forced captives, hostages are being tortured, and political evildoers or private tyrants are at their work. The dying are slowly slipping towards death. Human beings perish in accidents, soldiers are killed at this very instant by other human beings. At this very moment, all over the world, Christians are praying, Jews, Muslims, Buddhists are praying.

The continents are drifting, the glaciers are crumbling into the Arctic Ocean, the mountains are folding. At this very moment, in the night, the glimmer of grace is flickering nearly everywhere. This immense universe of darknesses, of suffering, of indifference, is scattered with these glimmers invisible to the naked eye, but known by me and by you in our prayers, when the grace of orison comes and brushes us with its wing. In this long night, the hard, intense sparks of thought are shining nearly everywhere, like those produced by striking together steel and flint: the clash of intellect against the mass of things. But it is not of this scintillation I am speaking, it is not this spectacle I am recommending. I am asking you to contemplate the faint glimmers, delicate and transparent, of souls touched by the grace of orison.

Wherever there are human beings, at this very moment, there are souls at prayer. 'The eternal silence of infinite space' trembles with the murmuring of prayers. This silence is not frightening. Or rather it is not only frightening: this silence is alive. And who dares tell me that in the infinite spaces whose silence terrifies me there are not other souls at prayer?

At this very instant, at five light-hours, Pluto is revolving round the sun, and its 'year' lasts two hundred and fifty of our terrestrial years. There are one hundred billion solar systems in our galaxy, and billions of galaxies in the universe. Everywhere, in those immense voids traversed by the mathematical functions of the Holy Spirit and structured by the logical universe, from logos, the Word, perhaps there are souls vibrating in prayer.

Each one of us is the culmination of a sequence of energy – matter – life – micro-organism – plant – animal – primate – human race – civilizations – Christian civilization; he shares with the latest virus the gift of being at home in the universe as the child in the womb – even in death, he is at home. And you and I operate a transmutation of that profound interrelatedness in the act of prayer. Perhaps at this very moment, on other earths, in other solar systems belonging to other galaxies, other beings are turning in the same way as we do, or in an equivalent way, towards God: the silence of the abyss contains, perhaps, an infinite murmuring of prayers.

I do not know. But I do know that human beings are praying at this very moment, and always have been. I do not believe there is one single second of time in which there is not one human soul at prayer.

I propose this meditation to whomever, among us, knows no more than I about it. I propose it to the sick, the lame, the depressed, the neurasthenics, the neurotics, those contemplating suicide, and the mad. I have found myself in almost all these categories, and I am the brother of all those whose sufferings I have not experienced. Let us think of the sufferings of God within us, and of all the atrocious sufferings taking place at this very moment, in God. Let us think of those who think of us without knowing us, let us think of those who pray, of all the silent multitude of souls at prayer. We are not alone. In solitude, silence, forsakenness, in the sleep of matter, the sound and the fury of suffering, of birth, of coupling, of despair, of evil and of good, there is everywhere the peace of prayer, everywhere glimmers of grace; there is the Church of souls.

I cannot forget one spring night, cold, transparent, the air sharp and motionless; midnight – suspended instant – the eve of Easter according to the Orthodox rite. The priest came out of the church that was too small to hold us all; he was holding a lighted candle; we lit those we were holding in our hands at his flame and then from one to the other. Soon the whole square in front of the church was peopled with those little motionless flames, all the faces were softly illuminated by those little radiances, so warm, so tender. An assembly, a people of little radiances.

Among other things, I love the Chinese, and with gratitude, because they call Christianity 'the religion of lights'. (Another reason for loving them is their reverence for the 'Heavens', that is, the universe that transcends the universe, as the sky, limitless, rises beyond the loess plain.) We are a people of calm little flames in the night, taking light from one another, and spreading ever outwards in the dark.

Perhaps solitude, sadness, forsakenness are nothing but a failure of attention to the multitude of prayers, of souls, of beings, and a failure to turn oneself towards them. For in my experience irreverence is nothing but a failure of memory, or a lack of consciousness of the ensemble of things, of the all. Solitude, sadness, forsakenness, absurdity, nothingness are truths of immediate experience, like the rotation of the sun round the earth. One must not be passive. Offering oneself, but not passively. Humble, but not inert. Unlike the earth that turns round the sun and turns round upon itself, we turn round God within us.

I am saying this in full consciousness of the Evil, of the ugliness, of the disorder in the world. My eyes are still smarting at the recent spectacle of a wild beast prowling through high, dry grasses, with his prey in his jaws. He was holding it by its broken neck, the head dangling on one side, the body on the other. A few feet away, another animal was accompanying him, gazing fixedly not at the wild beast, but at the prey, which it resembled. It was the companion of the victim, the male or the female, the mother, the playmate... Like us, they feel, and perhaps more strongly, the passions of love and friendship. It was its other self, he who kept him warm in solitude and in the cold of the universe, and now he was dead, inert, borne off by the wild beast who had snapped his neck with a single bite, and who is about to devour him – and begins by licking him as meticulously as he licks his little ones and licks himself. It will take me a long time to get over the sadness of that little creature left all alone. That cruelty, that sadness, that pain, that satisfaction, that slobbering appetite, and the whole bizarre stupidity of the thing – all that is part of the order of the world, and of God's will. And I do not say one word about human suffering, because it is even closer to us and even more insupportable, and because human cruelty is not innocent like that of the beasts. I know, I know. If I suggest a prayer, it is not because I pray at the drop of a hat. I see that God is also the God of pain, in a universe that is also a universe of suffering. And it is in that darkness that I see vibrating the souls of a people at prayer.

Darkness in broad daylight too. And in broad daylight too, the people of our human brothers at prayer. We are not alone. I am writing this, as I often do, sitting in front of the television screen. The day before yesterday I had found it marvellous and I had blessed it. Solitary, one who knows solitude all too well, withdrawn from all and everything, isolated like a sick man, like an insomniac in the night, I was working in front of the television, which was switched on; I was working as one prays. They were broadcasting, after the recent funeral of the Pope, who found such humility in death and grew in stature through it, the enthronement of the new Pope. I had witnessed the funeral ceremony at the house of friends to whom this book is dedicated, and I found in it an occasion for meditation. I was watching the enthronement in solitude, and in it I discovered consolation and joy of soul. I do not say jubilation, nor exultation, I say joy, sweetness of soul.

In this respect also, I am neither naïve nor blind. I know only too well display and *apparatchiks*. I know very well that the Pope is the chief functionary of a great and ancient organization, and that the cardinals who prostrate themselves before him are the Central Committee, and that the throne is a thing of wood, horsehair and cloth. But I also see, through all this, friendship, reconciliation, goodness; I see piety, prayer, peace. That square is prayer, that crowd is prayer, that cupola is a leap upwards to the beauty of God, an offering of all that is beautiful within ourselves.

Those vestments that our Protestant brethren find too sumptuous are signs: they signify solemnity, celebration, worship, and they are also prayer. Even the large tourist, yawning or chewing gum and taking snaps, is participating in the prayer, and the Highnesses in the front row with their baubles round their necks, and the Swiss Guards in costumes designed by Raphael. The thing is much more serious than one would think. There is no public human act more serious. How fine they are, the black cardinals and the yellow cardinals! One day, he before whom they will prostrate themselves will be as black or as yellow as these. The cardinalate purple elevates, magnifies and unites all races in its dignity. I love them, our dear delegates to the majesty of the Church, representatives of Christian peoples. The old gentleman seated on that chair, dressed like a woman and sporting a headdress as bizarre as that of a Buddhist or Shintoist priest, is our delegate towards God, placed as at the prow of a ship, towards God the abyss. How good it is to live, love, pray here, among the people of souls.

Chance, which is sometimes irreverent, and sometimes devout, made me write, in the book on which I am working at the moment: 'As if below sin there was

innocence, and at the centre of the criminal, a little child.'
At that instant exactly I heard the Pope chant: *In nomine
Patris, et Filii, et Spiritus Sancti.* My eyes filled with tears.
One should be a Christian. One should be able to be a
Christian. But how to be a Christian? Impossible?

11.

OF THE IMPOSSIBILITY OF BEING
A CHRISTIAN

How to be a Christian?

For about twenty years I asked myself this question, more or less explicitly, more or less consciously, and without finding an answer. The answer was given to me by someone else. I asked the question of someone else, only once in my life, and I received the answer.

It was on the pavement outside a big international hotel full of businessmen from every country in the world who were talking Basic English, much as the merchants of the Apocalypse talked *koinê*, Basic Greek.

In that hotel, later, the son of a man held hostage by terrorists had to deliver suitcases full of banknotes to the kidnappers' representatives; the journalists and press photographers were all ready, but it did not come off, and the hostage was assassinated – 'executed', as terrorists say, to give themselves the air of legitimate executioners.

A little further on was the headquarters of the world's most powerful steelworkers' trade union. A little further on was the banking district, hundreds of banks in one square kilometre, and whatever was not a bank was an insurance company or an advertising agency. Just next to it, the red light district, the drug pushers, and the highest level of criminality in the country and perhaps in the continent.

A very Christian situation, and certainly a good place to ask oneself the question 'How can one be a Christian?' In this century, what with our scientific knowledge of the universe, our technical mastery of the universe, our histor-

ical and philosophical critiques of all religions, the de-
Christianization of daily life, of souls, of spirits, of minds,
how can one be a Christian? How can one belong to that
religion, two thousand years old, born in the Near East on
the burial grounds of twenty or a hundred religions that
were born, developed, grew old and died there since
neolithic times – Jericho is the most ancient city on earth:
that religion with its strange dogmas, incomprehensible,
inadmissible dogmas? It was absurd, crazy, ridiculous to
be a Christian.

Being like the majority of my fellow men naturally
sociable, affectionate and faithful, I was not happy not
being a Christian. All my ancestors were Christians. I have
a sense of solidarity with my children, and with my
children's children and with all those who will come after
us: that is why, among other things, I cannot condone, or
accept, pollution, the desertification and the destruction of
our planet. But I also have a sense of solidarity with those
who died before us; I carry within me their genetic
message, I carry their thought and their languages in the
data processing code of my thought and the languages I
speak, with their emotional contexts of unknown pro-
fundity. I am only too familiar with the suffering of souls
and bodies that can be caused by a presumptuous breaking
with the past: one cannot break with the past, for the past
is always present, genetically and linguistically, in the
logico-historical continuity of space-time.

Therefore, I should have wanted to be a Christian, just
as I should have wanted to be a Muslim, or Hindu, or
Buddhist, or Jain, or Shintoist, or Taoist, or Confucianist,
if I had been born into another civilization. There, too, I
should doubtless have encountered the same insurmountable difficulty. For I love to love, but I have good sight and
I keep my eyes open, and I see what I see. Solidarity is not
enough. I could never be a Christian simply in order to feel
cosy and warm amid the crowd of my fellow-believers. I
could never be a Christian for the sake of sociability,

tradition, need for a hiding-place, fear of solitude. I must be honest; honestly, I saw the scientific critique of the Christian religion, and of all religion: and I saw the Christian reality, which some even call post-Christian. I knew how to address myself to God; but how to be a Christian? I was so small, lost, forsaken before God, alone before that terrifying God, that God-abyss, that God of suffering, but also of joy. If it had to be, I would remain alone.

What was there in common between me and that mass of dogmas – Asiatic, Hellenistic, piled on top of one another, stratified, sedimented for two thousand years, stretching across schisms and wars of religion upon earth that had created gods since the neolithic age? Between me and those ecclesiastical bureaucracies, the scores and hundreds of thousands of priests, pastors, monks, members of sects, the hundreds of millions of the faithful, the scores or hundreds of Churches and independent communities, all that dead, festering mass, alive and burning in parts, like earthly vegetation? Nothing, except the past. I was well aware that the past was mine. I bore the name of the Galilean fisherman Simon Barjona, Chimôn bar-Yonah, the Obedient, son of Colombe, to whom they had given the sobriquet 'Peter', just as in the pre-Christian North the Scandinavians were sometimes called Stein, 'Stone'. My family name originally signified the faithful of the Sea Goddess of Asia Minor: they were called Démétrios, sons of Dê-mêtêr, Gê-mê-têr, Earth Mother, just as the disciples of Christ called themselves Christian. My neuro-cerebral computer was the depository of information from two Christian millennia, and from Hellenic, Semitic, Sumerian and neolithic millennia. My place was here, and I could not change it, through pride, or ignorance, or folly, or barbarism. But I could not be a Christian. It was impossible for me to be a Christian.

So I put the question to two men with whom I was walking in the street. We were leaving the club we all three of us belonged to. On my right was the Protestant pastor of the Church I love best of all among Protestant Churches, and to which I would be converted if I were the sort of man to be converted, and if for a Christian baptized into the Orthodox Church Roman Catholicism were not much closer. The other, on my left, a plump little man with a pink and white complexion, a little blotchy, had an ecclesiastical air, and was in fact my dear and reverend friend Monsignor Walter A., archpriest of the cathedral.

I put the question to them briefly and politely, for that one time in my life, without expecting a decisive answer, not even an answer that I might take seriously into consideration. I was expecting nothing. But as I had found myself by chance together with them, I used the occasion to ask them the most serious question I had to ask anyone at that time. I did not want just to make conversation, I was not curious, nor idle, nor talkative; I was just taking advantage of the situation which placed me between two professional Christians. (The pastor later became a bishop, or superintendent, as they say now, which is the same thing, translated from Greek into Latin; recently, when a pastor made a protest by burning himself to death in a public square in a town in Socialist Thuringia, they said he was not a martyr, but a witness, which is the same thing, translated from Greek into German: I am willing.)

The gentleman on my right answered me first: 'You must have grace. For example, I have grace.'

All very well for him, but what if I did not have it? Was I therefore lost? Abandoned?

Mgr A. was walking along in silence beside me, a look of concentration in his eyes, self-forgetting in face of the problem, an admirable example of what the Church can make of one of its servants. He was there to answer the cry for help from a lonely human being, one who had perhaps gone astray, and who was asking him the way towards Christ. How can one be a Christian, I cried (in a tone of polite conversation), when it is evidently impossible?

He answered me in seven words. In German, they are nine.

'That depends on your attitude towards Jesus,' he said.

He was so precise, so undogmatic, so untheological, so lacking in solemnity or rhetoric that he had not even said 'Christ', not even 'Jesus Christ'. He had said 'Jesus', the personal proper name of the man of Nazareth, towards whom it was a matter of having or of not having an attitude, or if one were to have one, knowing which one to have. He had given me the answer. He had given me the key, opened the door. He had delivered me over to the Church of Christ. I was saved. For I had been very alone. Even when one is addressing oneself to God, there are still human beings, and I did not have a way leading both to God *and* to human beings, and one cannot have the one without the other. He had given me the answer I was looking for.

For in fact I may doubt everything, I may reject everything, I may lose everything, but I cannot doubt Jesus, nor reject him, nor lose him. It so happens that, for me, he is the highest summit humanity has ever reached, the point at which humanity and God come in touch. Apart, of course, from each prayer; apart from each instant of grace; apart from each soul, within its most inward heart and centre; apart from all the points or all the energy particles of the universe; if one considers the human race, and if one seeks a human being in whom God was fully present, I mean in the measure of and according to human capacity, then I could not give any other answer but: 'It is he.'

I know him personally. I know him better than any other living person around me. None has that intensity, that originality, that coherence, that prodigious unity.

There is only one person whom I think I may know in a similar way, but at a very great distance, and that is also a man whom I know through the writings of his disciples: Socrates, son of Sophroniscus, of the Alopecia tribe, citizen of Athens, former soldier, known for his calm bravery under fire, former member of the Tribunal of the Five Hundred, known for having uselessly opposed a judicial assassination, haunter of the palaestra, the gymnasium, freeloader at dinners of the 'in' people, an even greater maker of conversation than the nephew of Rameau and Dr Johnson together, and a man about whom those who knew him said that 'making his acquaintance shakes you like contact with an electric eel'.

I know Socrates through the narrative passages of the *Criton*, the *Phédon*, the *Banquet*, through the extraordinary discourse of Alcibiades in the last-named, through a few other passages in the dialogues of Plato, through two lines in Aristophanes' *The Clouds* and through a text by Xenophon which is not up to much, for Xenophon was a professional soldier, a sporting type, a country gentleman with a taste for horses and hunting: his masterpiece is that of a well-bred sportsman and soldier, and finally he was a man of property and a gentleman, all of which is sufficient to love Socrates, but not to understand him. We have read the historians and the biographers of antiquity, and it is obvious that those unforgettable texts are upheld by the active presence of a unique man, the wisest, the most just, the most whole and the most devout man of his time and of that world, and Socrates was certainly such a man.

In the same way, but to an even higher degree, to the highest degree, the unknown men who, one generation after the death of Jesus, wrote the Synoptic Gospels, writers of genius, assembled the witness of other unknowns who had the genius to see, to hear, to remember and to transmit what was something important, unheard-of, staggering; and all that is borne along, sustained, brought alive at a level of intensity that makes it cross the space-time of two millennia without having lost its impact, through the presence, the shock waves, the living memory, of a unique acuity, which marked a being such as there had never been either before or after him.

We know the biographies of antiquity, among them those of the great mystics, the prophets, the thaumaturges like Apollonius of Tyana and the suicidal exhibitionists like Peregrinus Proteus. In none of them, even in the fragments left by the existence of the greatest – Pythagoras, Heraclitus, Empedocles or bizarre Diogenes, the first and greatest of the beatniks – do we find that inimitable accent. Only the account of his master by Plato comes anywhere near it.

It is for me an inexhaustible source of astonishment that there should be erudite men who deny the real existence of Jesus. As if such a personality, such discourse, such details, could be invented! I accept, of course, the results of theological, historical and philological research since the Reformation and with their centre in Protestant Germany. I accept the relativity, the problematical, obscure or semi-obscure character of the texts of the Gospel, composed no doubt in Syria by Hellenized Orientals, sons of that ground so fertile in religions for so many millennia; written one generation, or in the case of the Gospel of Saint John, two generations, therefore respectively about thirty and sixty years, after the death of Jesus; written finally by people of whom at least one, Luke, never set foot in Palestine.

And yet, it cannot be denied: nowhere else does one find the sublime simplicity of narration linked with hallucinating detail and with the substance, unique in human history, of the reports given by the Gospels. Neither in Lucian, nor in Plutarch, nor in Polybus – I name the last because certain observations, as in Book XVIII, Chapter 53, could have been written by a man of the twentieth century, with our special sensitivity towards irrational behaviour – nor in Sallust, nor in Suetonius or Tacitus (to name the most important historiographers and biographers approximately contemporary with the Gospel writers, or more precisely 'contemporary as to the style of the events, the interest in the individual personality and the

narrative vision'). Nowhere else does one find that sobriety, that elevation, that purity, that energy – despite the bad
Greek. Except – and not quite to the same degree – in the
narrative passages of Plato consecrated to Socrates.

My thought and my taste are formed by two millennia
of Christianity. I am conditioned to associate religious,
ethical and aesthetic values with these texts which I judge
by criteria formed by study of the texts themselves and by
two thousand years of imitation (bungled) of Jesus Christ.
It is not a school of objectivity.

But the selection of the masterpieces of antiquity was
effected before the Christian era, between the first publication of the Homeric epic in Athens under Pisistratus, and
the choice of tragic poets in Alexandria during the last two
centuries before Jesus Christ. Cultivated Christians assimilated that heritage en bloc and did not think of submitting
it to a critique based on the style of the Old Testament.
The continuity of Hellenism is uninterrupted in Constantinople until 1453. Since then, it has been 'plugged in' to the
Occident.

So our criteria are not Christian, but from antiquity.
Moreover, we have at our disposal a table of Christian
criteria, and one of 'post Christian' criteria. Better than
that: we possess also systems of reference absolutely alien
and autonomous, to collate with our Hellenic abscissa and
our Jewish ordinate. They are homologous texts: fun-
damentals of religion, biographies, narratives of individual
destinies, narrative portraits of unforgettable people.

There is the canon of Buddha's discourses; there is the
Che Chi; there is Icelandic literature: at least three literary
sensibilities and three descriptions of man, complete,
perfect, created outside Christianity.

We find certain common traits in the great models of
narrative, whether in the historic texts of the Old Testament, in Herodotus, in the *Dhammapaddam,* in Sseuma
Tsien, in Plutarch or in the most ancient sagas. These texts
taken all together provide us with an aesthetic of biog-

raphical narration, and it is by relying upon this system of co-ordinates that I am speaking of the narrative passages devoted to Socrates in the Platonic dialogues, as well as in the Synoptic Gospels and particularly in Mark. (For the merits of John are mainly of a poetic and mystic order, or theological. Despite that, the most dramatic passage in the Gospels is found in John, and it contains in a nutshell the art of 'Dostoyevskian' dialogue: it is possible to recognize the same technique in John 1:45-50, and in the last speech in the Stavrogin-Tikhon scene: 'Damned psychologist!')

In so far as it is permitted to have a preference, Mark is my favourite. He is the reporter, sober and prosaic. He is not a theologian, not a metaphysician, not a mystic. With an unexpected effect, his lack of lyricism gives his narration an early-morning fragrance, a freshness, a humble and almost musical perfection.

The reporter: where Matthew and Luke say that Jesus was on the boat and asleep, Mark is more precise:'*And he was in the hinder part of the ship, asleep on a pillow.*' Mark often gives precise details: '*And that same day, when the even was come...*' In another place, he says: '*Six days later.*' Or again: '*When the even was come,* Jesus went out of the city.'

It is the same instinctive technique, characteristic of great narratives in all literatures, which I find in the first classics of narration considered as an art. I find it in Herodotus, in the last sentence in the Adrastus episode: 'When all had gone *and there was silence around the tomb...*' I find it again in this detail, just as useless yet just as decisive artistically, in the story of the crime of Gibeah in the Book of Judges: 'And behold, the woman his concubine was fallen down at the door of the house, *and her hands were upon the threshold.*' I claim that in these two fragments of sentences we can see the first examples of great prose narrative treated as an art. And that is precisely the art of Mark.

Mark draws with a single stroke, like a Far Eastern painter, the outline of 'a certain young man, having a linen cloth cast about his naked body; and the young men laid hold on him: *And he left the linen cloth, and fled from them naked.*' It is worthy of the brush of Hokusai. It is a simple touch, 'the single stroke of the brush', that Tao Chi advises in his writings on painting, *Hua Yu Lu*. And that Chinese ink calligraphy is so convincing, so striking, the scene is so visionary in its gratuitous character, that one is inclined to identify that unknown person with the narrator himself.

In Mark there is, I think, only one passage written by the 'omniscient narrator', the prayer in the Garden of Olives. All the rest could have been reported by one or more eye-witnesses. One other exception perhaps: the temptation in the desert, but this is strangely and characteristically pallid and abstract in Mark, the great journalistic genius in universal literature, and so much more beautiful in the other synoptists. This is because myth is not his forte. He describes concrete things that happened exactly as he describes them. His colleagues offer us a product that is a distillation of the human condition, with the three fundamental temptations, sensual enjoyment, which we today call consummation; power over the elements of the universe, called then miracle and magic and today technique; and power over men. In the history of humanity there has been only one man exposed to all of them at the same time: one man who inspired those that knew him with the feeling that he had the stature to be not just the Grand Inquisitor, or Faust, or Caesar, but to be all three at once. They understood even that he possessed still greater strength than that: the strength to survive temptation and to become again as a little child, without forgetting what he knew and had surmounted. The scene in the desert is the equivalent, in terms of mytho-poetic style and formal structure, of the scene in which Siddhartha Gautama leaves his palace and encounters a beggar, an old man and a funeral procession.

Mark does not speak of the origins of Jesus. Let it be said

in passing: how sad it is to see Voltaire, who writes prose as Mozart makes music, and who is always and infallibly on the side of reason and humanity, against fanaticism, folly and stupidity, playing the buffoon in his *Dictionnaire Philosophique* on the two genealogies which do not agree in their details, when Luke says, with such Hellenic politeness, and for once with better manners that Voltaire: 'And Jesus, when he began his ministry, was about thirty years of age, being (*as was supposed*) the son of Joseph, which was the son of Heli, which was the son of Matthat, which was the son of Levi...'

For Mark, Jesus is a man who comes from Nazareth and mingles with the crowd surrounding John the Baptist on the banks of the Jordan. And at the end, he is a man who is dead and buried; only something unusual happens: on the morning of the third day, the women find the stone blocking the tomb rolled away, the tomb empty, and a young man clothed in white seated *on the right side,* this reporter of genius makes clear. They are frightened and tell no one what they believe they have heard this young man say. Then, Mary, Mariam, Miriam, Amère (Bitter), Amertume (Bitterness), as in Spain they call girls Dolores, Dolor or Llagas, Wounds, the former local prostitute Magdalene affirms that she has just met Jesus. The disciples do not believe her. Jesus appears 'in another form unto two of them' – that must be on the road to Emmaus – but contrary to his custom Mark gives no details. Once again, the others refuse to believe what they are told. Right up to the last minute allowed by faith, Mark retains the sober reserve of a realistic narrator. So much so that even today his entire text, up the last six verses (16:14-20), which scholars say have been added later, could have been written by a neutral eye-witness, even an unbeliever, as well as by a man of our own century, provided that we ascribe to collective hallucination all the miracles, which a contemporary of Mark, for example, the highly cultured Tacitus, would never have doubted.

I do not speak of cures. In the presence of such an extraordinary being, one as overpowering as Jesus, it would have been miraculous if there had been no miraculous cures. The epileptics, the neuropaths, those who were ill with psychosomatic ailments were cured by his touch. He had a magnetism, an aura, a radiance, as we say, without being able to explain the phenomenon. The psychological ambience was one of waiting, of hyperacute tension; the crowd was in a state of moral, religious and political effervescence wherever he went, between two mystical crises and two explosions of political violence. It was a combination of Lourdes and the taking of the Bastille, an exceptional state of collective psychism, with all the repercussions that would entail for the individual neuro-vegetative system. Jewish national rebellions were continuous under the Roman occupation and were to lead to the great revolution, to war, to the destruction of the country and of Jerusalem. As for religious tension, the oneness of the Gospel is proof of that, the very existence of our religion lends it faith.

I have known Stalinists in my country, returning from Hungary in October 1956, transfigured by the experience of collective purification: the revolutionary crowd is good, and plunging into it one suffers a personal catharsis, as many Parisians can attest after having lived through the days of May 1968. The Stalinists of whom I am speaking were morally transformed despite their 'class interest', despite the mortal danger they would have encountered in a repetition of the events in Hungary in our land. After having seen that with my own eyes, I understood an observation by the Comte de Ségur returning to France after the unleashing of the new collective psychism: he no longer recognized his compatriots; they all had an air never seen before – grave, tense, resolute, intensely active (from his *Mémoires*, just after the portrait of Prince de Kaunitz). In the psychological tension of the country during the decades which preceded the war of the Jews, after the

appearance of John the Baptist, a man already extraordinary to the highest degree according to the testimony of
Jesus himself, who knew him, there can be no doubt that
cures were made. I do not know what happened in the
midday heat and the luminous haze of the Sea of Galilee,
nor during the night of the tempest, nor in the crowd
which was no longer hungry after having eaten crumbs of
bread and fish. I do not know how literally one should
take this or that miraculous episode; but I do not doubt the
cures.

As for the scenes or the discourses that I do not
understand, such as the malediction of the fig tree, or 'I
came not to bring peace, but a sword', I suspend my
judgement. I do not understand, I am waiting, I put
myself into the hands of the savants, we shall see.

I have nothing more to say, except this: that I know
Jesus as if I had been there among the crowd. I am there, I
am in the crowd. And if it is true that I prefer Mark, that
does not mean I do not find Jesus in the other synoptists,
and in John too, sometimes with a blazing presence, as in
the episode with Nathanael.

I feel I know Jesus; but that 'I feel' is only precaution,
politeness, humility: to be completely true, I must say I
know Jesus, I know him better than I have ever known
any man in my own time, encountered a thousand times in
my life, talked with a thousand times. I know Jesus better
than I know my wife and my children, and better than I
know myself. Perhaps because of the intensity, because of
the incredible force of his being. Perhaps because of his
coherence, his unity, despite also the variants, the impreci-
sions or contradictions of the information transmitted by
the two generations following him.

I feel also, and this time it is not a polite formula, it is
really true – I do not know, I just feel I know that even the
fact that I know nothing of his appearance helps me to
recognize him. Suetonius describes exactly the face, the
body, and the bearing of Caesar, and even his voice, which

was not, as one might expect, a big, virile bass, but rather shrill; I remember only the negligent way he had of fastening his belt in his youth, just as Edward VII neglected to fasten the bottom button of his waistcoat after dinner, or turned up the bottoms of his trousers on the beach at Brighton. Caesar remains an enigma, something Edward VII has never been.

The beauty of Alexander and his habit of keeping his head tilted towards his shoulder do not help us to know him better; one can guess something about him when one learns that he passed unnoticed amid his generals, because of the simplicity of his garments. The ugliness of Socrates is important, because the Athenians – sensual, aesthetes and bisexual – were discovering for the first time in the history of the Hellenic spirit an invisible beauty, not aesthetic and asexual, and what we call the soul. What does it matter, if we want to know Plato, that he was handsome, and with such broad shoulders that the palaestra nickname, Plato the Broad, stuck to him, instead of his real name, which only a few specialists know today? God himself becomes less recognizable when we look at the fragments of his visage accessible to us, and which frighten us by their strangeness; with eyes closed, we recognize him, we love him, he comes to meet us, and we go towards him. The disciples of Jesus and the Evangelists, all men of genius, beings who possessed the genius of piety, of love, of faith, could have handed down to us details about his physical appearance, a thousand times; but not one of them thought of doing that, not a single time. On the contrary, they show us him in life, acting, they show us his gestures, his expression, we hear the tone and the accent of his voice.

We see him continuously, we perceive his immediate presence, we are there, around him, he is here, among us. He reads in public a passage from the prophet Isaiah, in the house of prayer of his native town, Nazareth. It was what we should call today at once church and house of culture in that country place, and it bore a Greek name, in that Orient so deeply Hellenized: *synagogé*, 'meeting', like the tribunal of Jerusalem, the sanhedrin, a name apparently Jewish if there ever was one, came from 'council', *synédrion*. Apparently the participants in the service each 'Sunday', which was the Saturday, took turns in reading the day's text, or a text chosen by them, and had the right to comment on it.

'And he closed the book, and gave it back to the attendant, and sat down. And the eyes of all them that were in the synagogue were fastened on him. And he began to say unto them...'

We all have our eyes fastened on him, ever since that day, since that time. 'And he *began*': we sense the leap he is preparing. He was just beginning. At that very moment, he begins.

The book was a long paper scroll, fastened to two sticks at the two ends, and rolled up by beginning at both ends at the same time. The writing was set out in short, narrow columns of superposed lines, and the columns were parallel to the two sticks. They read aloud, rolling up one end and unrolling the other at the same time. The same book can still be found today, made in exactly the same way, in every Jewish synagogue. Jesus read aloud, rolled up the two ends until the two scrolls touched one another, held out the book to the servant of the community, and sat down. Everybody had their eyes fastened on him.

Everywhere he made his appearance, he spoke in the houses of prayer, after the Saturday divine service. 'And all bare him witness, and wondered at the gracious words that proceeded out of his mouth. And they were astonished at his doctrine: for his word was with power.' He had a strength that was felt by all. This strength caused passers-by to flock round him, and he was followed by the crowd. They pressed on his heels, they became worried if they began to feel they were losing him. 'And the people sought him, and came unto him, and stayed him, that he should not depart from them.'

'The pharisees and the doctors of the law', or what we should today call puritans and intellectuals, were 'sitting by, which were come out of every town of Galilee, and Judaea, and Jerusalem.' People read a lot in the villages, in that land; there were many people who questioned themselves very seriously about their moral life, so much so as to merit the name of pharisees, persons apart, or what might be called rigorists, and numbers of cultivated people who knew the sacred book by heart, that strange and fascinating book, as well-bred Hellenes of those days knew by heart their Homer, their Hesiod, their Pindar and the three great tragic dramatists. Those people obsessed by moral and intellectual questions had their eyes fastened on him, just as did the beggars, the vagabonds, the peasants, the artisans and the fishermen: 'The scribes and pharisees watched him.' All were silent and watched him fixedly.

'But he knew their thoughts, and said to the man which had the withered hand, Rise up, and stand forth in the midst.' He spoke that with a tranquil authority, with absolute authority; an authority so great that it becomes invisible, and does not know itself. We see him, we hear him, we listen to the command; and of course in the silence he is obeyed. The man 'arose and stood forth'. He had a 'withered' hand − rachitic, paralysed, dystrophic, attacked by muscular atrophy or by a chronic cramp of a nervous nature − which is the most probable, given the swiftness of the cure. The notables, the well-to-do, people leading exemplary lives, cultivated people, were watching: if this amateur preacher, this *Privatdozent,** the greatest of *Privatdozent*s among the Jews from the prophet Balaam to the doctors (of philosophy) Marx and (of medicine) Freud, was about to effect a cure on a Saturday, a holy day, a taboo day, when all labour, all effort, all activity other than prayer and meditation were forbidden by divine law: so they were about to accuse him of breaking the Sabbath.

'But he knew their thoughts.' 'Then said Jesus unto

★ *Privatdozent*: in German in the text, meaning an unpaid university assistant (Translator's note).

them, I will ask you one thing: Is it lawful on the sabbath days to do good, or to do evil? to save life, or to destroy it?'

On another occasion, he explained to them that it is not man who is made for the Sabbath, but the Sabbath that is made for man: not a man for structures, for society, for the homeland, for the Church, for the Party, for free trade, for liberty, for anything at all that is not he; but inversely, it is the structure, the game, the abstract schema, the mental schema, the context, which is made for the man of flesh and soul, for the computer gifted with a conscience of himself and of his liberty, and accessible to grace: the structures, society, homeland, Church, Party, trade, liberty, are made for the concrete, individual man, capable of suffering, of hope and joy (he alone capable, and only God in him it might be said, but let us pass over that last point – we shall never know).

He asked the moral question above the limits of culture, or civilization, or society, or socio-economic organization, the facts: save life, or kill? Good, or Evil? And even despite the taboo?

They were all silent, the ill-wishers as well as the indifferent, the somnolent as well as those who were beginning to feel an upheaval of the soul, the 're-programming' of their computer.

Then: 'And looking round about upon them all, he said unto the man, stretch forth thy hand.'

He often looked round upon them all. He looks round upon all of us, since we are in the crowd around him. I am there, at whatever instant in the day; you are there; we are all there together.

The 'good rich man' departs, 'sorrowful, for he had great possessions'. The disciples, astonished, asked one another: 'And who then can be saved?' *But Jesus beheld them,* and said unto them...'

Jesus 'looked round about on them with anger, being grieved for the hardness of their hearts', and he addresses his listeners severely: 'O generation of vipers!' 'He taught as if having authority, and not like the scribes', the tenured professors in the universities, socialized, trained to that profession. But more often, it is not the severe tone, nor even the authority that one notices. 'Beholding the crowd, he was moved by compassion for them, for they languished and were faint, like sheep not having a shepherd': like an idle crowd in an industrial megalopolis, like the millions of sorry creatures imprisoned in millions of boxes made of metal and Plexiglass emitting clouds of poisoned vapour at rush hours. 'Then Jesus called his disciples unto him, and said, I have compassion on the multitide.' He looks around him, and most often he is moved by compassion. A man suffering from a skin disease, frequently provoked by nervous syndromes, but called in those days 'a leper', throws himself at his feet and asks him in a pleading voice: 'If thou wilt, thou canst make me clean.' 'And Jesus, moved with compassion, put forth his hand, and touched him, and saith unto him, I will; be thou clean.'

He gives the same absolute attention to every individual being. A man comes to him, casts himself on his knees before him, and says: 'Good Master, what shall I do that I may inherit eternal life?' And Jesus said unto him, 'Why callest thou me good? There is none good but one, that is, God. Thou knowest the commandments.' – 'Master all these I have observed from my youth,' says the unknown man. Jesus beholds him fixedly, that look goes through him, illuminates him in every corner of his soul. *'Then Jesus beholding him loved him.'*

This look sometimes expresses a sort of technical curiosity. Jesus takes by the hand a blind man who had been brought for him to cure, leads him out of the village, puts spittle on his eyes and 'imposes his hands' upon him, which usually means that he puts both his hands on his head, but here he does it upon his eyes. Then he asks the blind man if he can see anything. 'I see trees as men, walking,' says the blind man, seeing dark, indistinct outlines. Then 'after that he put his hands again upon his eyes, and made him look up: and he was restored, and saw every man clearly. And he sent him away to his house, saying, Neither go into the town, nor tell it to any in the town.'

He did not want any publicity. He would have preferred to keep it secret. He was a healer, but he was much more than that. However, we see him examining attentively, questioning like a doctor when he is brought a 'dumb spirit', whom his 'demon' throws on the ground uttering howls and gnashing his teeth, and whom he has 'cast' even into the water and the fire – that is, the unfortunate creature has fallen senseless into the house's water tank, or on the fire in the hearth in the centre of the main room when the fit seizes him, with sudden loss of conscience, stiffening, loss of balance, convulsions: 'the spirit tare him; and he fell on the ground, and wallowed foaming.' And uttering a howl that I shall never forget, for I have heard it uttered by a high school friend who had an epileptic attack in public, and I was present. Then the man of Nazareth wants to know exactly: 'How long is it ago since this came unto him?' If it was a long time, the cure would be difficult.

The most extraordinary thing is his tone when unfortunates beg him with loud cries to heal them and he stops and questions them with critical curiosity: *'Believe ye that I can do this thing?'* And they howl: 'Yes, thou canst!' And he replies: 'Go, your faith has healed ye.' And he moves on.

In the crowd, he suddenly stops. He has felt his strength running out of him like a fluid. 'Who touched my clothes?' The disciples reply with stupid good sense: 'Thou seest the multitude thronging thee, and sayest thou, Who touched me?' But *he* knows; he knows that of which he speaks. 'Who touched me?'

It was a woman 'which had an issue of blood for twelve years'. She touched him, hoping to be cured; touched him secretly, trembling with emotion, hope, humility, love; and 'in her body she felt that she was healed of that plague'. In her belly she felt a sort of shoot of healing.

The crowd presses around him. 'The multitude listened unto him with pleasure.' 'There were many coming and going', the agitation of passers-by on a riot day. Passers-by, idle lookers-on, ask what is happening. 'It is Jesus, the prophet of Nazareth.' Blind men sitting on the ground, backs to the wall of a house, ask what all the noise is about. 'It is Jesus of Nazareth passing by.' Beggars bellow: 'Hosanna, son of David!' *Hôchî âhnnâ,* save me, I beg of thee! Help, please! They bring him the sick on stretchers. Other little groups in the crowd: intellectuals discussing, surrounded by little knots of listeners with craned necks. But here is the neuropath who 'always, night and day... was in the mountains, and in the tombs, crying, and cutting himself with stones.' Here is the 'unclean spirit' now, looking normal and respectable, 'sitting, and clothed, and in his right mind', listening to the preacher from Nazareth.

More blind people again, and people with speech difficulties, hearing troubles, deafness. 'He sighed, lifted his eyes to the heavens, and said: *Ephphatha,* that is, Be opened.' Then he departs again, followed closely by his little group, his team, chosen with the instinct of genius from among a population throbbing with instinct and genius, reaching out towards a spiritual event so far unheard-of and an imminent national revolt, for taxes are heavy, the Roman occupier is hated, his Quislings, Herod and others, despised. John is crying in the desert, gatherings have already been dispersed by the Roman shock troops leaving dozens of corpses on the ground. Something is going to happen, something they have been waiting for since time immemorial, something the whole world has always been waiting for, something that may happen at any moment now. It is perhaps he, the awaited one, let's run and see what he is doing, listen to what he is saying. Already everyone is in movement.

But he, sometimes, is silent. 'He did not answer one word.' 'Jesus was hungry.' 'But he was sleeping.' He walks in silence, and suddenly turns and asks his disciples: 'Of what were ye talking?' Another time he remains silent and writes with his finger in the dust of the public square. This is how Archimedes was killed during the sack of Syracuse: he was drawing geometrical figures on the sand or in the dust in front of him. (Archimedes, having discovered the principle that bears his name while he was taking a bath, leapt out and ran stark naked through the streets shouting: 'I have found it! *Eureka!*' Here again is 'the one stroke of the brush' which Tao Chi recommends, and which I admire so much in Mark: this one is by Plutarch.) Once again, at the dreadful news that John the Baptist had been executed in prison, Jesus 'departed into a desert place by ship privately'.

I know him, I am there, in the multitude. All films and 'musicals' about Jesus make me sick, with their approximations, their deformations, their involuntary falsehoods, their frivolity, their thoughtlessness and lack of reverence. They make the country and the people more Jewish than the Jews and more Arab than the Arabs. All the Romans are in breastplates, the temples hideous, the statues and 'idols' monstrous. All bogus! What one has to do is to reject idols, even if they are beautiful ones, and not make up falsehoods.

The Mediterranean world was 'antique' in the most natural way; it was the Hellenistic world, and today one can still see humans clothed exactly like the Greek orators sculpted by Polyclete or Lysippus; the peasants of Erythrea, who drape themselves in their length of white cloth like the Ancients in their himation.

Everyone wore the tunic, a short shirt of wool or linen, with brief sleeves or simple armhole slits, the 'cloak', the pallium, a rectangle of wool or linen covering the body, one end thrown over the shoulder, the other carried over the arm; and sometimes they wore only the pallium over their naked bodies. Light sandals on the feet, short hair, neatly combed, the face shaven or with a well-trimmed beard, for just like the jewels at the throats and wrists of the women, both comb and razor had been invented in the paleolithic age. The people washed frequently; they went to the public baths.

The most ancient images from the catacombs show us a youthful Jesus, without a beard, curly-headed, absolutely Hellenic. I do not believe he was like that; but nor do I believe that this world of farmers, artisans, civilized merchants – religious, meticulous in their alimentary and hygienic rituals, devoted readers of great literature, enjoying discussions on themes which they took with profound seriousness, knowing depth psychology, paying their taxes in drachmas, didrachmas and staters of gold and silver – were a gang of grubby, flea-ridden mopheads.

The towns had colonnades of corinthian columns. They were living under a Roman, not a Turkish occupation. The Orient and North Africa were rich in agoras, forums, doric, ionian or corinthian temples, in theatres, baths, stadia. In the ruins of the magnificent caravan metropolis of Baalbek-Heliopolis or Dura-Europos, bas-reliefs show patrician cameleers with their princesses, as unlike Bedouin as can be imagined. The Jews were sometimes named Aristobulus, Philippus, Achillas, Titus, Agrippa, Antipas,, Berenice, and spoke Greek, though of course with accents of Brooklyn or the Bronx.

We, too, have lived under an occupation. There was the Roman Empire, and the other superpower in the East, who with his army at Stalingrad had vanquished Crassus and taken him prisoner. Since then, the world has been divided into two parts.

The Romans were insupportable: hypocritical moralists, legalistic, liberals, wheeler-dealers, corrupt, prosaic and 'protestant' in comparison with the Greeks – in short, Americans, but excellent and disdainful colonizers like the

British, and with an army clothed in scarlet: the soldiers covered Jesus with one of their uniform cloaks: 'And they stripped him, and put on him a scarlet robe' (Matthew 27:28). The Romans: military like the Germans, as zealous in the repression of revolts as the Russians, technocrats and technicians like the Westerners they were, too much in evidence, with their heaven knows how many cohorts of rocket-launchers in the heavy-armoured legion stationed at Jerusalem airport; with their collectors of Roman taxes, hated by the natives as much as those who collaborated with the foreigners; their Roman dollar with the effigy of the president-generalissimo elected by the Senate, but in reality by the army, and belonging to the Bonaparte-Kennedy-Caesar dynasty. The Roman Empire was rotten to the core, rotten with abundance, luxury, conspicuous consumption, sensual pleasure, indifference, cruelty, hardened hearts. We know the graffiti found in Pompei, scribbled by a tourist, a carpet-seller or a 'guest worker' (but they called them 'slaves'): *sodoma gomora,* Semite translation of the Roman *la dolce vita.*

The country of the Jews was simmering with fury under their occupation, like Ireland under the British, Hungary under the Russians, Cisjordania under Israel, Paris under the Germans. The Jews: feverish, overexcited, superior and knowing their superiority, full of the faults of their genius, hysterical, fanatical. They had invented the One God, better than Amenophis IV, the one incorporate, transcendent, nameless God. They are not going to tolerate the graven images of these foreign brutes. Perhaps the 'sicari' or hired assassins are already mixing with the multitudes. *Sica*: dagger; they were terrorists who were to drown in blood Jerusalem and the entire country with their well-known and efficacious method: to provoke a reaction from authority and thus to lay bare the latent fascism of the Romans, which would then unleash the people's revolution that would bring the Kingdom of God upon earth.

This is why the 'publicans', farmers and collectors of Roman taxes, were execrated: they were collaborating with the occupier. Jesus ate and drank with them and with the 'prostitutes', the goodtime girls in the bars frequented by the Roman, German, American troops, by the tourists come to admire the Temple of Solomon, by businessmen, by uncircumcised foreigners: *they* had their heads shaved and were paraded naked through the streets, reviled and spat upon. Jesus kept some very bad company. He was caught between two fires: on the one hand, pious, cultivated, rich, patriotic and respectable people, but prudent, not wanting to get into trouble with the occupation; on the other hand, conspirators, violent agitators like Barabbas ('Son of the Father'), and future or actual assassins.

It was a universe of villages, small towns and hamlets around the great holy city with its enormous temple, which Jesus himself visited as a pilgrim and a tourist, along with his disciples, gaping idly: 'Master, see what manner of stones and what buildings are here!' They were villages and towns somewhat similar to those of medieval Italy, Spain or the South of France, with in addition, here and there, corinthian capitals, Greek frontons, the Greek chlamys, the *koinê* of civilized people. The Jews were invaded by the Hellenist influence and sometimes fought against it with fury, but at other times accepted it to the point of taking part in the life of the palaestra, the gymnasium, where men were *gymnos,* naked – something that did not suit them, because of their circumcision, which attracted pointing fingers and made them the butt of 'Hellenes' as Semitic as themselves. Sacred prostitution, matriarchal and fertility cults, with their phallic symbols, filled them with horror; 'happenings' with gladiators were unknown to them. The Jews were against all easy-going life, they were all for self-mastery, moral discipline, strictness in everything, and possessed, driven on by the desire to go beyond everything in the search for God, the thirst for purity, goodness, 'salvation'.

They had certainly felt the influence of Greek, Semitic, Cypriot stoicism, at once the culmination of Hellenism and an upsurge of things buried in the pre-Indo-European soil. They had learned this Hellenistic style of search for wisdom, probably unleashed by contact with India following Alexander's expedition and the installation of Macedonian dynasties with Greek 'courts' like Central Headquarters, Greek general staffs, municipalities, businesses and technicians; or finally, Hellenized, in Persia, Afghanistan, Syria, Iraq, and more or less everywhere in Asia Minor. The present town of Bet-Schaân, which also in the days of David was called Bet-Schaân as it is today, was called in Jesus' times Scythopolis! And the present-day tourist can see the ruins of the synagogue of Gennesaret, and its peristyle with corinthian capitals – but with smooth-shafted columns. A solecism, like the Hellenistic baroque of Petra, at the heart of Arabia Petraea...

But influences or none, what I remember is that the Judaea, Samaria and Galilee of the times of Jesus were countries where a wandering preacher could seriously tell some rich stranger, distinguished too, who came running to kneel before him in the street: 'If thou wouldst be perfect...' without the bystanders bursting out laughing, and without the on-the-spot reporter finding anything extraordinary in the scene. What is striking, and what also strikes the spectators, including notably the preacher's disciples, is the solution proposed by the itinerant rabbi, the 'visiting professor': to give away his riches (as, nineteen centuries later, almost day for day, Ludwig Wittgenstein renounced the great fortune he had just inherited from his father). The intense desire to be 'perfect', of course, had nothing extraordinary about it. There were obviously many people for whom this was a serious problem. Those Jews and Galileans and Samaritans were educating themselves, they meditated, they would have grave and passionate discussions, they read aloud the sacred and moral texts in the church on Saturdays, the

holy day, day of rest and contemplation, and they wanted
to be perfect. It was among such people that Jesus made his
appearance.

They certainly had the petty faults of their greatness:
they were impatient, finicky, irritable, excitable, intolerant. The people of Nazareth burst out angrily: 'Is not this
the carpenter?'... Everyone knew his family: timid, nondescript folk; Yossef ('Increase', but to save confusion, let
us translate into Latin: August, from *augere,* to augment,
to increase), his father; Mary, Miriam, Amertume, Dolores the mother; the brothers James, Yaakob, 'Supplanter'
(ever since the story of Essau), Yossef or Yosseh, Simon
or Chimôn, 'Obedient', as today we say Fidel; and then
Yudah, 'Praise', Eloi, Gottlob, 'God be Praised'; and
finally he himself, Jesus, Yéchu, that is to say Yéhochuah,
Joshua, 'God is Salvation', or, in our modern tongues,
Salvatore, Salvador.

The people of Nazareth, overwhelmed by unexpected
emotion, which they did not understand and were not
even conscious of, saw him roll up the book, give it to the
servant of the synagogue, and listened to him. But at the
incredible audacity of his words, they burst out with:
Blasphemy! Heresy! Brazen insolence! Insult to religion!
They were just like the reactionaries of the Athenian left –
for Socrates was not assassinated by the oligarchy, but was
the greatest victim and martyr of a democracy if there ever
was one, and there are many such victims, though too few
true democracies... Out with him! Expel him from the
town! To the precipice! Stone him! So they 'chased' him
out, they dragged him out of the town to throw him into
the void. Nazareth is constructed like those small Italian,
Spanish and southern French towns, on a hill, and there is
on one side a steep drop, precipitous enough to break the
neck of a man thrown over the walls.

I have seen the same thing happening in the street, in
1944 and 1945: people howling and drunk with rage, to
left and right of a man they were dragging by both arms,

stretched out as if on a cross, and whose nose and mouth were bleeding, probably smashed by his assailants' fists. At Nazareth they were furious, but puzzled, and despite all that hot raucous anger, hesitating – for they were a people of genius, and he had spoken to their souls. They did not really know what they wanted. They dared not, they would not really kill him. He was one of them, the son of the carpenter, the son of Mary, the brother of James, Joseph, Simon and Jude. But he had shaken them. For one silent moment, they had forgotten everything, there in the synagogue; they had known nothing but his presence among them. There was an uneasy indecision, no one struck him, there was a disturbance somewhere in the crowd, people pushing in contrary directions. 'But Jesus, passing through the midst of them, went his way.'

He was their son, their brother, really one of them. When a woman of Samaria spoke to him, he did not answer. It was the accent, the style of speech of a Protestant as heard by a Roman Catholic, or of a Shi'ite for a Sunnite, of an atheist for a believer. But he gives as an example of humanity the Samaritan – the heretic, the Jesuit, the *curé,* the communist, the 'nigger', the Boche, the Yankee, the 'wop', the drop-out, the 'Nip', the homosexual, the traitor, the untouchable, the one-eyed man in the country of the blind or the blind man in the land of those who can see: the Other. Here, too, man is not made for the Sabbath, nor for his own people, Israel or Samaria; it is the world that is made for man. Another time, Jesus rejects the request of a Syro-Phoenician woman, a foreigner. But when she cries out: 'Yet the dogs under the table eat of the children's crumbs,' he is moved to compassion and grants her request.

He was strength, power, energy itself. But even more than that, he was compassionate. All that terrible energy melted into pity and tenderness. He was a Jew, he knew nothing of the world outside his land. When a Roman centurion, that is, an officer risen from the ranks, shows he is devout, Jesus 'admires' him, he was all astonishment before this man whom we must imagine as being probably a Semite, or Berber, or German, or Celt, or Iberian, naturalized because of his bravery in face of the enemy, speaking Latin badly – the Latin of the barracks and the Greek of the great Mediterranean ports, like the American in airports all the world over in this twentieth century. I can see his fellows in the street: white helmet, freshly-pressed uniform, silk scarf at his neck, six-barrelled Colt on his hip in its white leather sheath, and his name on the left of his chest: Pulaski, or Santamaria, or Giumbalaitis, or Tomasek, or Jimenez: all old Roman names, in the hundred-and-first airport legion. And when by chance he is called really Marcus Martius, or Cassius Smith, he is a black. Very tall, very beautiful, but black. Jesus loved that soldier, obedient and patient as an ox under the yoke, and said to the disciples: 'Verily I say unto you, I have not found so great faith, no not in Israel. And I say unto you, That many shall come from the east and west, and shall sit down with Abraham, and Isaac, and Jacob, in the king-dom of heaven.' During the decades following the death of Jesus, Saint Paul, also a Roman citizen, having paid for his naturalization in staters and tetradrachmas, realized that all human beings, not only Jews like him, Chaul of Tarchich, disguised in Latin as Paulus, corresponding to the Celtic 'Petit' and the Germanic 'Little' or 'Klein', were to find one another in Jesus.

Jesus, the man himself, alive, in his body of flesh, with the warmth of his flesh, the softness and fragility of his flesh – that is the man I am speaking of here. I know his anger, his severity, his wisdom, his penetration, his look – of which it is said that only Giotto and Titian were able to paint it, and each only once, and only the look he fixed upon Judas: but that look contained so many expressions – penetrating, compassionate, moved, sombre, distressed, flashing with indignation. I have seen Jesus angry, chasing people before him and whipping them with a handful of ropes. But what has made him unforgettable to those who have known him is his tolerance, his good nature. I seem to hear him, see him half-smiling, when he tells his friends – and they were all exceptional beings, those fishermen, that tax collector, those peasants, those artisans, those middle-class folk, all men of genius, extraordinary personalities, capable of resisting his presence without perishing, without running away, without reactions of hatred and negation. Well, it was those men, those who would in future be crucified or stoned for their faith in him, those people who loved him because he was as he was, and because they were as they were, to whom Jesus said 'If ye then, *being evil*... Or what man is there of you, whom if his son ask bread, will he give him a stone... If ye then, being evil, know how to give good gifts unto your children, how much more shall your Father which is in heaven give good things to them that ask him?'

This is the only time when I seem to see him smile, a little, just a very little, and so fleetingly! *Being evil*, those beings steeped in self-abnegation, and who, even though still confused, impure, their brains polluted and stuffed with disputes about precedence in the Kingdom of Heaven, were already open, accessible, malleable to his unexampled teaching, proof of which is that they transmitted it, and that they transmitted precisely that which was unexampled, and that we are Christians.

It is true that he was a just Jew and that he came to fulfill exactly the Jewish moral law, the highest, the most noble, the most humane and the most gentle that had ever existed until his times. I am not ignoring the tribal ferocity of the Hebrew past, nor the love of good and the hatred of Evil among the Zoroastrians, nor the radiant abstract purity of Buddhism, nor the half-Heraclitean, half-Christian morality of the Tao, nor the morality of love in Mo Ti (I am naming them in order of their geographical distance from me); I am not unaware of the marvellous resemblance between Buddhist gentleness and Christian gentleness, nor that the words 'I am the way' can be translated as 'I am the Tao'. But I do not wish to mix things up, nor to keep them separate, and even less to oppose them to one another. I am trying to say, clumsily, humbly, that I know him, that I perceive his presence as if he were here before me, as if I were before him, as if he were in me, as I am in him, at the centre of my heart, and there, only as gentleness, kindness, love. I leave it to the theologians to solve the riddles of the texts, on which I have already had something to say. I am not going to get myself entangled in something I do not understand. I close my eyes – I who keep them open before really great and essential problems; I pass, I wait in patience. And I am attached to Jesus the man who was goodness itself, gentleness, purity itself, a human being with body hair and warts, and I do not know what else – did they blow their noses with their fingers in those days? But a human being who introduced into the course of human history and into the duration of the universe a germ, a spark, through his person, through his being, through his manner of being. Since then, nothing has been the same any more.

I am not trying to draw Jesus, nor to expound the teachings of the Gospels, nor to add anything at all to what the world already knows. The Gospels are enough, there is nothing to be added to them; in any case, it is not for me to append my commentary: I have only to follow his teaching, the most difficult and important task I have ahead of me. What I am trying to do here is to explain to whomever will listen to me, or to whomever it may be of some service, that Jesus is present, accessible, so close we can touch him, see him, hear him. Perhaps that sensation of direct, personal knowledge is communicable. Perhaps there are beside myself one or two persons to whom the question has presented itself in the same terms: how to be a Christian? And to whom salvation, the open door shall be offered, as they were to me, in the words: 'That depends on your attitude towards Jesus.'

One can love that Jesus personally, above all other beings in the universe. As can be seen, I have no need to think of his resurrection, nor of his divinity, nor of his divine descent, nor of the virginity of the Virgin, nor of him as Saviour, awaited as the Persians awaited Saochyant. I do not need anything; I can see him passing in the street, looking at our faces encircling him: I can hear him speaking. He sometimes begins abruptly: 'Listen. A sower went forth to sow.' Someone has just told him: 'But if you can do something, come and help us, have compassion on us.'

He gives an exasperated shrug, despite the pity burning within him for these people: 'If you can!...' he repeats. 'With God all things are possible.'

I love him. I am amazed that such a person should ever have existed, that he should have been possible; for he was not imaginable, if we look at all the literature of humanity before his coming, in which all sorts of beings are imagined, have been imaginable. And he says what he says – something even more unimaginable, in comparison with what was said before he came, and which we have still not completely understood, sometimes not even begun to understand.

But all that can be read in the Gospels.

He, too, personally, is in the Gospels; there we meet him, he speaks, we see him, we touch him in the midst of the multitude, with his disciples, with the intellectuals giving him trick questions, the rigid moralists without heart, without pity, the self-sufficient who think 'I am better than my neighbour', the Roman military police in the background, and poor Mary Magdalene who felt she had become a human being again after having been just a body offered up in a common market full of satisfied consumers. Here are the 'publicans', the collaborators, the sympathisers with the terrorist Barabbas, the sympathisers with John, already decapitated. Here are the rich ladies needing a guru, they too have souls, they too are children of God, poor things, poor dears – 'And Joanna the wife of Chuza, Herod's steward, and Susanna, and many others, which ministered unto him of their substance.' And the beggars and the lame, as in the etchings of Rembrandt, and the pilgrim-tourist Simon, come from Cyrene, in North Africa, and who was to be requisitioned in the street, because he was big and tough, to carry the too-heavy beam of the cross.

Now comes the last day, with the so-human pleasantries of people who are hitting him after having crowned him with thorns: 'Guess who hit you, seer!' And the jokes of the spectators at the execution: 'Perform one of your miracles, unhook yourself – it's now or never!' For we are so charming, we humans, who pass judgement on God.

The inscription up there is the ferocious sally of some Soviet general, but written by someone not wholly bad, who uttered the most civilized, the most *sophisticated* words in the whole of human history:'What is truth?', shrugging his shoulders, of course. The upright beam of the cross: the two feet nailed separately, for they did not forge nails long enough to pierce two feet and sink deep enough into the wood – the demand for them was not all that great. Long agony. Death by cardiac collapsus. Terrible torture, intended for slaves, ultimate abjection, absolute humiliation. Up to and including his reproach to God, like that of a child to a grown-up, without denying him, without doubting him, without accusing him: he is complaining simply of having been abandoned.

He knows it is in the rules of the game, that it has to happen so; but that interjection, in all its pain and sorrow, is a part of the game too. He, the best human being who ever existed, the strongest, the most courageous, the most noble, the most gentle, the most pitiful, has to die thus, knowing full well he must die, and asking the childlike question of all creatures who are dying, men and beasts: 'Why? Why me? Where are you?' It is the same question in all its various forms, that of the separation of the being who is not, or who is no longer, or not yet, reunited with God: 'Why do I exist, why does the world exist, why is there only God, unity, joy, good, light, peace and nothing else?' He died for us, we die with him; he is crucified endlessly and the whole world is endlessly crucified, asking endlessly through the mouth of Jesus and of all suffering beings: 'Why hast thou forsaken me?' It is not a cry of revolt, anger, defiance, rage, but a cry of pure pain, carrying within it its own strange 'going beyond', of which I dare not speak.

I do not know if he was resurrected, nor if he will come back at the end of time; all I know is that he is present now. Having read the Gospels, it is henceforth impossible for me to reject Jesus. It is henceforth impossible for me, knowing him, not to love him. It is unthinkable that I should not orient my existence and my being upon his person. Having known him, I am following him, as far as my feeble strength allows, humbly and insignificantly, in the multitude, at the tail end of the crowd, in my room all alone, praying, at the tail end of a crowd of generations throughout space-time. In other words, I am a Christian. It appeared to me impossible to be a Christian. It is impossible for me not to be a Christian. I knew where to look for God; but I did not know how to be myself, how to act; how to exist in this world and among these human beings. *How to be*: I can find that only in following Christ.

In that sense, I understand even the 'parable' – as Wittgenstein would call it – of the 'Christ', of him who was awaited. 'Is it he we are waiting for?' I do not doubt it. I did not doubt it, but I did not understand and so I suspended my thought. Now I can see that, however strange it may seem, he was the one whom we awaited, and is still the one we await, and whom we shall await as long as there are human beings to pass the Good News on to one another.

I am following him, badly, staggering, stumbling at every step, in a way that would make him blush for me,

and makes me blush for myself; a wicked, a miserable
follower of Christ – but I would not know how else to call
myself, for that is what I am, a follower of Jesus Christ, a
Christian. One may refuse Jesus one's love, one's adoration, one's compassion, but only if one has not read the
Gospels, or if one has only pretended to read them. As for
myself, I have read them badly, and only in fragments,
and I am of no value as a reference source. I know what he
was like, I know he died on the cross, and I do not know if
he rose again. But I know that he is present, here and now.
I can see him, I know him, and I love him.

12.

THE IMPOSITION OF HANDS
OR CRITIQUE OF THE CHURCH

It is impossible to be a Christian. It is impossible not to be a Christian. It is impossible to be a Christian outside the Church, and the Church is 'impossible'.

Jesus is crucified, but he has left us, too, torn to pieces, torn between what we are and what we are called to be. I do not understand how he could have told me: 'My yoke is light.' He is asking of me no less than the impossible. But I feel and I know that his yoke is light, because in the love and sweetness of Christ, difficulties, hardships, contradictions and impossibilities melt like wax in a flame.

Tertullian wrote that one is born pagan, that one becomes Christian. The 'natural man' arouses my deep suspicions, because he is less whole, less innocent, less 'antique' than one thinks. The fault is still there. The crack – what Wittgenstein would call 'the parable of sin' – is already there: the tension between the individual Me and the moral commandment of the group, between oblivion and all that is not me, and fundamental amity, in Christian terms, love of one's neighbour.

Adam australopithecus already knew loss of innocence and nostalgia for regained integrity. That is what the natural man is: that tree split by lightning. Or, in animal terms, the sick beast: the guilty beast. Wretched Nietzsche dreamed of man as an innocent beast. He did not even know that beasts are capable of guilt, when their instincts conflict and do damage to one another. We, having lost the machinery – if not infallible, at least quite reliable – of the instincts, are guilty as soon as we take the first step out of paradise. And that is when Jesus smashes his second lightning bolt into that twisted and mutilated tree: the desire to go beyond. Man already felt the pain of that desire, but Jesus told him: 'You shall go that way, in the direction I point out to you', and he shows him how to go beyond the human condition in the love of God and the love of one's neighbour.

If there is a superman, or a man as man should be, or a happy man, it is he, the one he invites me to become. It is impossible to be a Christian, and it is impossible not to be one in the desire to follow Jesus, and in the love of Christ.

I am a Christian, not a Nazarene. I take words for what they are. For example, 'socialism', from *socius*, 'companion, comrade, partner, team-mate, ally' – the essential meaning. Expropriation, class struggle, bureaucracy collectivism, envy, intolerance, police despotism and all the rest we know all too well have nothing at all to do – except by fraudulent imitation – with that profound impulse, having its foundations in the instinct of friendship inherited from our animal ancestors, and that I would call the Christianity of the industrial era. In the same way, 'Christian' does not signify a being who follows Jesus of Nazareth, but a follower of Jesus Christ.

He who follows Jesus Christ thinks of Jesus as the man of Nazareth, but at the same time as the one who was awaited, and whom we await once more at every instant: Jesus, Yehochuah, the itinerant preacher executed in Jerusalem as a consequence of a judiciary error, the concrete, individual man, the biological and historical being, the human person of inexhaustible interest, of unlimited appeal, with a strength, a purity, an originality, a creativity and a goodness that are unique; and God become man in Jesus, like the lightning flash that links heaven and earth in the one discharge of energy: the culminating point of human history, and at the same time the always-actual, always-present point at which human history is beyond time.

The Jews awaited the Messiah. They taught us the transcendent and immanent God, and the saviour always awaited. One imagined him as a hero at once religious and political, and one called him the Anointed of the Lord, among other names, because in the ancient Orient the supreme luxury was to pour on one's hair an oil in which those 'aromatics' of Arabia had been macerated, a precious oil bought against its weight in precious stones. We would say 'the bearer of the crown', after that circlet of precious metal furnished with points, introduced into Europe by the princes of the Germanic tribes, who had received it from the steppe, where for the first time it had been admired among the Parthians. As far as I know, the first crown such as we understand the word is seen on the great bas-relief of Chapur; before that, one knew only the 'diadem', a fillet round the brows, or the crown of olive or oak. The crown with points was for fifteen hundred years our equivalent of the 'unguent', the magical oil, *chresma*, the chrism with which one anointed the heads of the princes of the Orient.

In the *Memoirs* of James Bruce, a Scots doctor who lived for many years in Ethiopia in the second half of the eighteenth century, at the court of the emperor, king of kings, *negus negesti,* is found the scene of a visitation made by the sovereign to one of his provinces. All the local kinglets came to do him homage. All at once there arrived the chief of an up-country tribe, in ceremonial attire: he was stark naked, and covered with butter, a precious substance, from head to feet. He was an Anointed One, and it was no joke, for he probably had the power of life and death over his subjects, and used that power, and his subjects were human beings, our fellows, our brethren.

From the Jews, we have learnt that God is not in a statue, nor in an oak grove, nor in the storm, nor in the sexual organs, nor in the wild or domestic animal. Ever since Christ, we have realized that the one we await, the one we await at every instant, is not a chief surrounded by his personal ministers and his dignitaries, his secret agents, bodyguards and motor-cycle outriders. We still use the old term, taken from the Greek, which is a translation from the Hebrew, because its essential meaning still has value; it is not a question of the distinctive sign of sovereign, social, religious or political function, it is a question of that waiting we all experience, that waiting within each one of us, the waiting of someone who will orient our being towards God.

He himself is oriented towards God in a unique way, with supreme intensity and simplicity. That is why he is *par excellence* the Son of God. For us he is the Christ, and, if I may venture to paraphrase the words of Wittgenstein, 'we may attach to him the parable of God as Son'.

I 'know' that he is God the Father. That 'know' is, I am not forgetting, a stammered word, a blink of thought, as I grope my way round the inaccessible... In that derisory measure, I 'know' that God the Father is the abyss, what Jacob Boehme called the *Ungrund,* 'that which is without bottom', the Deeps, the Bottomless. He is the one of whom one should not speak, and about whom one should be silent, for even his contemptors are incapable of holding their tongues, and repeat endlessly that he is dead. He is the one towards whom our thought is directed, as well as our words and our prayer, our being. My dictionary says under the headword 'prayer': 'invocation, solicitation'. That is curious: I do not invoke God, nor solicit him; I confine myself to turning towards him and thanking him for having given me joy.

I do not know what the Holy Spirit is. It seemed to me that it is the intelligible structure of being, a pure relationship, that which relates or links, that which makes the multiple one. Perhaps, I do not know, I do not even seek to know. I 'think' God and Christ, that is, I direct myself, from infinitely far away, by means of thought, towards God, who is so close by means of love; and I strive to follow Christ, my well-beloved, the human being I have loved the most in my life, in whatever way I can, as best I can – which is usually not good enough – staggering, stumbling, crawling.

I am a Christian. I am one of those who follow Christ. No one can force me to deny Jesus Christ, as they can force me to say that two and two make five. They can even make me doubt Christ, probably after having disintegrated my personality, with doubt and denial springing up like weeds in the ruins of what I was. It is obvious I am a man of the twentieth century, born in East Europe, and so I have to think to every eventuality. But when I am in my right mind, in good health, with a clear head, I can think of Jesus spontaneously, freely, in this way: I think of Jesus Christ, son of man, son of God, God become man. I think according to the Gospels and the teaching of the apostles and of the Fathers of the Church, the synods and the Christian theologians.

As for what I cannot think, for example, that third person of the Trinity, and the Trinity itself, I accept it blindly, humbly, patiently. It seems to me that I am beginning to be able to think of the virginity of Mary: the mother is virgin in the sense that sexuality is burned away, consumed by maternal love, and in the male, by infinite tenderness, humble and protective, filial and paternal, towards the mother – as also towards the young girl still permeated with childish frigidity, before the awakening of sexuality. This 'chivalrous' reaction must also come from a great distance, from the reaction of the protective beast, either head of the pack, or sentry of the tribe, or the greater of the two hunting together.

That is why I like to look, thinking of the mother of Jesus, at those pieces of wood or sculpted stone, painted, enveloped in precious cloths and covered with real jewels or false ones, exhibited in churches, and looking like a grave young Italian or Spanish peasant girl: 'Hail, Mary, I like you, Madame, mother and virgin, young peasant girl who knows nothing of face powder or anything else much for that matter, unless it be to give life and to give her own life for that life she has brought into the world. I like you, Madame, bless me, wherever you may be, whoever you may be; descend upon me, my God, here in front of this piece of wood which is placed here to remind me of the mother of Jesus Christ and of all mothers and of all the children who later will be mothers, the poor little things; hail, Mary, full of grace.' It is because of the cult of Mary that there is so much non-narcissism, non-exhibitionism, so much suave beauty in the expression of women and girls in Catholic countries, and of which for me the most recent and most astonishing example was an innocent, irresistible and blooming young Italian student – a communist.

But in truth, I suspend my thought in the expectation of the grace of being able to understand more, and I follow blindly the teaching of the Church. For I cannot be a Christian outside the Church. Jesus tells me: follow me. I am following him, badly, with difficulty, at a distance, but I am following him. He tells me: love one another. I am trying to love my neighbour, or at least not to hate him, or at least not to be indifferent. Jesus tells me: withdraw to your room and pray. I withdraw to my room in local council housing or a rented suburban house on the fringes of the Megalopolis, and I pray. I try to pray as he taught me, or more simply, or with greater effort, as he prayed: 'Nevertheless, not my will, but thine, be done.' But as soon as I am in the presence of another human being, I have to act according to the teaching of Christ. If the other is not a Christian, I am a witness to Christ, I represent all other Christians. If the other is a Christian, 'there where two or three of you are gathered together in my name, there shall I be with you'. He is here, present, he teaches, he touches hearts, overwhelms souls, dies on the cross, dies under torture, dies at the stake, dies against a wall, dies in the cells and basements of public and private torturers, and lives, resurrected, immortal, immediately present, grants us salvation, gives our existence meaning and direction, puts it in order, however chaotic, troubled, muddy, clapped-out, and done-in it may be. He is present to each one of us in our hearts, in our thoughts, in the Gospels, and in the Church.

I take that word also for what it means: *ekklesia,* assembly.

I cannot be a Christian outside the assembly of Christians. I am one of the lowest, the least brilliant, and there are only too many who are no better than I, we follow Christ wretchedly, lamentably, but together; he is here, and we follow him.

I accept the dogma blindly, when I cannot think it; but I do not blindly accept the Church. I accept it knowing well what I do. I acccept the Church with open eyes.

Before accepting the Church, one must read Gibbon and Voltaire and take as our own their just criticism of the folly, the stupidity and the crimes of the Church; and accept the Church afterwards, if one can. Everywhere I have lived, including exile, I have carried with me the dossier of the trial of the Templars and the *Manual of the Inquisitor* by Bernard Gui. The dossiers of the Moscow trials were not necessary, I knew them by heart. They resembled one another so much, at five hundred years' distance and at opposite ends of the continent, except that the torturers and judges of the king of Paris allowed the condemned to retract their confessions and to complain of having been tortured. One must also read the trial of Joan of Arc; her replies radiating innocence, intelligence, grace, with a touch of humour, make me think: here is a child of Christ, the family resemblance is unmistakable, no one could be so blind as not to see it. But no, the ecclesiastical tribunal had decided to burn her alive, to have her examined by midwives to make sure she was still a virgin, to have her manhandled by executioners; and if the soldiers were weeping in front of the stake, perhaps it was because the smoke got in their eyes. Or were they

Christians? Where was the Church? Where was the assembly of Christians, the assembly of those who follow Christ?

One should read the monumental *History of the Inquisition,* by Lea, and the more recent *History of the Inquisition* by Kamen. I found in it the cry of a French sailor tortured by the Inquisition in the Canary Islands – in that remote province, the archives of the Spanish Holy Office of the Inquisition have been preserved more intact than elsewhere: 'I was no heretic, but you have made me so.' That reminded me of something. How many times have I not heard the same words, or guessed the same thought behind faces masked by fear, or thought the same thing myself, before what marxist bureaucrats were doing in the name of socialism.

The Spanish Inquisition was above all the instrument of the centralized State against local freedoms, and of the grand aristocracy against the middle classes, just like the pomp and circumstance of the Party at odds with scientists, technicians and administrators who had no Party. But that does not diminish the responsibility of the Church. I have also read the trial of Giordano Bruno, and that of Michel Servet. We reproach the Catholic Church with its crimes; but if the English Catholics burned Protestant saints, the English Protestants burned Catholic saints, Jesuit or not; and Catholics and Protestants in all countries have burned innocents of their own persuasion – 'witches', 'madmen', hysterical women, neurasthenics or simply unfortunates who did not know how to defend themselves against those who wanted to get rid of them. The assembly of Christians bears responsibility just as much as the *ekklesia* of Athens, the Chamber of citizens, which killed innocent Socrates. It was the Helia and not the *ekklesia*, but the Five Hundred had been recruited from the body of the citizens, as priests are recruited from the body of Christians – the body of Christ, they say, and it is the truth.

But the experiences of the two last generations have taught us, if the third will lend an ear to its elders, that the great crimes of human history are, in the first place, the effect of technological and social changes. Ibn Khaldun had already understood this five hundred years ago, when he was taking part in the eternal conflict between the nomads and the agriculturalists. In our country, people still used to exclaim, on the occasion of any sudden agitation: 'It's not the Tartars coming back, is it?' Farmers armed with rifles exterminated the nomads, societies with even more murderous techniques at their disposal have subjugated or destroyed others. The Church has never committed as many heinous crimes as have States, empires, tribes, administrative authorities, soldiers and all sorts of non-religious organizations.

The crimes of the Church are crimes of authority. They are not Christian crimes, that is, crimes committed according to the teaching and example of Jesus Christ – an absurdity and a glaring contradiction which one must nevertheless place before the eyes of the detractors of the Church and of Christianity, in order to explode the nullity of their main argument.

It is not the assembly that has sinned, but its delegates, against the teaching of Jesus Christ, that is, against the spirit itself and the very meaning of the assembly through the ages. And finally we have discovered that we must learn to brake, muzzle, dam and counterbalance by opposing forces, also kept on a leash, the power of Authorities, of administrations, general staffs, organizations and the ravages of abrupt technological and social changes.

The understanding of the functioning, the specific defects, the innate dangers, the correctives in any giant organization is just as important for humanity as were the discoveries of bacilli and the antidotes for rabies, cholera and the plague. We cannot do without organizations in human society; we cannot exist without them; but we can and should control them so that they may no longer do the evil that makes them execrable, and so that they may only fulfill their beneficent functions. That is as difficult as making a heart transplant and even more urgent than finding a cure for cancer.

The Church has never, and no religious bureaucracy has ever, even among the Aztecs, caused the orgies of destruction and suffering unleashed by the City of antiquity, by the national States, by economic liberalism, by marxism in power, by nazism, equally anti-Christian, and by a simple restructurization in what paleontologists, anthropologists and ethnologists glibly and hypocritically call 'tools', that is, the fabrication and the use of arms.

The Christian church, the assembly of Christians, with its delegates and its priests, has always been the Church of its epoch and of its society. It has not committed crimes, because crimes are not Christian. The criminal does not follow Jesus Christ, he crucifies him once more. But the Church bears a heavy responsibility for those who have sinned in its name. And I believe it expiates those sins. All through the miseries of humanity in our time, which rub off on the Church, Christian bureaucracy, ecclesiastical bureaucracy follows, imperfectly as we all do, the teaching of Christ, more or less well, usually less, like all of us, follows it wretchedly, lamentably; but above all – and this is its essential function – the Church transmits the Gospels, teaches the Gospels, spreads the Gospels.

I seek Jesus Christ in a Protestant Bible bought twenty years ago in a Parisian cafe, *Les Deux Magots*, and distributed for a few small coins by a Calvinist church organization. The first Bible I had in my hands, when still a small boy, pretending to read it though still hardly able to talk, sitting beside my mother, both of us with little hoops fixed to our heads to represent haloes, for we were obviously devout as saints, was the Bible of Luther. It was the Organizations, the Organization of the Church that put the word of Christ in my hands, and which put into my head and my heart the person of Christ. Without the

Organization, I do not know if there would still be the assembly of Christians, the body of Christ. It is that bureaucracy which transmits the Gospel, and keeps us gathered in its net. 'I will make you fishers of men,' said Jesus. The meshes of the net are also – I will not say exclusively – but they are also the meshes of the organizational chart or flow sheet of ecclesiastical bureaucracy. I know that the meshes in the net are, truly, the words of the Gospel, the words of conversations between Christians, and the daily acts of Christians. But they are also those of the complex of organizations called – the part for the whole – 'the Church'.

For twenty years I wondered how I could be a Christian, and I could not find the answer: it was an *apparatchik* of the Church, that dear Mgr Walter A., who reflected for a moment in silence while walking beside me, and who gave me the answer. After twenty years, I who was devout and attached to God, but not knowing how to go beyond the God of Spinoza, heard a militant of the Church, my very dear and reverend brother and father in Jesus Christ, Jean N., tell me: 'One must be *almost* pantheist, but not stop there', God being immanent and also transcendent, and the *Deus sive natura* not being such that one cannot think of something greater. The immanent God, but not transcendent, is still beyond the limits of my thought.

And again, it was he who told me – who called myself devout, but who loved my neighbour with somewhat violent nuances and parentheses: 'One cannot love God, without loving human beings; otherwise it is a falsehood'. It was those two men who listened to me when I either had to talk about it to someone or suffocate. They tell me that the Church is turning away from the practice of auricular confession, and that it offends the ideas and sentiments of non-Catholic Christians. But when I feel myself in danger of sinking beneath the burden, with whom can I share it? To whom can I open my heart, when there is no longer anyone to listen to us, and when we sometimes just want to talk to another human being? And even if we have someone to confess ourselves to without betraying ourselves as human beings, without degrading the confession to the level of a shameful and dangerous confidence imparted in secret, and which poisons and destroys it? To speak as one soul to another, as if alone together in the void, in the desert, in the night – with whom can one do that, if not with another Christian: Christian to Christian, layman to ecclesiastic? And it is difficult for me to believe that, if I were a Lutheran or a Calvinist or a Baptist, and I were crushed by my burden, I could not go to see the pastor and speak with him as I speak with my Orthodox or Catholic confessor: we are Christians, and despite my ignorance I venture to assert that the pastor would not reject me, and that no matter who – a married, bearded pope* or the Catholic priest, or the Protestant pastor, would welcome me, even if I were not baptized in his Church. We are Christians.

True, I can also go to see a psychoanalyst; but the one does not stand in the way of the other – it is not the same thing. I hope with all my heart that they will allow the layman to confess, and the ecclesiastic to listen to him, soul to soul, man to man, alone together in the presence of Jesus Christ.

I take words for what they mean: *laïkos,* from *laos,* the people; I am one of the Christian people. The ecclesiastic belongs to the assembly, he is my delegate, and I am not his. I call him Father, because I want to, and because I have delegated him to pray when I cannot pray, to study the Gospels when I cannot, to look after my neighbour when I am unable to do so: he is the delegate of my weakness. And he calls me Son, because I allow him to do so, and I ask him to do so; he speaks in the name of Christ, awestruck, when he thinks of him, crushed by his responsibility. I share my burden with him – but what a sharing, and what a burden! Poor priests, poor pastors.

*i.e. Of the Greek Orthodox Church (Translator's note).

I do not consider priests to be better than they are. I can image what it is to look at the assembly of Christians from the 'bad' side, from the altar towards the door, the reverse of the perspective seen by the faithful, which is from the door to the altar; and I can see the whole thing. I imagine the temptation of routine, the temptations to take the divine service and the ritual and the symbols either too lightly, or more seriously than one takes the human souls, each human soul. I can imagine the awful temptation of the priest to surrender (render oneself, give in, capitulate) to the evidence and to think: 'But what a bunch of wretched ninnies they are. There's nothing here!' I can image what it is like to perform so many times every day, all one's life, the motions, the ritual gestures, to handle the objects of worship, when Adam, the primate, is accustomed to dominating everything he takes in his hand – he manipulates, he kills, he even treats living things as dead objects, he handles, trains and tortures the living for his pleasure, he shoves things around, creates them, destroys and repairs them: and is he to be suddenly different now, with these other objects? Or on the contrary, is the poor priest compelled each day to perform the creative and almost superhuman task, and be alive, burning, in soul and spirit, present and awake to the prayer and to the meaning of the symbols? It would kill me; and I think they only make it through the strength of humility, of wisdom, of habit, and the strength of knowing that prayer, the collective organization constructed around prayer, the symbolic objects gathered reverently together, the sacred edifice constructed around prayer, are more than the priest, that vehicle, that bearer, that servant, that functionary of prayer. I know well why I love Church people and why I admire them and why I pity them: because they carry a cross heavier than my own.

Oh, no, I do not consider priests to be any better, and above all, do not consider them to be any other than what they are. One of those I am talking about here is a being so marvellous that I would not dare to speak about him, for fear of embarrassing him. The other confessed to me that he had come to God, not through gratitude, like me ('I envy you, you were really lucky,' the dear man told me), but through ritual, and indeed I have seen him celebrating the 'mass of Charlemagne' with a childlike fervour. The third, with whom I sometimes speak on the telephone like two castaways with walkie-talkies, separated by the nocturnal ocean, suffers because he is living maritally with his housekeeper, and has admitted it to everyone, greatly scandalizing people who hasten to pass judgement and condemn (I would never have believed there were so many judges in the world as I have seen since I came to the West, where freedom of speech, and therefore freedom to condemn one's neighbour, reigns supreme). And the one priest to have given me the imposition of hands, a pope of my native church, asked me: 'How can you, an educated man, believe in such things?' At that time, I suspended my judgement, I neither believed nor disbelieved, because I do not like just to 'believe'; but all the same, it was not for him to be surprised. The *apparatchiks* of our assembly are of all kinds. But for sixty-six generations they are the chain that links us directly, personally, to Jesus Christ.

I do not believe in some magical contact, nor in the transmission of a fluid, from Jesus Christ to me, through the imposition of hands. Nor do I deny it. I do not wish to know. Perhaps, later, I shall want to know, or I shall give up thinking about it completely. But that is not what is important at the moment. It is enough for me to know that this personal and physical contact existed. I do not even know why it warms my heart to know that the man of Nazareth, the Christ, God become man, placed his hands on the head of one of his disciples, who in his turn placed his hands on the head of a Christian, and so on, through two thousand years and sixty-six generations. It makes me happy; I am moved, deeply touched.

When the priest 'imposes his hands', it is as if he were laying a pound of beefsteak on your skull. It is neither light nor heavy; it has a certain weight, and an animal warmth – and I detest non-sexual physical contacts! The imposition of hands is a non-sexual, non-utilitarian physical contact. It is a little dirty, a little sickening, like any non-sexual contact, and even alas, sometimes like sexual contact too...

But the flesh is like that; that is how a human being is. There are no humans without animal warmth, without smell, without secretions. There is no disincarnate human being: we have to take him as he is. Even the word of Christ, the Gospel, is passed from hand to hand for twenty centuries, in the form of a book – blackened paper – and it is thus that it will pass into the future. Communication by word of mouth is material, and electromagnetic waves are also – to the imperceptible stages where matter, flesh, weight begin to go on the skids, become particles, waves, discharges, emanations of energy, and, perhaps, at the very limit, pure thought – but I do not want to speculate on that. What is important is that physical contact, the hands of the human being, an animal with hands on the skull of another human being, a cerebral animal; the warmth, the presence, the asexual intimacy, the immediate proximity of Jesus Christ to you and to me, a living chain of living beings, the Church throughout all the duration of time, the assembly of Christians, the body of Christ in space-time.

It was when the unbeliever pope imposed his hands upon me that I sensed and understood that it is not the individual person of the priest, nor his faith or lack of faith, nor his sins or his purity that count for the Christian kneeling before him and receiving the imposition of hands, but simply the continuity of the chain. And it seems to me that it is not a chain, but a web, a net made of an immense number of chains joined together, a living mesh, which stretches out endlessly, and whose holes are mended, and which is restored to life wherever we destroyed it, or thought we had destroyed it.

The relatively inactive intellectual life of my maternal Church (the one into which I was baptized, and not the Calvinist church to which my mother belonged), its ritualism, its contemplativeness inadequately supported by intellectual preparation, its humility, not to say its servility to the State, have often embarrassed me. The wall of icons also often annoyed me, hiding the essential ritual of the mass. (On the other hand, I realize that, compared with that mysterious operation, the Catholic mass is prosaic and cold and one might almost say Protestant, just as the Lutheran mass is, compared with the Catholic liturgy, and Calvinist preaching compared with the Lutheran mass, and, probably, the Quaker meeting, compared with the Calvinist preaching...)

I have been pained by the primitivism and the bad manners of our popes, by the grossness and stupidity of the sacristans, by the infinite distance away from us of bishops and monks. Yes, I know the popes smelled of mice, wax and stale incense, I know that their accoutrements, transmitted from the Byzantine Middle Ages, are strange, and that the texts have not had the benefit of an *aggiornamento*. We bought the Protestant Bible. I am pained by the intolerance of our church towards Catholics and Protestants, whenever it can catch them. It is not satisfactory. It is, as I said right at the beginning of this chapter, 'impossible'.

But it is the Church into which I was baptized, and I am staying in it. Moreover, I could not leave it. It would not even be necessary for me to love it: it is my homeland, and even more, it is my place, and I could not leave it, for I have no other. Even if I were to deny God and Jesus Christ, I would not leave it. One cannot escape what one is. I should simply be an even worse Christian than I am already. We see, or rather we used to see, when there were still authentic communists, communists who had lost their faith: in their very opposition to the Church, they remained all their lives centred on that lost faith. In a Christian, it is even stronger: one does not become anti-Christian, even repudiating one's faith, one remains Christian, only one is a little more of a sinner than before. There is no apostasy possible. The faith one loses is a faith one has never had (among ex-communists turned anti-communists or abstentionists, a gap remains). One is born pagan. One becomes a Christian. And remains one. That is, one cannot tear from one's flesh and soul the sign that the word of Jesus Christ has branded upon one's whole being. Oh, yes, he really branded us for life.

I love and admire the Catholic Church. It is active, tireless, close, more alive and younger than mine – which it offended with brutal barbarism in 1054, shortly before the massacre of Christians sheltering in the cathedral at Jerusalem, to the cry of 'God wills it'. God wills everything that happens, but Jesus Christ does not want murder. The crimes, the sins, the errors, the blunders and the stupidities of the Roman Church – another 'impossible' Church – are ever-present in my mind.

But even more present are Saint Francis of Assisi and Catherine of Siena, John of the Cross and Theresa of Avila, and the hundreds, the thousands of ascetic saints, learned saints, mystics, silent orders, the imitators of Jesus Christ, the erudite orders, the teaching orders, the tilling and cultivating orders, the nursing orders – I prefer not to insist too much upon the preachers and to pass with averted eyes the converters and the persecutors of heretics: Christ was not just crucified, he was also burned a thousand times at the stake.

Yet the Catholic Church expiates its sins, in humility and even in humiliation. Despite everything it is the major star in the constellation of Christian Churches: it is the most numerous, the most active, the most efficient, though many a Protestant Church can rival it admirably in that respect. When I have the choice, I enter a Catholic church – regretting that at the same time I cannot also be in a Lutheran church. For I cannot do without the pure beauty, truly angelic, of the liturgy and the Lutheran hymns, words and music, of a childlike innocence and a virile energy, that upraise the heart and the soul with them, towards God. There are the very purity and strength of the Gospel, as in the religious etchings of Rembrandt, the *Crucifixion,* the *Lesser Centaury.* If I were not an Orthodox Christian, I should be a Roman Catholic, and at the same time regret not being able to be an Evangelical Lutheran. But after all: why should one not be able to belong to all three?

I believe – I do not know: I believe – that there is not one useless or superfluous Christian Church, nor a single one that does harm. As soon as we are two or three gathered together in his name, he is with us. It is a matter of loving Jesus Christ and of loving one another. Everything that distracts us from that, everything that separates us, should be attenuated, suspended, passed over in silence, pardoned and forgotten. The one thing we must not forget is Christ's gentleness, and that the Church is the assembly of Christians, bodies, souls and minds, together with their actions, their sins, their remorse, their expiation, their hope and their joy, all existing through space-time. I cannot think without pain of a church – I am speaking of a meeting place, of a house of prayer – in which I would not be welcome, even if I were to be welcomed badly, or even chased away, despite my love of Christ, because of ritual, tradition, dogma, race, civilization, nation, social group that happen to be mine, or because of my personal bizarrerie. And yet this has happened to numberless Christians. But the walls fall, they become transparent, they disappear. Christians are becoming less and less intolerant and more and more conscious of what unites them – the love of Christ and mutual love. Jesus also loves the freaks, the handicapped, the cretins, the monsters, the mutants, just as he loves the vicious, the degenerate, the criminals, the aliens and all those who are in some way or other 'different'.

And now, may I be permitted to dream a little.

For fifty years I have listened to and sometimes repeated, under pressure, without laughing, the dreams proclaimed by others, without laughing, to be the truth: the death of God; the end of religion, that illusion; the unending sequence of societies – slave-owning-feudal-capitalist-socialist -communist – the last being the ultimate and supreme form of human organization, all too imminent in certain lands (too) close to mine; the superiority of the Aryan race, the final solution and the Jewish question and the coming of the millennary Empire; the anticommunist crusade of that Empire, with its two allies, two backward little countries of Eastern Europe that have a mortal hatred of one another, one of which was my father's, the other my mother's country; the anti-Nazi crusade, 'Crusade in Europe', of the American, British, French and Soviet democracies, aiming at transforming Germany, a wilderness of scorched ruins, into an agricultural and pastoral land with a small population; the historical relativity of all morality, for all morality expresses class interests, and the one true morality is the revolutionary morality, according to which good is what hastens the overthrow of present society, for example Russian society in 1878, or Italian society in 1978, and evil is anything that stabilizes it, even if it is progress; the intellectual infallibility of Mussolini (*Mussolini ha sempre ragione* – Mussolini is always right), Lenin, Hitler, Stalin and Mao Tse-tung; the universal scientific geniality and in fact the omniscience of Stalin; the coming of socialist man, a new type, qualitatively superior to the man who preceded him; school without regulations, without punishments, without rewards and without lessons; total sexual liberation, with male brothels and houses of discipline and torture for sadistic and masochistic clients; unlimited growth; zero growth; and finally the liberation of humanity by means of the kidnapping and assassination (so-called 'execution', in a dark hole, so-called 'people's prison') of politicians, wealthy people, plane passengers, travellers in trains and in buses.

By comparison, my dreams are modest. There is one which concerns the future of the Church.

Since it began, the Church has three or four times been old, decrepit and dying.

The contemporary texts on the sack of Rome by Alaric and on the fall of the Roman Empire in the west breathe an oppressive air of belonging to an aged, tired, dying world. This feeling again becomes evident with the approach of the year 1,000.

In that interval, oriental Christianity was torn by a long war of religion known as the quarrel of the images, then almost utterly beaten by Islam: Asia Minor, Syria, Egypt, North Africa, Spain were lost to Christianity. At the same time, the succession of Fathers of the Church, of great scholars and Christian philosophers, came to an end for several centuries. It was towards the end of this period that Germania was Christianized, and, right at the end, Russia. Towards the year 1,000, the Normans besieged the wretched little town of Paris and Swedes proceeded to make what were to be their last human sacrifices, including that of their king because of a bad harvest; the altar was at Uppsala.

In the midst of this period of anguish, the conversion of the Germans, the Slavs and the Hungarians, the romanesque and gothic flowering, the 'white mantle of cathedrals', among them the Cathedral of Uppsala; the University of Paris, centre of European philosophy all through the Middle Ages; the other great European universities, the theological summaries (*Summae Theologicae*), the great ascetic orders, preachers or scholars, 'little' Francis of Assisi, Catherine of Siena, Bruno, the Cistercians, tillers and cultivators of Europe: all that, in the year 600 or 700, was unimaginable. And yet, the Church, the assembly of Christians, came to life again, was rejuvenated and gave birth to that first marvellous era, from Kiev and Novgorod in the east to Ireland in the west, from Trondheim in the north to the Sicily of the Normans in the south.

After which came the crusades, the sack of Constantinople, a Christian metropolis, by Christian crusaders, the horror of the crusades against the Albigensians and the pagan Slavs, the exile of the Popes and the schism, a whole epoque of decadence marked by the burning of heretics at Montsegur at one end, and by Savonarola at the stake – or, if one wants to extend the period of degradation, the expulsion and the executions at the stake of Spanish Jews and Moors at the other. During those few centuries, the oriental Church was tolerated and despised as a cult of the subjects of the Golden Horde and of Ottoman military authority. And the Christian intellect went into a decline.

I know that such broadly-outlined sketches are not allowed; I know that the curves of growth and decline intersect, and that each date taken as the beginning of an evolutionary phase can be replaced by another, and contradicted by a concomitant regression, or on the contrary by a germ of development. I know that only those great arbitrary simplifications are allowed which have the backing of the secret police or that of pressure groups and entrenched interests for which they provide a totem and a rallying sign. But I am dreaming, in all humility, and it seems to me that the great crisis of the end of the Middle Ages was also a period of defeat for the Church, which was obviously obsessed by the need for reform, something felt by all ecclesiastics and all laymen. The Pope informed the inquisitors that Savonarola, already tortured at great length, should be put to death, 'even were he a second John the Baptist'. He was – of the Reformation.

Running the risk of only dreaming, and of being guilty of generalizations without the slightest value, it seems to me that at the moment when Constantinople had just fallen into the hands of the Turks, when, a hundred years after Hus, Savonarola had just been burned at the stake, when humanism triumphed, and when the Papacy, totally corrupt, disgusted a pilgrim *ad limina,* the monk Martin Luther, the Church was dying. At that moment, the Reformation of the Church, called Counter-Reformation in Catholic countries, the creation of a vast Protestant theology and its Catholic counterpart, the Catholic mysticism of the sixteenth and seventeenth centuries, the Protestant piety of the same centuries, a new Catholic continent and a new Protestant continent, new religious orders, Protestant societies and sects no less admirable for piety and fervour: all that, from the days of the Popes and the antipopes of Rome, Avignon and Peniscola, and above all the Borgia Popes, the della Rovere and Medici Popes, was unthinkable, hidden in the night of an unimaginable future. It was not even a dream: it was nothing.

For a third or fourth time the Church is dying, the Church has been dead, before our very eyes, for more than two centuries. The age of Enlightenment in the eighteenth century, the age of progress in the nineteenth century, the age of darkness and relapse into barbarism in the twentieth century, seem to have killed it off. The French Revolution and the Goddess Reason, the Russian Revolution and marxist-leninism, technocracy with Nazi myths, technocracy without myths, 'pragmatic' and 'liberal', the triumph of science, the defeat of science in the face of unexpected after-effects, the triumph of scientific ideologies like fascism and pseudo-scientific ones like marxism, the misery and poverty of the Industrial Revolution which put the masses off Christianity, the de-Christianization of the Russian empire, of Eastern Europe, of Africa, the de-Christianization of the West through material consumption and sensual satisfactions, the relative sterility of Christian thought for two centuries, at least in comparison with the great centuries of Christian thought, and finally the priests and pastors turned atheists, marxists and freudians: all mount up to a sure proof of death. That the Church should be reborn from such degradation, and, which would be even more difficult, from this almost total enervation, would be more than science fiction, more than any dream – it would be absurd.

Within two centuries, between the birth of Origen and the death of Saint Augustine, the Church absorbed and assimilated Platonism, Stoicism and Neo-Platonism. Then, for five hundred years, it grew old, and died its first apparent death. For four centuries, between Johannes Scotus Erigena and Occam, it absorbed and assimilated Aristotelian, Arab and Jewish philosophy. Then the Christian intellect became that caricature mocked by Rabelais, and even he did not lay it on thick enough. Again, from Erasmus to Luther, until that night in November 1654, in which Pascal scribbled 'Joy, joy, joy, tears of joy', the Church absorbed and assimilated the Renaissaance and the first scientific revolution, from Copernicus to Galileo. Pascal, the geometer, the precursor of differential calculus and the theory of aleatory games (*De Alea Geometrica*), the physicist, and, with his calculating machine, after Raymond Lulle, the precursor of cybernetics and data processing, the man of 'the eternal silence of those infinite spaces that frighten me', is the living example of the fusion between Christian piety and scientific knowledge of the Copernican universe.

One might add another day in November, the one on which, a generation earlier, English emigrants drafted and signed, off Provincetown, on the North Atlantic coast, the principles by which they desired to live together. It was the date of the foundation of modern democracies, until now the least evil States in the history of humanity. They were Christians, Protestants, men and women for whom the earth was round and situated somewhere on the edge of the solar system, in 'the eternal silence of those infinite spaces'.

After this last apogee, in the seventeenth century, the Church fell into decrepitude, God died, and the Pope became infallible. I could not say what became of Protes-

214 TO THE UNKNOWN GOD

tant Christianity, and I do not have much to say about oriental Christianity for the same period of two or three centuries, ending with the present day.

It would doubtless be unimaginable that, in some unknown future, the Authorities of the various separated, but *conciliable* Churches – conciliable in the double sense of 'reconcilables' and 'capable of sitting down together in an oecumenical council' – should put to use our accumulated experience of the laws, the specific defects, the specific crises, the modalities of permanent reform and control of all great organizations, of all bureaucracies, in order to bring it about that the Sabbath be made for man, not man for the Sabbath. Too much of a science fiction fantasy, no doubt, to hope that the Church might absorb and assimilate the second scientific revolution, that of relativity, the quantum theory, the plurivalent logics and geometries, genetics, and ethology. It would be absurd, because it would be something never seen before, and even if it had been seen before and repeated several times, and from then on unrepeatable; it would be absurd to expect that new monastic order, new societies or Protestant sects, or the already-existing old ones, rejuvenated, should absorb the thrust of devotion, of mysticism, of ascesis, of sacrifice, of voluntary poverty, of fraternity and community, even chastity, of the young, of women, of all those passionate ones that the world as we see it leaves unsatisfied to the point of screaming, of dying, and who cannot or will no longer believe in those things that our thought could conceive even greater, nor in guides such as Jesus Christ.

(On the subject of chastity, not obligatory, nor magical but voluntary and simply as an ethical decision, we must note the first signs of reaction, in America, always in advance of the movements in the modern world, against the cult of youth, of sexuality and sensual pleasure in general.)

It would be absurd to expect that Christians, Christian orders, Christian societies should imitate, at almost a

thousand years' distance in time, the Cistercians, the tillers
and cultivators of Europe, and teach humanity the techniques of ecology, of an agriculture that would not destroy
the habitat, of non-polluting industrialization, and go out
into the third and fourth worlds as doctors, teachers,
technicians and farmers, to help their fellow men to drive
out famine, disease and death as far away as possible
without the soul being damaged.

It would above all be unthinkable that the Church
should reform once again, starting from the discovery, the
study and the critique of the bureaucratic and organizational phenomenon. It would be unthinkable that it should
find mechanisms of equilibrium and security *with* liberty,
and that one might be able to sing the mass in Latin as well
as in the language of the country, or that jeans should be
allowed as well as the cassock, without either of them
having to be forbidden. I dream of an Authority at once
efficient and liberal, which would develop new methods to
replace the inertia, the intolerance, the spiritual sloth, the
soulless discipline, with activity, friendship, an intelligent
and deeply-considered entente between Christians, and
between the clergy and Christian people.

And it would probably be absurd to expect Christian
thought that would not be expressed in *baralipton*, the
jargon of the experts, but in *koinê*, in Basic Human,
accessible to the assembly of the faithful, following the
example of the Evangelists, of Saint Augustine, of Saint
Francis of Assisi, of Saint Martin Luther, and of Saint
Blaise Pascal (who was so unjust to the Jesuits).

Yes, I know I am indulging in daydreams: a poor
visionary, a poor fool, a poor wretch who imagines that a
thing which is repeated three times can also be repeated
four times, and that the Church dying of its dead God
would be capable once more of making one of those great
steps forward, towards the City of God, perhaps (but in
truth he does not dare to dream with such precision).

Yes, I am daydreaming, instead of reflecting like a

serious grown man on future society, in which each one
will give according to his limited strength, and will receive
according to his limitless needs, or at any rate very
extensible requirements; instead of thinking of unlimited
growth, of the total emancipation of all, and of total
sensual satisfaction through all the exterior and interior
organs, all the surfaces and all the orifices of our bodies;
instead of thinking of zero growth, of the stabilization of
needs and resources, so that washerwomen will always
have washerwomen's hands, working mothers of families
will always have, at the age of fifty, the bodies of working
mothers of families at the age of fifty, and that the walking
skeletons of the Sahara and Bengal will always remain
walking skeletons. And to put these reflections into a
language for accomplices, and season them with a few
justifications of violence (historically necessary), and with
a few stylistic flourishes, such as: 'trashcan of history,
dunghill of history, wheel of history, imperialist pigs'.

I am bitterly conscious of my inferiority, but also I make
no pretension to be taken seriously, unless by one or two
unfortunates like myself. The autist character, the compensatory character of these daydreams is not unknown to
me, and I only go on dreaming even more, and ever more
irresponsibly. I dream of a black Pope, of a Protestant
Pope, of a Russian Pope, of a Jewish Pope. Instead of
thinking in a responsible way of the de-alienation of the
mad through violence, I tell myself that if a miracle was
possible after the year 500, after the year 1,000, after the
year 1,500, it should still be possible once more. It will
soon be the year 2,000. The terror of the year 2,000 is
already there, insidious. *A bello atomico, a fame, a frigore, a
peste atomica, a pollutione terrae, a multitudine nostra immani,
libera nos, Domine. And preserve us from our own folly, my
God, Amen.*

13.

THE ROSE WINDOW OF THE SOUTH TRANSEPT

The rose window in the south transept was shimmering with radiance, illuminated by a shaft of sunlight: chakra, mandala, rose-mallow, mystic rose, numinous nenuphar, lotus of the West, emblem of God, configuration of the universe, symbol of the relative transparence of the world around us.

It had been designed, constructed and placed in position by arthitects, stone masons, stained glass craftsmen who died seven or eight centuries ago, but who live on through this window. They had suspended it up there, enshrined in the wall, intermediary between the interior space filled with prayer, and the exterior space, 'the eternal silence of those infinite spaces', extending as far as those zones where electromagnetic fields distort Euclidean geometry, where space itself becomes rugged and uneven and straight lines begin to bend and twist, where galaxies go speeding by to the tune of Hubble's constant, in the absolute cold of absolute zero on the Kelvin scale and the radiophonic roaring of quasars, until space-time curves inwards and turns back in upon itself, as in the Apocalypse, where 'the heaven departed as a scroll when it is rolled together', one of the double scrolls that were used when giving public readings in the synagogue at Nazareth.

We stood there without moving, heads raised towards the hearth of iridescent light, shot through as if with a spear of brilliant gold: my friend Jean de B., who had taken me with him to pray together in Notre Dame in Paris, and I, who at that instant conceived the absurd

desire to live and have my being in that radiant flower, and
to have it before my eyes at the moment of death.

I have never understood why Europeans should now sit
in the lotus position to meditate, instead of falling on their
knees, or standing, to pray; why they should shave their
heads, leaving a crest or lock of hair on top, instead of
wearing the tonsure; why they go barefoot, instead of in
coarse sandals; and why they put on dirty jeans, or an
orange chlamys, instead of a habit of sackcloth. Why
choose a guru, when one has a priest, a pastor, a confessor,
a director of conscience? Why an ashram, where there is La
Trappe, the Chartreuse and some thousands of other
houses of retreat? Let us be beatniks: Diogenes was the
first, the stoic itinerant preachers were beatniks, the
Fathers of the desert and their disciples were, the first
Franciscans were also. But Christians who despised their
century – and I can well understand that one might want to
reject one's century, particularly the twentieth – were all
that, with a decisive something else: their orientation
towards God, through the love of Christ.

It seems to me that we have to breathe life into what we
have around us, instead of going to the ends of the earth
for inspiration. I say this precisely because of my profound
veneration for all other avenues towards God, and of my
perfect friendship for our brethren born into other civilizations, into other religions.

For besides my encounter with the rose window, there
was my encounter with the Buddha, in the Grand Lamas-
ery in Beijing.

One enters it through a succession of deserted court-
yards, as in all Chinese palaces and monasteries. Next
there is a stone-paved walk; a young man in trousers and
his shirtsleeves, very clean, with blue-black hair, was
prostrating himself on those paving flags, rising, lowering
himself again, flat on his stomach, without stop. Very
young: as young as the Russian soldiers in the crowds at
the convent at Zagorsk, the young Armenian soldiers in

Soviet uniform in the cathedral of Etchmiadzine, or the young French pilgrims on the road to Chartres.

Next there was a colonnade, an elaborately-decorated peristyle; inside the colonnade, sitting cross-legged on rectangular cushions, each with his book beside him, the monks, in chlamys, one shoulder and arm bare, exactly as in Greek statues, the head shaven, sometimes covered with a sort of antique crested helmet, but made of felt, no more outlandish than the tonsures, the mitres and cowls of Christians, than Jewish prayer shawls or the prayer bands which are rolled round the arm in the synagogue. They were saying their prayers, their deep voices making a loud buzzing sound, like a swarm of steel hornets. More remote from us, but not more outlandish than the Muslim cantilena, or the tragic Jewish recitative, or the undulation of plain chant, which to us sounds angelic, childlike and celestial. Two pebbles and two white flowers; or *amor intellectualis Dei;* it would be interesting to know how Albert Einstein addressed himself to God.

Prayers in a sacred tongue, two thousand five hundred years old; traditional vestments, which existed, identical, in the days of Alexander the Great. Familiar to us, though a little younger, later in time. We passed through, and entered the temple.

Inside, a patio, a sort of cloister, but covered, with several storeys, surrounded by galleries one on top of the other. And in the centre, immense, clothed in silk, sculpted from the trunk of a single gigantic tree brought from the forests of Indochina, probably by river, the Buddha looking straight in front of him, at an unknown remove, half raising his hands bearing a silken band, the sign of peace, of amity, of salutation. He is present; he is intense, he tears you out of yourself, he drags you forth out of yourself, towards transcendence, the elsewhere, the beyond.

I am not confusing the significant with the signified, nor the images with what they represent. The Christian God with his long beard carved in stone and Jesus Christ in wood painted a faded pink and with chocolate-coloured blood are signs, one of the unthinkable, the unspeakable God transcendent and immanent, the other of Jesus Christ, God become man in the person of the carpenter of Nazareth. I am not one of those wretched creatures forever ready to mock 'idols' or destroy them (they are always the 'idols' of others, but *eidôlon* simply signifies image, and image simply signifies a thing which represents or makes allusion to the thing it is the sign of). I knew well enough that this tree trunk was only a sculptured sign, and I knew that it signified the historical personage of Siddartha Gautama, of the Shakya clan, called by his disciples and by all those who follow his teaching, and by us also, who do not follow him, the Buddha, that is, the Enlightened One, the conqueror of the suffering of existence.

An old monk greeted us. He offered me on his out-stretched hands a band of silk, as a sign of friendship, and as a memory of my visit.

They offer a band of silk, cheap, I think, price being immaterial in the nature of the gift. We put our hands together, or extend the right hand. The silken band, like our joined hands, is the gesture of the vanquished, who surrenders, offering his hands to the noose, or already offering himself the band that will be used to bind his wrists. It is a gesture of peace, intended to deflect the other's aggressive impulse, to make the enemy a friend. Sublimation, transfiguration of ancient savage behaviour, of primitives who hunted in the wild: one can read about it in Lorenz, Eibl-Eibesfeldt and their friends. Adam the ape was capable of conciliation and peace, as are wolves, tigers, fish and birds.

I saw a girl, still very young, on the campus of a Bangkok university, putting her hands together in the Hindu and Christian fashion, in the midst of a crowd of young right-wingers who were busy massacring their communist university comrades. Some were beating frenziedly, with wooden staves pulled out of the fence and crimson with blood, a small youth hung from a gallows and already dead, his face smashed to pieces. Others were howling at the young girl who was hoping to survive thanks to her gesture of peace. It was the communists, that day, who were being crucified, those who usually make arrangements for the crucifixion of others. But we Christians, barely escaped with our lives from pagan persecutions, did we not hasten to persecute the pagans, the Arians, the Montanists and so on during the last two thousand years? Jesus Christ is always on the side of the crucified, and I believe he changes sides in the twinkling of an eye: he is not loyal to the person, and even less to the group; he is loyal to suffering.

Piety, peace, contemplation and harmony of the soul, serenity, were just as perceptible in the Buddhist temple in Beijing as before the rose window of the south transept in Notre Dame in Paris, and the Tibetan monk who offered me the silken band of friendship was as close to me as my friend Jean de B. And twenty years later my very dear and reverend friend Father Jean N., told me, on his return from Benares: 'I felt myself to be at home with the Brahman mystics on the banks of the Ganges.'

For we do not have to wonder if it is they who feel close to us; we have to give, before receiving, and without expecting to receive anything whatsoever in return, except simple, pure friendship and amity.

On my return from China, at once I found the pairs of pointed steeples of western gothic cathedrals very strange. I cannot forget Chartres far off on the plain, a pale grey silhouette between the green fields of Beauce and the light blue sky; nor the cathedral of Lübeck on its Baltic plain, in the cold furnace of a winter sunset. Why pointed? Why two? Why not superimposed roofs, towers of superimposed roofs piled upon one another like pagodas? Why not roofs tilted at the tip like tents? Why not construct towers like pairs of ribbed melons, as in India, or pairs of massive stone constructions, as on either side of the entrance to Egyptian temples? Why not a peristyle with a Greek fronton? Even Orthodox churches seemed bizarre to me, and the priests, the monks, with their beards, their black veils, their gilded mitres. I felt more at home in Saint Michael's in Hamburg, with its air of a vast salon of the Sun King, as grave, sumptuous and frigid, and with the same childlike purity, as a composition by Bach. And I liked the sermon by a lama in a black cassock, with the white ruff of the Renaissance at his neck. He was speaking of Jesus Christ.

There is a Christian sobriety, a prosaicness, an odour of poverty or at any rate of sobriety that I love and find everywhere, and which comes to us out of the mists of time. In the house of my dear Mgr Walter A., there is that odour of poverty, as there is in the palace of the Katholikos of Etchmiadzine, head of the Armenian Church – I believe they are monophysites, and that they think of Jesus Christ only as God and as the son of God, and human only in appearance: but I hasten to turn away from questions of dogma, essential as they are, if they separate me from my Armenian brethren. It is enough for me that they pray to God and that they love Jesus Christ above all else. One must first love them, forgive them, and ask them to forgive me; concepts, thinkable faith, speakable faith will come later, and if it is to separate us we had better remain silent and stay friends.

The Christian odour of poverty. Monophysite priests still wear the cowl, the penitent's hood, now made of watered silk, but exactly the same shape as it was original-ly: a bag, split down one side. Beatniks. Christians have always been the proletariat, workers, artisans, slaves, intellectuals, doctors, peasants, small income people, sol-diers; polite, thoughtful, wise and worthy of confidence. They did not participate in the great pagan orgy, the gladiatorial combats, the happenings at the fertility rites. They were against dancing in circles, kill-joys, protestants, a sort of poor people's priests, trade unionists, social democrats. The great expense of luxury in Nero's time, the great sexual liberation of antiquity, the great orgiastic feast were not for them.

The Venus of Cnidus and peoples massacred or sold at public auction; the Hermaphrodite of Naples and the squad of soldiers with the gracious order to open your veins; the Platonic Eros and the lamentable sigh of a young male slave, labourer in a factory making sandstone vases, who engraved on the flank of a hill in North Africa – one can still read the inscription – that he loved a young girl, but had to submit to the sexual demands of his fellow-workers in slavery: *hic Dorus paedicatur amans Laviniam.* The gracious and impressive fresques of Pompeii and five thousand slaves crucified all along the Via Appia; the gigantic marble phallus – it can still be seen on the agora of a town in Asia Minor, the shaft broken, leaving only the testicles one metre in diameter – and the sentence of death for whoever, as the Christians did, refused to declare with all due solemnity before the constituted authorities that Caïus Jules Joseph Vissarionovitch Bonaparte Caesar Neron, president of the Senate, Generalissimo of the armed forces, tribune of the people, president of the Trade Unions, secretary general of the Party and Pope, was God. The Christians were annoying, insupportable, filled with ill will, obstinate, and they smelled of poverty. I love them. I have read Celsus, attentively, or rather those long passages, which make almost a whole book on their own, collected by Origen in his *contra Celsum*; Celsus, who is so right, and who understood so little of what it was all about. They rejected the relaxation of all sphincter muscles; they rejected dissipation, frivolity, they were all for meditation, concentration, edification, all those words which one must look at as if one were reading them for the first time, and understand what they really mean: to edify, construct, build, collect oneself, collect oneself around one's centre. Or again: to rise up, to take flight: the

Christians said *sursum corda*, and not 'off with your knickers!'

If you had been with me in the German churches – yes, German – at Christmas in the year 1942, during the winter in Stalingrad, or in the Cathedral of the Trinity Saint Serge in Zagorsk under Stalin, there in the dense mass of Russian peasants, with a handful of young soldiers, stocky, blond – I think there were even some in the uniform of the pretorians of the MVD; if you had experienced the Nativity eve in the Orthodox churches of Eastern Europe during the construction of Tartar socialism in those countries, or at least in French churches during the Nazi occupation, you would know what it is all about: the upward leap of the soul in pain, humanity crucified upon itself, sending out its whole heart to the unknown God.

It is enough to find oneself at the Buddha's feet in Beijing and to receive the silken band of friendship held out, with the same gesture as that of the giant statue, by a very sweet old monk, very humble and very much a master of himself; it is enough to enter any mosque – shoes off, no camera, leaving behind the avid, empty eye of the tourist: to enter as a respectful brother, and discover the sublime piety of Islam; it is enough to pray with Jewish friends, head covered, addressing the prayer to the transcendent God they taught us about.

It is enough to receive a visit from a pair of Mormon missionaries, or Jehovah's Witnesses, to find piety other than in the Christian Church. My father was imprisoned under socialism, without having done anything wrong, and left prison suffering from the illness from which he was to die; but also filled with admiration for his prison companions, Jehovah's Witnesses, the most courageous, the most firm in their faith, and who gave hope and confidence to the others. When they visited me, their missionaries began by saying bad things about the Church, and I turned a deaf ear, for the Church is the assembly of Christians, including themselves; we all are the Church; I preferred to love them as the prison companions of my father. But all this is simply to say that we have it within us to feel and sympathize very strongly with the piety of non-Christians, just as much as that of Christians who do not belong to our Church. It is impossible for human beings to love God without loving one another. It is impossible for one piety to give offence to another without ceasing to be piety. I strive to follow Jesus Christ, he whom we await, he whom we have been waiting for, the son of God: that does not oblige me to deny God, nor to deny that Mahomet is the Prophet of God. That does not oblige me to deny that Buddha is the Enlightened One, nor that his teaching can deliver us from the suffering of existence. That does not oblige me to deny the law of Moses, or the election of the people of Israel.

I well know that there are essential points in faith as thought, speakable faith, faith that is declared in words, that separate our religions, born and developed in distinct civilizations, with their thought and sensibility different from those of others.

Wherever I may feel a conflict is possible, I shall say nothing. I shall suspend my thought. I shall allow only friendship, good nature and patience to remain in my presence. I know that if I were a good Muslim I should deserve to be called a good Christian. I know that if I were to fulfill the Five Commandments of Buddhism and of Hinduism I should be fulfilling also the Commandments which God gave to Moses, and I should be following the teaching that Jesus Christ gave us all.

Theologies have been and are creative. They evolved in historical time. They can evolve again, in living religions. It should be conceivable that the theologies of living religions would progress, in all prudence, with infinite delicacy, with the supreme reserve of speculation, the sovereign economy of means, exacted by love, amity, serenity, wisdom; that they would progress in a convergent manner, not towards fusion, not towards confusion: but towards conciliation.

14.

THE THIRD RESPONSE

For many years, I have been conducting a little conversation with him, a conversation within the great conversation. We see one another once every three or four or five years, but the thread or our exchange is never lost. It happens each time in the house or the friends to whom I dedicate these pages, and much more than these pages: they are miracle workers, who perform miracles of friendship.

He arrives, in his ordinary everyday clothes, wearing his ordinary tie, which had once been stained and imperfectly cleaned; for evening wear, he has a dark suit, and another tie. I have only seen this indifference to external things in militant communists, in the days when they were real militants and real communists.

He was a prisoner of the Gestapo. He comes of a good family, and possesses nothing except a bad painting of Saint Ignatius, a gift from one of the faithful, and which his superiors always send on after him each time they send him to one or other of their houses. Father Jean N., hopes each time that he will be relieved of this daub; but his superiors send it on after him with great expedition, and then he grits his teeth, smiles, relaxes and says nothing.

He has a virile air, grey hair close-cropped, but he has a very soft, caressing voice. Only once have I heard him raise his voice, angrily, almost threateningly: that was when he gave me the third response. The first response was that of Mgr Walter A., to 'How to be a Christian?' – 'That depends on your attitude towards Jesus.' The second, which I received from the same Father N., was: 'God is the God of Spinoza, but he is not just the God of Spinoza; he is everything that can be thought, yet he transcends thought.'

The third response, given without my having to ask him: 'How should I behave? What should I do?' was: 'One cannot love God without loving men; it would be a falsehood.' He spoke roughly. His gentleness stopped there – before the supreme, and the worst, dishonesty.

It took me years to understand and to make up my mind. I am not speaking of the mental decision, all cut and dried: 'I want to do such and such a thing.' I am speaking of a decision which would become a part of my being; a decision which is already an interior disposition, an inclination.

And then all of a sudden the pieces of the puzzle fall into place all on their own. Situations in daily life take sudden and unexpected turns, which transform them, which reorient all their valencies. It becomes more and more easy for me to be affable, thoughtful, kind, and more and more difficult to be cold or indifferent or aggressive. I discover the great pleasure of being inoffensive. I discover the pleasures of politeness – the real, sincere politeness that comes from the heart. All around me, people pass by without looking at one another, or they look at one another with hard, impudent expressions. Strangers do not greet one another, do not say good morning when using the lift; they do not say thank you, and hold their breath so as not to smell the hateful odour of one's fellow man. And the young yell, hyperactive and threatening, in a constant lather of aggressivity and aggression.

During my youth, I still knew the politeness of country ways now extinct, the good morning between strangers, reactions acquired during centuries in which people walked abroad armed, or at least with a cudgel in the hand and a knife stuck down inside the boot. The bowing of the head – 'Look, I am exposing my head to blows, do not hurt me'; the hand extended: 'See, my right hand, the hand which handles the murderous tool (*implement*), is empty; I am not armed: let's be friends.' The smile: 'I do not hate you, I like you, I am in a good mood, act the same way with me, let us be of good cheer together, let's be friends.' We shall learn, I hope, in the streets of Megalopolis, to behave like civilized human beings, as if we were living with dignity, liberty and amity.

I know how naïve and mawkish those words sound. But they should be read against a background of children hacked to pieces with an axe, old people robbed in dark alleys, human skulls with big irregular holes made by pieces of metal. I do not like pain and suffering. I am not looking for trouble. But I keep my eyes open, and I see everywhere around us the vibrations of demonic behaviour, impatient, ready to unleash itself. That is what makes stories of demonic possession and pseudo-diabolical films unbearable for me: they are a spiteful trick of the devil, who makes us believe he does not exist by showing himself on film and paper, with horns, hairy body, horrid yells and borborygmic rumblings. Then it is he who is at the wheel of the car that speeds away after knocking you down; he possesses someone next to you in the office or the machine shop; he is within yourselves, within myself, during a moment of ill will, envy, anger, hardening of the heart, refusal to pity, ferocious appetite, sullenness or impoliteness. Suffering is much closer, Evil is much more immediate than we in our superficiality would like to think. We can learn, we shall learn, and teach our children, social behaviour, and prudent, delicate and good-hearted contact between humans.

Animals give us an example of this. In the country, many years ago, my youngest daughter, who still had not started speaking, was always treated with especial gentleness by our dog. He would come close to her, turn away his head and look elsewhere, until she patted him on the back or stroked him; then he would go on playing. That arc of a circle formed by the spine, its convexity turned towards the child, seemed strange to me; there was something tense, compulsive in that movement which forced the dog to look away. It was not until long afterwards, when the good beast had been dead for years, that I discovered in Lorenz and Eibl-Eibesfeldt the significance of that gesture. The dog was offering his jugular for the child to bite. He was making peace overtures. 'See, you can kill me with one bite, I'll let you, so give up, and let's be friends.' He was imputing to the child another kind of behaviour, his own innate behavioural reaction. In the same way we can impute to ever vaster groups, teams, tribes, nations, continental unions, Judeo-Christian civilization, all humanity, the entire biosphere, the instinctive behaviour of human friendship.

To abstain from giving offence is already a great deal. To be aware of the existence of one's fellow man, of one's neighbour, and to let him know, just between ourselves, that we do not hate him and that he is not supremely indifferent to us is already a good beginning. All is possible, and we are living, through relapses and perversions, that grand mutation which widens the area of affectionate behaviour between a mother and her child, between parents and children. (I have rarely seen anything so charming as the behaviour of a South African bushman holding a baby at arms' length, talking to it and then kissing it all over, with open mouth.) Family, little horde, tribe, city, State or nation, humanity – so it goes, and already naïve daydreamers like me are preparing to join friendship with beings on other solar systems. We are obviously half way there. It is not an easy road, but we can see where it is leading.

One can see where it is leading: I say that without forgetting half my high-school class fallen in the war, without forgetting my father who almost perished in socialist prisons, and my father in Jesus Christ who was incarcerated by the Gestapo; without forgetting that I myself was knocked senseless and almost killed by Soviet troops looting our homes, and that my best friend has just been mugged in the street by looters in New York.

I am not forgetting suffering, especially the suffering of others. But I have seen Hitler passing by in the street, all-powerful, all-evildoing, and I see now that there is nothing left of him, not even a place to mark his grave. I have seen Stalin deified, and I see now that his name has become a term of abuse, so that even those who deserve it indignantly object to being called Stalinists. I have seen the Arabs passing from the condition of slaves to that of masters, and masters more wise and more moderate than others would have been in their place. I have seen the emancipation of the black peoples, and I was happy to see black judges in the grey wigs of English judges, and I said to myself that after all there is something good to be learned from us whites – law, fairness, the rights of man and of the citizen. I have seen Jews in the streets of German towns, branded with the yellow star; I have seen the survivors finally found, two thousand years after the fall of Jerusalem, the State of Israel. All that happened in my lifetime – the quasi-extinction of a people bearing the law of God, and his salvation: a people once more threatened.

I was a child when Gide was writing his *Voyage au Congo* and his *Retour d'URSS*. Forty years afterwards, the left in the West is finally about to return also; meanwhile, humanity has adopted black music and black art, and perhaps we shall learn something from the Blacks – kindness, cordiality, piety – perhaps even dignity and sexual modesty, for if we ask Africans, celebrated for their sexual vigour, what they think of Western eroticism, their replies will astonish us.

I have seem Mao Tse-tung standing, almost divine, on the Gate of Heavenly Peace and the wild applause of visiting Western leftist dolts; meanwhile, I was exchanging ironical hints and winks with the Chinese, making byzantine pleasantries about bureaucracy, our absolute, stupid, dangerous and ridiculous sovereign ruler: I had come from Byzantium, and I could recognize in Tartar socialism the bureaucracy of the Tsin, the Han, the Mongols, and the Manchus.

I was a child when the whole world heard of Gandhi; I saw his great soul, truly the Mahatma, triumph, and then I saw his poor thin little body riddled with bullets by a young man with good intentions, who believed, as he had been taught, that violence is good and that the end justifies the means; then, Gandhi vanquished, forgotten; and once more triumphant, in the greatest democracy known to humanity.

As children, adolescents, young people, adults, we have known hunger, epidemics, war, terror. We grew up, and in places still live under either open or hypocritically disguised tyrannies, of a barbarism either primitive or refined; but there are entire countries, entire continents, which are free and in a position to make good use of their liberty. We are no longer so afraid; but we shut our eyes, our ears and our hearts to the fear suffered by others. We no longer suffer so much from hunger; but we are destroying what we cannot eat, instead of giving it to those who are starving. We no longer suffer from the plague, the typhus or cholera; but we are poisoning ourselves by eating too much, we are poisoning ourselves with alcohol, tobacco, drugs and medicaments, not forgetting automobile exhausts. We allow the deserts to spread and encroach upon polluted and devastated lands; but at least we know how to go about it in order to make it flower again. Perhaps we shall do it tomorrow. All is not yet lost. All is still possible, even good.

The world is full of marvellous discoveries still to be made, as I know from experience. The piety and devoutness of Muslims, their capacity to link all the points of their existence to the centre of that existence, which is submission to God. Jewish uprightness, Jewish attachment to the moral law. The sublime religiosity of the Hindus, the inward thrust towards all other human beings. The Chinese inclination towards civilized coexistence, their fundamental patterns of the art of living, politeness become identical with our very being. Truth, the immediate humanity of negritude. I shall love them all, I shall respect them all, I shall open my heart to them, without attempting to unsettle them, even less to convert them; but according to the measure of my strength, I shall work to see that they have freedom of choice and a chance of salvation. I even believe that I shall end by accepting the communists, in so far as human solidarity – what Christians call loving one's neighbour – can raise them above hatred, so that they may learn to show less of the clenched fists and more of the wide-open arms. If they renounce intellectual trickery and deceit, and the usurpation of political power by violence and intrigue, then even they may participate in this miraculous convergence which is taking place now before our very eyes. We must unlearn hatred. The great civilizations which, all together, make up the civilization of human life, are drawing closer without being confused with one another, without losing their individual identities: Judeo-Christian civilization in its two variants, Western and Russian, Islamic civilization, African civilization, Hindu civilization and Chinese civilization (I am still naming them in the order of their geographical distance from me, which has no actual importance).

We must unlearn hatred also in daily life. Lately, I have noticed that it is becoming easier for me not to hate. One of my sins was resentment, and I was vindictive: when one has a good memory, one does not easily forget: one remembers all...

A dozen years ago, at the end of that summer in which my friend Paul C., the German Jewish poet, and my friend

Marek H., the Polish writer, died, and when I was considering, after their example, the quickest way out, the shortest and least painful, I received a telephone call that saved my life. They wanted to entrust me with the publicity for a huge enterprise, and it was the son and principal collaborator of the founding president who was telephoning me. It brought tears to my eyes, tears of gratitude and relief. So my family and I were going to survive.

The negotiations took a turn for the worse. There was a sudden chill in the air. Then, ill will, and even impoliteness. Finally, on the occasion of the presentation of competitors' ideas – the Old Man, the big boss, at the end of a ten-metre-long table, twenty directors all tight-lipped, frigid, cautious, seated around it – I understood, when the boss leaned towards me with a sarcastic snigger: 'Well, you attacked me in the past; speak up, we're all ears.' I had not attacked him, but, by chance, at the club, I had given him a rather sharp reply. He had fifteen thousand wage-earners under him, he was famous, and his vanity, or his pride, had taken offence at my remark: now he was going to teach me a lesson in respect for one's superiors. I had fallen into a trap. I had to witness the triumph of my rivals: those artful dodgers had made themselves rich for the rest of their days, along with the firm's director of publicity, whose palm they had greased; and I dropped back into the ranks of the unemployed, and into the temptation to commit suicide.

Meanwhile, after having built an empire on three different markets and left his onward and upward path strewn with the corpses of his competitors, the great man went bankrupt in his turn. Above the figure of a billion dollars worth of business a year – I am not talking of funny money, but of hard cash, commensurate with the actual work done to produce it – bankruptcy today is called fusion, concentration, takeover bid. He was bought out by one of those monsters of oligopoly, and shown the door without even a purely formal say in the matter, without even being offered a seat on the board of directors: nothing, nothing but a monthly remittance, enormous for people like my reader or myself, but a bitter mockery for a great captain of industry. He and his son are finished, retired, nullities. I meet them at the club. For a long time, I kept wanting to tell the Old Man: 'You are petty, you are vain, you are cowardly.' Today, I do not even feel pleased at his fall. He does not seem to have understood anything. I am left with a sort of sadness, a remoteness, a regret at having had anything to do with him. But perhaps soon I shall be able to go up to him, my hand extended in friendship. All is possible, even good.

The revelation of amity is, how easy it is to be good-tempered; what a pleasure one takes in being thoughtful, what a satisfaction in being kind. We are not forbidden to be either good and resentful, nor good and stupid. There is the joy of ingenuity in good. Intelligence is indispensable in Christian love. Nothing, in Evil, is definite or definitive, for all can be modified by amity; the limits, the parameters, are movable, without using force, by simple patient pressure. The great secret seems to be productivity, creativity in the field of the good: to add to the sum of things a gesture, a word, a look, a smile. One does not wipe out Evil, or the sorrow and the ill temper that are so frightening in this world, except by replacing them with something else. Once again, the great secret seems to be inventiveness: an unexpected word, an initiative, an invitation, a common enterprise; nothing makes us such good friends – we, the descendants of the little hordes of paleolithic hunters – nothing unites us more than an enterprise undertaken together, from a simple diversion to navigating the earth or the moon, from a simple but successful conversation (which is in itself a work of art like chamber music), to the construction and exploitation of a nuclear *fusion* factory, without radioactive wastes.

In the humdrum mediocrity of my existence, therefore,

I shall ingeniously devise ways to spread around me good humour, moderation, gentleness, and to deploy a patient and tireless activity, at the same time remaining open to accept, on the part of one's fellow, a pause, an interruption of contact, and to withdraw, to plunge back into myself again, in order to emerge once more refreshed and fortified, to recommence that life in common, of which one might say that it, too, is – in the sense of 'turning oneself towards another' – a conversation, the other face of the unending conversation that we conduct with our unknown interlocutor.

15.

LOVING ONE'S NEIGHBOUR
AS ONESELF?

Does one love oneself? I have detested myself, I have despised myself; I have got to the point when I could not bear the smell of my own sweat, and when I could not look at my face in the glass: I have hated myself for my weakness, for my sins, for my failure. Until one day my friend, my brother in Jesus Christ, my priest told me: 'Jesus loves you, even if you are a sinner; he loves you despite your faults. Do not hate yourself.' I replied: 'One must be very strong in order to be so soft.'

I was pretending to joke, but I was overcome. No one had ever spoken to me in that way. I am the child of a pitiless century, of a pitiless world, and at home I was taught to be proud: to be hard on myself and others, to despise softness and weakness; and to win, or to survive when others perished. I have done all that, yet I find myself a failure. But now I understand.

Working for my family, for friends, for my neighbour, for everyone. Making them see, and understand, that it is for them I am working. Inventing, creating, producing things or attitudes which give them satisfaction of joy, which are useful or agreeable or both. Cultivating a friendly tone of voice, gentleness, tolerance, gravity not lacking in good humour, seriousness without ill temper, persuasiveness – but also the art of listening, taking an

interest in the person who is talking to us. Being a
Christian and spreading good will all around one, in
ever-widening circles and ripples. Loving God in the
person of fellow human beings, beginning with those
closest to me, my wife, my children, my friends, and from
them moving outwards and outwards to the ends of the
inhabited world.

I have just been reading a declaration by a working man.
For him, there had never been anything in common
between his work and his religious life. He was not
working for his neighbour. The life, the health, the
well-being of his fellow man was not dependent upon his
work well done. Now we are three hundred million
Europeans and two hundred million Americans, an eighth
of the population of the earth, sternly chained to exacti-
tude, correctness, punctuality, to the finish of our work or
the skill of our performance; we are known for our
'conscientious' work: and he thinks that is not Christian! I
know of course that work badly done is not rewarded, and
that one soon loses one's job if one turns out rubbish; but
that is not the centre of gravity in the matter. The centre of
gravity is that we naturally love good work well done,
because we are conscientious, because we have a conscience, a moral conscience, a Christian conscience – even
atheists; we are all shoots from the ancient root of Adam
the maker of tools in well-trimmed flint, quite perfect,
nicely polished. And doubtless what we hold of value is of
value for the other seven-eighths of humanity.

Loving one's neighbour as oneself also means being a
member of a working team, member of a factory collective or of some enterprise or organization or of other
forms of social activity; that means being a citizen of one's
village or of one's town, of one's region, of one's country,
of one's federation of States, and citizen of the world. Man
is possible, as is good, and it seems to me that man is
imminent. This creates a desire to associate, to act as a
group, to spread all around one good will, thoughtfulness

for others, affability, deference, and to seek in common friendship and confidence new and practicable solutions, to explore neglected or unknown paths. And to practise those marvellous 'techniques' of life in common, the delicate and subtle art of helping one another, sympathy, understanding. Beginning with our nearest and dearest, all are happy to find themselves necessary, wanted, for they too live as we do on this earth that shakes with the movements of the imminent future and under the possible wrath of God. It is necessary to have imagination, to find the right word, the prudent, expected phrase, the necessary gesture or initiative; but also, it is necessary to know how to be silent, or to withdraw at the right moment, how to accept a rejection, which will prove to be increasingly rare and all the less hard to take as one develops a lighter touch, a less egoistic initiative, concern more centred on one's fellow.

I am living in the midst of happily changing situations, of transmutations in human relationships. God knows I do not shut my eyes to Evil, and that I am suffering at this very instant, after several days, from the vision of a suffering that I would have been helpless to prevent. But God also knows that I do not reject the evidence of good. One must be happy; and often we are. One must be grateful; and often we are not. Or not enough. One must know how to be happy and grateful, in all humility, without forgetting the suffering of others; without forgetting the fear of God; but accepting whatever he grants us.

That is why I also conscientiously exercise my rights and try to do my duty. The first time I voted there were, as I have said, armed and helmeted soldiers in front of the local polling station, and the one list of candidates. I ought at least to have wanted to choose between two candidates of the same party, whom I shall not name here, to spare their blushes. But no – one had to give one's approval, or be silent. And they called them elections, as if in those tongues 'to elect' did not mean, as in all other human tongues, to choose between two or several things, persons or solutions. It was one of the profoundest humiliations I have ever suffered, and after all I could well pardon it, now that I am free; but other human beings are still suffering it. And here, there are people who have the frivolity, not to say the villainy, to talk about 'formal liberties'. Do without them just once in your life, and you'll see if they are merely formalities!

But I prefer to support good, rather than vituperate against evil. Wherever I see people who are mad, violent, the enemies of my liberty, I turn aside. Wherever I see poeple who are inert, self-satisfied, not even half awake, I turn aside. I go to the aid of people who want controlled growth of the economy, abundance shared with those who have nothing, and for it to be changed from the idol it was, to the servant it ought to be. I shall lend my assistance to people who want man to be the master of his technology, not technology the master of man, who long to see the earth green once more, blossoming and fertile. I shall give my support to those who want private enterprises to be possessed and directed by the employees, enterprises to be the property of the wage-earners and directed by specialists in management, enterprises the property of shareholders and wage-earners, and managed as above, enterprises the personal property of their creators, a talent as rare and as precious as that of a great violinist, the talent to create new things, new benefits, new goods, new methods, new techniques, and situations where there were none before.

I shall support those who are in favour of collective enterprises, organizations, collectivities of all kinds, whose members are all known to one another at least by sight: nothing is the measure of man that cannot enter a man's field of sight, exist in a normal and moderate memory for names and faces, and in the comprehension of an individual man.

I shall turn away with horror from people who speak of important things, and who even sometimes claim the right to decide my destiny, in a language I cannot follow. Jesus Christ spoke like everybody else. Einstein spoke like everybody else; and he who does not make the effort to find a common language with me perhaps does not want a common power with me, nor a common liberty, nor a common destiny: and I doubt very much that he would be my friend, my fellow, my brother. I shall distrust, because of my experience of Tartar bureaucracy, all monster organizations, bureaucratic megabeasts, State-controlled, nationalized, privately-owned, the supertoads, giants composed of hundreds of thousands of human beings reduced to a few elementary functions, with a few nervous ganglia, little gangs of *apparatchiks,* neurotic, crazed with arrogance, and sick of sterility. I shall be for all auton-omous operations – local, regional, collective enterprises – and for all federal co-operations between autonomous unities, and in favour of all the mechanisms of preserva-tion and defence of the individual against collectivity, and of the small collectivity against the big. What a program-me! But all that is possible, all that is feasible, all that is already sketched out, all that already exists in part, more or less well realized, and all that is perfectible; and only a tiny fraction of it falls to me, to the measure of my strength: but I want to know what I want, and where I am going.

Small is beautiful, but also, to be is beautiful: how beautiful it is to exist, how good it is to create, to be productive, efficient, fertile in ideas, comprehensible, identifiable. How beautiful it is to be a man working alone, and to be in a team, and to have personal responsi-bility, or a responsibility to a team, to be a human being with a face and a name, a clearly-defined human group, with a team leader, elective or nominated: there must be many mansions in our house, as in that of the Father.

Henceforward, life will be very good. It is very good to love, both one's nearest and dearest and those far away, human beings separately and all together. It is so good that

God gives us the grace to be able to love.

And it is so good if he gives us also the grace to be humble, not to be puffed up, not to despise, nor detest. Our enormous flops, some of them almost mortal, are ever-present, and leap to the eye; our colossal blunders, the orgies of presumption and effrontery which I do not need to name, nor to point at disparagingly. I shall work humbly, to the measure of my limited means, at what seems to me to be the observable progress of humanity since I was born and even since known civilizations have succeeded one another and have been piled upon one another like the waves on the shores of the oceans.

I shall not forget of what body I am such an infinitesimal part, nor in what direction we are oriented, pointed, directed; but without forgetting, for all that, to be humble; without thinking myself more than a grain of sand on the shore, a drop of water in the sea, a particle of energy in the infinite universe, a tiny, a faint glimmer soon to be fused with the absolute radiance of God.

16.

WORDS AND SILENCE

A famous quotation, and a little-known one: 'Every word is the epitaph of a feeling' – it is by Nietzsche or La Rochefoucauld, I have forgotten which; and 'Theology is the subtlest form of atheism' – that is by a Viennese cafe metaphysician whom I know very well. I do not know if they are both right, but I know that I cannot go on for long talking about things that spring from the most intimate part of my being, from my 'heart', as we call that central point of the computer, where the conscious mind coincides with the deepest depths; that I cannot go on talking a long time about what is most secret in me, without the spring running dry.

I do not know if our most intense and durable feelings are not those that one never admits to; but I know that I could not go on talking very long about God without moving away from him. Theological discourse is certainly threatened by the mortal danger of unconscious impiety: thinking in cold blood is to manipulate a concept as one manipulates an object with one's hands; manipulation means mastery. As soon as one speaks of God, one manipulates, not one's being, but the verbal signals which make allusion to him, the approach instruments; manipulation excludes piety; speaking can only be reconciled with the love of God at the very limit of thought and all its acrobatics. I have spoken too much about God.

The conversation I have been conducting with him since I reached maturity is not the gallery. I do not speak with God for all and sundry. It is a three-sided conversation. The exception being – and it is the only time – when speaking of God to my neighbour which is almost (never altogether, but almost) as if I were praying to God. It is what I have been doing in this book. God knows I wanted to avoid it, and that I thought I was too weak, incompetent, primitive, naïve. But I found myself forced into it, pushed back step by step towards it. I have done it; and now after having spoken so much of God, I must say no more. I did well to speak of my conversation with him, but now I find I must take it up again. I was never again to open my mouth to speak of God. Once is enough. This time will be enough.

The word is there, it is the word of Christ. The Evangelists are there, Mark the reporter, Matthew the Jewish historian, Luke the Greek historian, John the mystical poet. Jesus is there, one can see him, one can hear him, one is a witness of his look, his silence, his slightest gesture, his tolerance, his pity, his indignation, his weariness, his despair. He is there, he is speaking, as always, today and tomorrow and when I am long dead and buried; he is still saying the same things and they are always new, always alive, similar to that tiny little glimmer, so delicate, so transparent, so fresh, as if it had never been here before and could never return. The word is with him: love God with all thy heart, with all thy soul and with all thy strength, and thy neighbour as thyself. Blessed are the humble, the weak, the sorrowing, the simple, the peacemakers. All that comforts, all that relaxes the grimace of suffering, of anger, madness, is Christian; all that comes with open arms, holds out loving hands, and gentles life, gives back hope, is his word. We have to follow God, and not speak about him. We must speak with God, and wait patiently, in silence, until he is willing to reply in silence.

As for me, he had pity on me, I am happy: those few

instants are sufficient to justify this existence, it was worth living. And I have the hope of seeing those instants return. Yesterday again, I was able to give thanks to God.

Nevertheless, I admit that I should like to have a conclusion that would put me in my place again, put me where I belong, where I must be: to die surrounded by my family, and loving them; helped, to pass out of time into I know not what slumber and I know not what awakening, by friendly doctors and human beings, who would treat me as a human being, their friend, their neighbour; and by the good sisters of those admirable orders who devote themselves to the sick and the dying; and by the priests who would recite for me those Latin or Greek poems composed very long ago by Christians speaking with God. I should like to fall asleep in the continuity of the Church, and that a priest impose his hands upon me even as someone imposed his hands upon him, and on him before him, from generation unto generation, down to the hands of Christ himself, and hence forward in time for as long as the word of Christ shall be passed from man to man.

A dog squashed by a passing car also sleeps with God. Before the pity of God the squashed dog and myself surrounded by my nearest and dearest and by the Church are perhaps the same. But it was to me that God gave Jesus Christ upon his cross. I am a human being, living at a certain point in this human history which converges and rises in a certain direction; I should very much like my existence, as obscure, mediocre and unsatisfying as it has been, to be placed in that current, or placed in the context of Christian civilization and of sister civilizations, civilizations that are one with it in amity: to feel myself swept away by that rippling of living waters, like the cataracts of Iguacu, but falling upwards. I should wish for a civilized death. And it would be wonderful to gaze, with my dying eyes, upon the shimmering rose window of the south transept.

But I also know very well that I could make a civilized ending in absolute negation, in absolute forsakenness and sadness, the total desert. I know only too well the ghastly savour of the absence of God, what is called loss of faith. To die like an animal – but that is not even true, for an animal has not heard of God, he loses nothing because he has nothing. To die from within, by desertification, like certain more and more extensive regions on our planet: absolute devalorization, the feeling and the proof of a lack of meaning, lack of value, of beauty, of savour and of the fragrance of everything: there where grace should leap forth, there is only dry sand, like the parched bed of a stream, a well run dry: cold sand, flat desert, the bush of thorns, the empty wind, the horizon void, no one, nothing, and the planet frozen in a glacial universe.

I would accept to be the last man on earth, if I could make peace and draw the bottom line: as there was prayer, the grace of orison, we are in the black, thank you, God, now I can take to my bed and go to sleep.

But – not to be able to pray. No longer to sense the presence of grace. To hope no more, to wait no more with confidence and patience, accepting humbly the fact that grace might never touch us again. No longer to be able to be like that: that is what frightens. I can be so ill that I would no longer know how to reconcile myself with God; or be rich and cynical, determined never again to fall into the trap of words, images and rituals, to never again be the dupe of men or of God or of myself. To die of sorrow, struck down in the very thing I love most; but as I would no longer love anyone, invulnerable, armoured, dying of boredom, of obesity, of scorn, of amused disgust, without God, without love, surrounded by money-grubbing quacks who would treat me like some data processor on the blink, and by world-weary nurses. To die in the stupefaction of drugs, a cadaver whose functioning is maintained by machines plugged into the flesh, until the time comes when a doctor decides to flip the switch off.

In this second example of civilized death, I should like to have a friend who would be there in time to give me a euphoriant powerful enough to put me to sleep quickly, agreeably and without any possibility of wakening again. A civilized ending. We are still barbarians, talking of injections given by a doctor playing the part of a charitable executioner: but even poor little cats and dogs should be spared that injection. In Athens, they were civilized: they handed you a bowl full of hemlock juice, freshly squeezed; you only had to take it and quaff it down yourself. It ought to be possible to offer hopeless cases – condemned by barbarism or by hopeless suffering and pain – the final euphoric potion, in response to a request solemnly repeated before a magistrate and a lawyer. Civilized death, in the sorrow of being without God. Nothing is; all that is, is nothing; nothing has value; nothing has meaning; let's put an end to it all, and no pulling of nasty faces; let's sleep.

But among all the possible ends, a third is perhaps reserved for me, one similar to the course of my life: effort, unceasing fighting, gradual loss of everything, then unexpected gain, unhoped-for grace, divine goodness of God and of God in men. Perhaps I am going to climb and crawl, right up to the last instant, towards that unknown hearth of radiant brightness, drag myself on hands and knees towards God, doubt in my heart and ignorance in my numbskull brain, forgetful of those few instants of grace, but from time to time remembering them, hoping for I know not what, if not those instants of gratitude, going towards him without knowing where he is nor who he is; tirelessly continuing the conversation as I have been doing until now.

A painful, difficult death, filled with uncertainty, but as it were still in movement, as if passing through a dividing partition, leaving here, or entering, even in nothingness, even in absolute sleep, as if one were simply returning home, as if one were returning to base, to oneself.

Then, down there, 'one' is another and the conversation

is consummated in reconciliation, love, peace. But all this is just words, gropings, approximations – there is nothing more to say, there is nothing more to do, I must put an end to this and return to silence and to him with whom I talk in that silence.